Christianity in Rural China

*Conflict and Accommodation in Jiangxi Province,
1860–1900*

Alan Richard Sweeten

CENTER FOR CHINESE STUDIES
. THE UNIVERSITY OF MICHIGAN
ANN ARBOR

MICHIGAN MONOGRAPHS IN CHINESE STUDIES
SERIES ESTABLISHED 1968

Published by
Center for Chinese Studies
The University of Michigan
Ann Arbor, Michigan 48104-1608

Grateful acknowledgment is made to the following publishers for permission to reprint copyrighted material:

"Catholic Converts in Jiangxi Province," originally published in *Christianity in China*, edited by Daniel H. Bays. Used with the permission of the publisher, Stanford University Press. ©1996 by the Board of Trustees of the Leland Stanford Junior University.

"A Village Church in Jiangxi," originally published in *Tradition and Metamorphosis in Modern Chinese History* edited by Yen-p'ing Hao and Hsiu-mei Wei. Used with the permission of the publisher, Institute of Modern History, Academia Sinica. © 1998 by Academia Sinica.

"Women and Law in Rural China," originally published in *Late Imperial China* (formerly *Ch'ing-shih wen-t'i*), edited by William Rowe. Used with permission of the publisher. © 1978 by Late Imperial China.

Library of Congress Cataloging-in-Publication Data

Sweeten, Alan Richard.
    Christianity in rural China : conflict and accommodation in Jiangxi Province, 1860-1900 / Alan Richard Sweeten.
        p.   cm. – (Michigan monographs in Chinese studies, ISSN 1081-9053 ; no. 91)
    Includes bibliographical references and index.
    ISBN 0-89264-146-0 (alk. paper)
    1.   Jiangxi Sheng (China) – Church history. I. Title. II. Series.
BR1295.J43 S94 2001
275.1'222081—dc21
                                                    2001028316

To Carol, Cynthia, and Monika
with love

and

to the memory of my parents,
brother, and sister

There is a time for everything,
and a season for every activity under heaven.
—Ecclesiastes 3:1

The end of a matter is better than its beginning,
and patience is better than pride.
—Ecclesiastes 7:8

Contents

Illustrations

Maps

Figures

Acknowledgments

How do I properly thank all those who have contributed in important ways to a book that has taken many years to research and complete? Special people have accompanied and helped me as I strolled along the path that brought me to this point. Graduation from high school in 1965 led directly, I thought, to either military conscription or college. I chose the latter because of the influence of Jamimah Sweeten, my dear mother. Earlier, while still raising a family, she first completed high school, then attended college. She became a very successful businesswoman and an intrepid world traveler. Besides demonstrating perseverance, toughness, and self-sacrifice, my mother showed me through personal example the importance of a higher education. Little did she know, as she encouraged me to go to college and get as much education as possible, the extent to which I would go to achieve satisfaction.

Yet, it is my wife Carol who has always been beside me and has sacrificed the most during our numerous moves and our five years abroad. Hand in hand, Carol supported me—literally, figuratively, and, most of all, lovingly. Without her understanding, tolerance, and patience I would have been unable to continue, let alone finish, this book. These few words of gratitude seem insufficient to express my feelings for all that she has freely given me.

My daughters Cynthia and Monika grew up during a time of frequent family trips related to my China career. Sometimes these moves were difficult for them. Fortunately, they can now chuckle about pointed questions such as "Whose idea was this anyway?" posed by eight-year-old Cyndy as we dragged thirteen pieces of luggage through Hong Kong's Kai Tak Airport while in transit for the third time to live in Taiwan, and "Daddy, do they have American food there?" asked by five-year-old Nikki as we moved from Taiwan to yet another "foreign" place, Delaware, where I began teaching. I am relieved that they love soy sauce as much as I do and am blessed to have them as part of my life.

My interest in history dates to my youth, and my study of China to my undergraduate years. In 1968 Carol and I left California in order to participate in a study-abroad program in Taiwan. The next year Mr. Lü Shih-chiang of the Institute of Modern History, Academia Sinica, led me to the fascinating subject of Christianity in China. A paper written for him evolved into a graduate school research topic and, eventually, a published article. I did not fully appreciate the complexity and significance of the topic, however, until I began my doctoral work in 1974 under the supervision of Professor Kwang-Ching Liu at the University of California, Davis.

K.C., as his friends and colleagues address him, compelled and propelled me along the way. Although neither of us knew what the facts would be nor how the story would come together, K.C. recognized the Zongli Yamen archives on cases involving Christians as an untouched treasure trove of information. Each step in the process from seminar paper to dissertation chapter to manuscript version has been in some way influenced by K.C.'s desire for logical organization and probing analysis. Moreover, the publication of this study would never have materialized had he ever lost faith in the importance of the subject or in me as the author. When I left academia in 1982 to pursue a full-time career in the business world, K.C. may have felt disappointment if not unhappiness regarding my decision. Whatever his feelings, he continued, in the finest tradition of the Confucian gentleman and teacher, to encourage me.

Gladly I mention as well the invaluable feedback provided by Professors Daniel H. Bays, Britten Dean, Harry J. Lamley, Charles A. Litzinger, R. G. Tiedemann, and, especially, Ernest P. Young. Several other people have assisted me far beyond the call of duty. Acting on behalf of the Congregation of the Mission, the following archivists opened up for me files of fascinating materials: Rev. Paul Henzmann (Maison-Mère), Rev. Stafford Poole (De Paul Center, Western Province), Rev. Louis Derbes (The De Andreis-Rosati Memorial Archives, St. Mary's of the Barrens), and Rev. John Carven (The Brother Bertrand Ducournau Archives, Eastern Province). For the Missionary Society of St. Columban, the vicar general, Fr. Noel Connolly, and archivist, Fr. Patrick Crowley, generously extended their help to me. Likewise, Frs. Luke O'Reilly and Pat Sheehy warmly shared their memories of mission work in Jiangxi. During the production process I benefited from association with Mr.

Brian Duggan, Office of Information Technology, and Ms. Vicki Eden, University Communications, California State University, Stanislaus. Thanks are also extended to Ms. Terre Fisher at the Center for Chinese Studies Publications, University of Michigan, for her valuable editorial assistance.

Financial support during one year came from the History of Christianity in China Project, sponsored by the Henry Luce Foundation of New York. In addition, funding for research leading to this publication was provided by the Research Enablement Program, a grant program for mission scholarship supported by the Pew Charitable Trusts, Philadelphia, Pennsylvania, and administered by the Overseas Ministries Study Center, New Haven, Connecticut. The Vincentian Studies Institute provided assistance to visit the Congregation of the Mission's archives in Paris. These grants, each coming at crucial junctures in my work, made it possible to continue my research and writing. I appreciate not only their generosity, but also the trust placed in me as an independent researcher.

Whether institutional, personal, or psychological, I cannot begin to repay all the support provided me over the years. If there is any merit to that which follows, I willingly share it. Any deficiencies present in this study remain the author's sole responsibility. After all, "it was my idea."

Wangxiang xuan
Denair, California
June 15, 2001

Foreword

L ocal conflicts in the late Chinese empire at the expense of Western missionaries and their Chinese converts have hitherto been seen as indications of Confucian intolerance, of the reaction of local elites and even responsible officials to the intrusion of a new religion backed by imperialist power arrogating the prerogatives of the Chinese gentry and officials. Historians usually assume that there was a pattern of Chinese anti-Christian movements actively promoted during the last four decades of the nineteenth century by the gentry elite with the connivance of officials, reaching a climax in the court-sponsored Boxer Uprising of 1900.

Examining the marvelously well-preserved archives of the Zongli Yamen, the Qing dynasty's office of foreign affairs established in 1861, Alan Sweeten has opened up relevant portions of this invaluable source, which includes reports from officials and functionaries at the county and subcounty levels and depositions of the Christians and non-Christians involved in legal cases arising out of the conflicts that took place in the province of Jiangxi in the period from 1860 to 1900. Sweeten offers a comprehensive and careful review of the cases and a remarkably fine and balanced analysis of the forces at work, of the protagonists and the villains (if such a term applies), and of the characteristic setting of local Chinese communities, especially small towns and villages in the countryside.

Chapters of this work present intriguing vignettes of well-documented incidents, viewing church life as part of everyday life and in relation to lineage and family, marriage and widowhood, property transactions and disputes, rituals and laws, crime and violence. The result is not only a new and realistic portrayal of the Sino-foreign disputes in the Christian "sectarian cases" (*jiao'an*), but also a fresh look at Chinese state and society, offering many insights from an unexpected angle, as it were, on the nature of rural Chinese communities and of the bureaucratic machinery at the subcounty level. Sweeten's well-researched observations are of important concern to Chinese social and cultural history.

Sweeten has worked on this book over the years as a labor of love. He not only covers the Chinese sources for his topic, but has incorporated letters and reports from Jiangxi found in the archives of European mission societies. Through the writing of this book, Sweeten has perfected his sinological skills and developed a style of historical writing that is factually precise yet reflects his careful and judicious interpretation of all the forces underlying the cases at hand. This work testifies both to the author's thoroughness and informed insight and to his genuine interest in the common people of China, not from the viewpoint of a Christian missionary, but from that of a sympathetic though sometimes skeptical friend.

Kwang-Ching Liu
University of California, Davis

Chapter 1

Christianity in Late Imperial China

Christianity will forever be associated with the problems and clashes that its presence in China produced. Many missionaries labeled such conflicts "persecution," while most gentry probably saw them as self-defense or retaliation. Whatever the slant, missionaries and Chinese Christians in large cities all over China suffered throughout the late nineteenth century. Blood flowed and property burned in or near Nanchang (1862), Yangzhou (1868), Tianjin (1870), Fuzhou (Fujian, 1878), Chongqing (1886), cities along the Grand Canal and Yangzi River (1891), Chengdu (1895), and other places. These urban-area incidents demonstrate the scale, intensity, and ongoing nature of that conflict.

This sanguinary record has not been ignored. Scholars who have studied it conclude that the gentry were anti-Christian and the populace in general was strongly opposed to Christianity. Kenneth Scott Latourette and Paul Cohen, for example, note that gentry often incited disturbances against missionaries and Chinese Christians. The gentry easily succeeded because the allegedly insincere and untrustworthy Christian rabble used their missionary connections to obtain special treatment from local authorities and to bully their neighbors. Constantly in strife with those around them, Christians either sought to live apart or were forced to live in their own enclaves—enclaves that existed as *imperia in imperio*.[1]

In fact we know very little about Christianity at the grassroots level and the daily interaction between ordinary Christians and non-Christians. No one has documented in detail over an extended period of time how Christianity fared in the small towns and villages of even one province. To address this gap, my study focuses exclusively on Jiangxi Province during the crucial time from 1860 to 1900, when the number of rural Christians, along with various problems involving them, increased noticeably.[2] I will examine the assumptions that Christians in the countryside regularly faced gentry-led harassment, that rural Chinese Christians were marginalized troublemakers who deserved the treatment they received from their angry neighbors, and that Christians voluntarily or involuntarily segregated themselves.

These assumptions may be challenged with new information from neglected government records about Christians in Jiangxi's small towns and rural localities. Files of the Zongli Yamen, the Qing dynasty's office for general management of foreign relations, include important materials about Christians who lived in rural Jiangxi. This source clarifies three key points: First, the gentry were not usually involved or implicated in cases that involved Christians. Instead of being gentry-led and targeting Christians, the so-called anti-Christian cases generally centered not on religion, but rather on specifically secular or personal matters. The content of these cases also provides a different perspective on everyday life, with Christians in regular contact, but not in constant conflict, with fellow Chinese. Second, Chinese Christians were not the flotsam of society. They came from various backgrounds and engaged non-Christians in a wide range of social and business affairs. Even if these customary relationships sometimes created problems, the problems were nothing out of the ordinary when viewed in the context of local society. Third, daily and regular contact with non-Christian kin and neighbors indicates that rural Christians did not form enclaves. To the contrary, most Christian Chinese continued to live side by side with ordinary Chinese. In fact, since Christians were such a small component of the communities in which they resided, they needed to find ways to practice their religion within the confines of normal community life. They apparently succeeded, although sporadic problems did occur.

Problems involving Christians in Jiangxi over four decades, with the exception of Nanchang during the 1860s, did not solidify into either a gentry-led or a mass-based anti-Christian (or anti-foreign) movement. Evidence presented in the following chapters strongly suggests that rural people accepted, or at least tolerated, Christians as members of the local community. Was this a small step towards an indigenous church and unique to Jiangxi?[3] What sorts of situations prevailed elsewhere in China? What bearing does this have, if any, on the emergence of forces that eventually led to the consequential changes of the early twentieth century and later? These are questions still awaiting exploration. Christianity's growth in Jiangxi's rural areas did coincide with increasing gentry exploitation of the people there. Moreover, whirlwinds of discontent and protest from the countryside eventually became storms of revolution that swept along everyone. The survival of Jiangxi's Christians during these tumultuous times cannot be explained by either missionary protection or the power of faith. It came, I believe, from widespread mutual accommodation between Christians and non-Christians within rural society. From my study of Jiangxi, I conclude that before 1900 Christians were, in the main, an accepted part of the rural landscape.

Scholarship on Christianity in the Confucian Setting

Previous generations of scholars of Christianity in late imperial China have studied the subject from many different angles, but the most provocative seems to be that of cultural impact and reaction. One view holds that all missionaries, by virtue of their very presence and purpose in China, "posed a revolutionary challenge to the traditional culture."[4] Chinese culture, at least that represented by the gentry during the nineteenth century, rested heavily on the traditions and values of Confucianism. Missionaries, however, found Confucian China grossly deficient and morally inferior to the Christian world. Their criticisms of Confucianism necessarily included the gentry since the gentry enjoyed the greatest benefits of the Confucian-based system. From this view, missionary efforts to propagate Christianity went beyond arguments about religious doctrine to a direct frontal assault on the gentry's position in society as community leader.[5]

In many ways missionaries represented the gentry's worst critics and greatest rivals, and the gentry perceived them as such. With extraterritorial status and special treaty privileges, both granted and assumed, missionaries directly engaged local government officials or circumvented them by appealing to Western diplomats. Missionaries established orphanages and schools, helped with famine relief, and otherwise assumed gentry-like responsibilities in social, economic, political, and moral realms. No wonder the gentry reacted strongly in word and deed to the missionary presence. Most sources agree that during the nineteenth century the gentry, for a variety of reasons, became obdurately opposed to missionaries and close-minded to Christianity.

These postulations, taken together with the gentry's supposedly near-total domination of local society, mean but one thing in the context of a dispute or conflict involving Christianity: the gentry must somehow be enmeshed in surrounding events. The author of *China and Christianity* has persuasively argued precisely this point. Paul Cohen finds for the decade of the 1860s a pattern of gentry-instigated conflict with Christians in three urban centers: Nanchang (Jiangxi), Changsha (Hunan), and Guiyang (Guizhou). He concludes that in these cities an already enervated officialdom found it necessary "to cater to the [anti-Christian] prejudices of the gentry and populace" in order not to alienate them from the dynasty.[6]

Others presume the situation in the rural areas to have been similar to that found by Cohen in the cities. Frederic Wakeman reasons that the "lower" gentry, most of whom resided in small towns and villages, had their control of local affairs undermined by the arrival of politically powerful and socially influential missionary rivals. This then accounts for their anger and hostility.[7] The "lower" gentry presumably sought to protect, as did the "upper" gentry in the cities, their political power and social position by leading the way against Christianity in the countryside and among the common people.

Many blame the gentry, urban and rural, for either instigating or directing the many anti-Christian incidents of the late nineteenth century. Proof in one form is abundant: a variety of printed materials ranging from books to anonymous placards and scatological drawings reveal the gentry's perception of missionaries as sociopolitical rivals and their predisposition to treat Christianity as a heterodox doctrine. These materials inflamed anti-Christian feelings and circulated at places, mostly cities, where missionaries and Christians became targets. Considerable evidence points to the gentry as the authors, sponsors, and disseminators of anti-Christian materials.[8]

Local officials often appear to have done little or nothing to halt the plethora of anti-Christian literature from circulating. One explanation for this is simple: officials after all were gentry, too, and for many of the same reasons opposed Christianity. Like the gentry, officials probably misunderstood many Christian beliefs and rites. However, officials did understand—and certainly resented—missionary aggressiveness. Many officials felt that missionaries too frequently interfered in lawsuits on behalf of Christians and too often claimed exaggerated indemnities for specific cases or demanded that uncooperative officials be cashiered. Any evaluation of officials' actions or inaction must also take into account a bureaucratic structure that at the local level made them sensitive to gentry opinions and dependent upon gentry assistance for fulfilling basic government functions.

When officials supported and protected the treaty rights granted to missionaries and Christians, they ran the risk of alienating the gentry. Alienated gentry could easily disrupt local government activities and hamper if not cripple officials' effectiveness. On the other hand, if local officials sided with the gentry against Christians, then complications abounded for those at higher levels of government responsible for Sino-Western relations. Local officials faced difficult choices.[9] Few it seems chose overt anti-Christian action. Instead, they either turned a blind eye to gentry activities and gave them "almost complete liberty to carry on their propagandistic and organizational activities" or protected them from repercussions, thereby providing an "operating framework for anti-Christian action that was relatively free of obstacles or risks."[10]

Given gentry and the government officials' influence on society and the manner in which they reacted to Christianity's presence, it has been argued that naturally they contributed to the common people's hostility. In addition, scholars assume that commoners had very concrete reasons of their own for feeling resentment or hatred toward Christianity. For example, when missionaries intervened in lawsuits on behalf of Christians, and when Christians used their religious status to influence judicial decisions, their adversaries had to shoulder the costly legal and settlement expenses. This affected only individuals or families, whereas entire neighborhoods and villages bore a proportionately heavier fee burden for periodic local temple festivals and theatrical performances (*yanxi*) when Christians took advantage of the fee exemption granted to them by the Zongli Yamen in 1862.[11]

In places where anti-Christian disturbances resulted in large monetary indemnities, officials sometimes hit the populace of whole counties with special levies or with higher taxes to raise the money. The common people resented any extra financial burdens and those associated with Christianity simply exacerbated existing feelings about missionaries and Christians disrupting key sociocultural activities.[12] Christian discontinuation of ancestor veneration was viewed not only as a challenge to a central cultural value, but also as a threat to the ideals of generational continuity and patrilineal lines of descent. Additionally, many non-Christians found certain rites, particularly those performed inside Catholic churches, to be strange or even immoral, and this helped create an environment easily filled with wild rumors.[13] All these tensions disturbed societal harmony, as did missionaries who built churches at locations where some people believed the structures disturbed geomantic forces (fengshui) and deleteriously affected the fate of the entire community.[14]

People's attitudes toward Christianity carried over into the political realm as well. In various parts of China, commoners sometimes linked Christianity with heterodox sects or secret societies.[15] Confusion of this sort prevailed especially in central and south China because of the Taiping Rebellion (1851–1864). A wide range of people had trouble distinguishing between the Christianity of the rebels and the religion preached by Western missionaries.[16] This fueled suspicions about the political reliability of all Christians. Many Chinese only knew that the Taipings practiced some sort of Christian faith and that the dynasty intended to suppress them. Since the rebellion caused increased suffering among the common people, many mistakenly blamed Christians. People thus had various reasons for their attitudes toward and reaction to Christianity. These came from personal or community experience rather than from prejudices passed on by the gentry. Consequently, it is not surprising that many Chinese reacted in overtly hostile ways to Christianity. Cohen concludes that since statistics indicate Chinese Christians to have been only a minuscule percentage of the total population, the vast majority of common people wanted no association whatsoever with Christianity.[17]

A corollary to this deduction is that the relatively few Chinese who followed Christianity did so for ulterior motives. Missionaries, by interfering in lawsuits, attracted prospects interested only in a potential legal advantage; by helping the needy with a gift of money or food, they gained adherents who simply wanted a handout. "Rice Christian" became the derogatory label for these people. But missionaries also proselytized among opium addicts, the homeless, the starving, the orphaned, and the abandoned. By virtue of their efforts to seek any and all for Christ, missionaries are said to have brought to the fold "the least law-abiding elements," "the seedier elements," and people from "the most disadvantaged classes—poor peasants, shopkeepers, merchants, vagabonds—the very people whose stake in the existing Chinese order was most tenuous."[18] For those who agree with the sweeping condemnations of the character and "class" of people who converted, Christians indeed appeared to be pariahs, literally and figuratively on the outskirts of society.

Whether Christians came from the bottom of the kettle or not, missionaries made certain behavioral demands of them. When converts followed missionaries' instructions and renounced ancestor veneration, for example, they risked severing family and lineage ties and losing the benefits that came from being a member of a larger social group. Likewise, when Christians refused to contribute money to support local temple celebrations and activities, they risked alienating themselves from their neighbors. These and similar actions, some scholars believe, split communities into separate Christian and non-Christian entities. Cohen words it succinctly: Christians, specifically Catholics, were largely "a community apart, isolated and often estranged from their fellow Chinese."[19]

Research on Christianity in Jiangxi

Research for this book focused exclusively on Jiangxi, and mainly its Catholic residents. Jiangxi makes an appropriate case study for several reasons. From the start, Catholic missionaries were trailblazers who regularly traveled through and worked in this province. Father Matteo Ricci visited and then lived in Nanchang, establishing the first Roman Catholic mission there during the mid-1590s.[20] Over the next two centuries Catholics survived the political turmoil and warfare of a dynastic change, periodic government opposition, the Rites Controversy setback, the Qing emperor's official proscription of Christianity in 1724, and many other problems. Unfortunately, not a great deal is known about missionaries' day-to-day work or about Christians' activities in this period. We do know that somehow many Christians remained committed to the faith.[21]

Through the seventeenth century, missionaries faced countless difficulties as they sought converts wherever they could find them. They achieved most of their success in the provinces of Zhili (Hebei), Shansi, Shaansi, Shandong, Zhejiang, Jiangnan (Jiangsu and Anhui), and Jiangxi. According to one estimate, thirteen thousand Catholics resided in these provinces in 1627.[22] By other estimates, the number of Catholics in all of China circa 1700–1703 range from 196,200 to no more than 300,000.[23] None of these figures can be confirmed with any precision now, but the fact remains that Catholicism had, in spite of many difficulties, firmly rooted itself in most provinces. In Jiangxi and elsewhere Catholics maintained their beliefs as individuals, bolstered by family support or the backing of their small congregations (*chrétientés*).[24] The Catholic presence and gradual numerical growth during the seventeenth century means that while some Chinese turned to Christianity, others probably accepted its presence. During the eighteenth century, however, Catholic population totals decreased to perhaps 120,000 due to government efforts at suppression. Counts vary for the period 1800–1815, but by then there were between 202,000 and 217,000 Catholics in China.[25]

The number of Catholics remained relatively stable until the concerted economic opening of China by the West during the 1830s and 1840s. From then onward the situation changed rapidly. By 1901 the Church claimed close to 720,000 followers in China.[26] During the last half of the nineteenth century, Catholic missionaries worked in every province. Most missionaries and Catholic Chinese lived in Zhili, Jiangsu, Sichuan, Guangdong, and Shandong while the fewest were found in Yunnan, Hunan, Gansu, and Guangxi.[27] In terms of the number of its priests, Catholics, churches, and chapels, Jiangxi was neither a leading nor a trailing province. In 1832 one French missionary and six Chinese priests watched over an estimated six thousand Catholics who lived in Jiangxi.[28] Ten years later that number had increased by several hundred. Dispersed among 160 congregations, Catholics worshipped in home oratories or in one of eighteen chapels.[29] By 1898–1899 the numbers had changed to thirty-six European priests, eighteen Chinese priests, 23,338 Catholics, and 105 churches and chapels.[30]

Protestant missionaries also proselytized in Jiangxi. In 1867 the Methodist Episcopal Church sent two men to establish their first mission at the newly opened treaty port of Jiujiang.[31] Joining the Methodists in 1869 were missionaries from the China Inland Mission and later other smaller mission groups. Through the rest of the nineteenth century, the China Inland Mission was the largest of all the groups and was active throughout the province.[32] In addition to preaching and seeking converts, Protestant missionaries established schools and boarding houses for students, gave medical aid in clinics, dispensaries, and hospitals, and provided special refuges for opium addicts. As a result of such work, by 1906 the China Inland Mission had through its ninety-two missionaries (including wives and associates) baptized 2,192 Chinese and established fifty-five organized churches and ninety-one chapels. The Methodists counted five missionaries, 1,018 baptized converts, and ten churches and chapels.[33] Protestant work in Jiangxi, and in most provinces, fell far behind that of their Catholic counterparts. Thus, given their numerical importance, my discussion will concentrate mainly on Catholics and their interaction with other Chinese.[34]

Besides the long history and moderate success of missionary work in Jiangxi, another important reason for concentrating our attention on this province is the basic one of availability of source materials. On the Catholic side for the period under study, it was priests from the Congregation of the Mission (Vincentians or Lazarists) along with a few secular priests and Sisters of Charity who worked in Jiangxi.[35] Their numerous reports provide background, statistics, and details on Church work, and their published letters, dating from 1833, provide first-hand accounts of traveling, living, and ministering in Jiangxi.[36] They also offer insightful comments regarding both Christians and non-Christians. Two priests had careers in Jiangxi that spanned six decades: Father Antoine Anot worked there from 1844 to 1893 and Father You Daoxuan (Joseph Yeou) from 1844 to 1896.[37] These two veterans and other experienced priests provide useful infor-mation regarding a variety of important issues within the scope of this study. Although priests tended to write about problems they encountered and conflicts in which they became involved, they occasionally jotted down nuggets of information about ordinary times and affairs.

On the Chinese side, primary source materials on Jiangxi from 1860 to 1900 are plentiful and evenly distributed chronologically, which is not true for all provinces.[38] Moreover, we have for reference one study of a large-scale anti-Christian disturbance in 1860s Nanchang; this so-called model case has done much to advance our understanding of the back-ground and dynamics of the mid-century conflict.[39] A second serious incident in Nanchang in 1906, when a magistrate mysteriously died shortly after being alone with a priest, caused rioting and culminated in the destruction of Catholic and Protestant property and the murder of several missionaries. This case, too, has been carefully studied.[40] Jiangxi, therefore, has received its share of Western scholarly attention, but the spotlight has remained focused on the large city of Nanchang for both of these periods.

Nanchang, the provincial capital, had particularly active and strong gentry leaders, judging from organized militia (*tuanlian*) activity there during the Taiping Rebellion and from anti-Catholic incidents during the 1860s.[41] Does this mean, following one scenario for anti-Catholic activity, that Nanchang's gentry exported their biased sentiments to other Jiangxi cities and to the countryside, thereby setting the stage for future conflict? Or is it possible that the weakness of the gentry's leadership and influence outside Nanchang allowed sectarian activities, including those of Catholics, to expand, creating conflict with the orthodox order?[42]

Evaluation of either of these possibilities requires examination of the content and identification of the participants in the various cases that occurred in Jiangxi's small towns and villages. When problems or conflicts ended up in court, if Christians were involved, ecclesiastical inquiries often, but not always, followed. This sparked a bureaucratic chain reaction.[43] Chinese officials forwarded relevant county records, additional investigatory reports, and higher-level official endorsements to the Zongli Yamen for review and instructions. At the same time, Western authorities also sent statements and petitions from Christians, reports from missionaries and consuls, and communications from various ministers to Zongli Yamen officials for appropriate action. These documents, along with Zongli Yamen replies to all concerned parties, constitute the *Jiaowu jiao'an dang*, the archive on Christian affairs and on cases and disputes involving missionaries and Christians.[44]

On one level the *Jiaowu jiao'an dang* allows us to see the standpoint of staunch Confucian officials and gentry. They considered heterodox activities, including those of Christians, a potential threat to both social mores and Qing political authority and therefore gave full attention to the investigation and settlement of all "sectarian cases" (*jiao'an*).[45] *Jiao'an* not only alerted low-level representatives of the central government and county subbureaucratic functionaries to local problems, they also motivated local supporters of the sociopolitical status quo to solve them. The problems made apparent in *jiao'an* thus help define the issues of the day and also help us understand the presumptions and actions of those involved.

From government officials and gentry we essentially see conflicts from the top looking downward. But the *Jiaowu jiao'an dang* also preserves a contrasting view. Transcribed oral depositions from litigants, usually illiterate common people who left no other record except in these cases, reveal key features of local society—its organization, its stress points, and its contact with the gentry and the county bureaucracy. A view from the ground floor, that is, from the common people's perspective, also provides significant new insights into Chinese-Christian relations.

The *Jiaowu jiao'an dang* also includes valuable materials written or supplied by missionaries that help in the accurate reconstruction of the cases. Letters and reports sent directly by missionaries to Paris and Rome provide additional information. Neither the Chinese nor the European sources, however, yield a complete account of the problems that occurred. Officials dealt with cases that went unmentioned in missionary accounts, and missionaries wrote about situations that officials did not report. But this is not necessarily significant. County magistrates had a difficult task governing large, densely populated jurisdictions. Officials sought to settle disputes locally and tried not to involve their superiors. When they succeeded, case materials remained in the county yamen files, files that no longer exist. On the Catholic side, priests also served large jurisdictions whose congregations were widely scattered. Their annual visits did not allow the missionaries to learn about, let alone intervene in, every dispute involving Catholics, and their records contain lacunae as well. Nonetheless, these voluminous Chinese and Western materials are the best available. Given their unique content, and in an effort to present as representative a picture as possible, I will refer to virtually every Jiangxi case mentioned in detail in the *Jiaowu jiao'an dang* collection.

The *jiao'an* materials, to be sure, emphasize problems and conflicts in the lives of some Chinese Christians. But this skews our view, leading to a focus on why hostility existed and how it led to conflict. Details within the *jiao'an* record that point to a generally peaceful coexistence between Christians and non-Christians in Jiangxi are sketchy and easily over-looked. Western accounts usually neglect normal, peaceful times, but not always. From missionary materials that shed light on one village in Jiangxi I try to provide another side to the story of relationships between Christians and non-Christians. This account, I believe, reveals a previously ignored aspect of local history and suggests that our views of local conflict— however extensive or important it may have been—must still be balanced by the fact that a process of accommodation was also in progress.

Although we can count the number of cases and the number of Christians involved in these cases, we still have no way of determining what percentage they represent of the total local court cases. This is because the Jiangxi county archives for this period are simply not extant. On the other hand we could try to quantify by page count and volume, or by percentage, the number of conflicts associated with Christianity versus the total number involving Westerners.[46] However, as Cohen notes, to appreciate fully Christianity's post-1860 threat to Chinese society means more than counting Christians and, by implication, cases. Since just a few missionaries or Christians could disturb a community's existing power structure, it is probably better to recognize that "qualitative factors, such as high visibility and external political support were vastly more important."[47]

Emphasis on qualitative factors, which I believe includes underlying issues and causes, leads to the question of how typical or atypical the Christian cases were when considered alongside non-Christian cases and taken in the context of what we know about Chinese society and the legal system.[48] Based on my research in all available *jiao'an* materials for Jiangxi, I believe that the broad categories of cases that emerge, and the specific issues prominent in these cases, fall within parameters that are representative, rather than exceptional, for rural China. Yet, since the cases involved only certain Christian congregations and relatively few individuals within them, one could argue that the problems and conflicts that occurred were extremely limited.[49] In addition, it is clear that no particular locale gave rise to a steady stream of cases. Why not? I believe the very nature of rural society—the particular sources of conflict, the parties involved, how participants resolved their problems, and how Christians and non-Christians came to accommodate one another in the communities where they lived, worked, and died—precluded it.

The cases in this book, drawn from the *Jiaowu jiao'an dang* and supplemented whenever possible by Western sources, indicate that problems involving Christians, which occurred in both urban and rural locales, usually centered on discrete secular matters such as unpaid debts, property transactions, and personal affairs. Given the mundane nature of many cases, and the fact that Christianity was not itself a central, irresolvable issue, local officials usually settled them easily. Overall, the cases tend to be isolated from one another in terms of their causes, issues, development, and timing. There is simply no evidence that gentry-class masterminds attempted to or succeeded in linking them together.

The absence of an organized gentry opposition is significant given their open hostility to Christianity and their dominant position in local society. To be sure, we find the gentry involved in some of the cases. Yet gentry problems with Christians, like those of the common people, were often of a non-religious sort. Even when the gentry did attempt to link Christianity to heterodoxy, this rarely became a central cause of conflict. After considering all the cases in Jiangxi before 1900, it is difficult to argue that, except for Nanchang in the 1860s, a gentry-led movement against Christianity took shape either locally or provincewide.

Since there appears to have been no coordinated movement, but only isolated and scattered cases, government officials dealt successfully with most *jiao'an*. Local officials deserve some credit for their management of these cases and for preventing their escalation into larger diplomatic problems for the dynasty. This becomes clear in the following chapters as I develop and elaborate on the theme that most problems between Christians and non-Christians pivoted on specific secular or personal matters.

In the next chapter I present an overview of Catholicism's arrival, establishment, and growth in Jiangxi, as well as the nature of Church life. A close look at Catholicism at the community level reveals that neither European missionaries nor even Chinese priests served as the everyday leaders of most congregations. Instead, we find catechists and local lay leaders guiding local Catholics. Coming from a variety of occupations, Catholics were no different from ordinary Chinese with whom they lived and worked. Nor were Catholics individually or collectively islands unto themselves; they maintained family, social, and business relationships with non-Christian relatives and neighbors.

In chapter 3 I determine where, why, and how missionaries established churches, chapels, and oratories. The vast majority of these places of worship were located in the countryside where rural Catholics played an important role in financing and supporting them. However, new operations and buildings led to problems, as did the ongoing contact between Christians and non-Christians. Examples of the problems that occurred are drawn from several counties and illustrate their multi-causal and mundane nature.

Chapter 4 focuses on tensions among lineages and families. The case studies show clearly that problems could arise for almost any reason and become very complex for those involved. Within lineages and families we find the involvement of women, and especially widows, to be a complicating factor for everyone concerned. Cases that involve widows' property "rights" help us understand not only the economic, but also the personal dimensions of contact between Christians and non-Christians. We need to remember that those involved were motivated and affected by love, hate, jealousy, anger, and "face." People's emotions sometimes led them to actions that resulted in personal tragedy, but had nothing to do with their station in life or religious beliefs.

Property transactions and disputes are the subject of chapter 5. After examining treaty arrangements regarding property purchase rights and procedures for missionaries and Christians, I delve into several cases. The prominent issues here include competition for land resources and improper or fraudulent transactions. Where geomancy emerged as an issue, the parties involved, interestingly, did not highlight cultural beliefs or attempt to make religion the main basis of their opposition.

Chapter 6 concerns the dynasty's local security concerns as they related to Christians. Many provincial and local officials had private doubts about the political reliability of Christians, yet somehow they had to maintain law and order and keep everyone under control. Whether a conflict was caused by a Christian or a non-Christian, officials all took suppression of disorder as their foremost duty. This meant, at least in the Nanchang area during the 1860s, eventually reining in the gentry and dampening their enthusiasm for anti-Christian activities. Elsewhere it meant using the gentry according to the dictates of local circumstances, and either closing or opening militia bureaus. It also meant using the *baojia* (local mutual responsibility or security) system and *dibao* (local agents of the county bureaucracy) to deal with conflict. The case studies in this chapter show Christians as both malefactors and victims and demonstrate that security problems usually had secular roots.

The last chapter considers a case in which rural Catholics lived peacefully with their non-Catholic kith and kin. At the village of Jiudu in eastern Jiangxi we find an unusual opportunity for extended observation of Christianity in the countryside, of residents resolving their differences over religion, and of life lived during normal times.[50] At Jiudu Catholicism seems to have been in tune with the rhythms of rural society. There and elsewhere in the countryside, Catholic mission work appears to have been carried out pragmatically and flexibly, especially in terms of contact with non-Catholics. Priests often allowed baptized girls raised in Catholic orphanages to marry non-Catholics, and welcomed non-Catholic involvement in the care of children in their orphanages. Ordinary Catholics were flexible, too. How they managed to accommodated their faith, and how non-Catholic relatives and neighbors accommodated them, are among the untold stories of Christianity in China.

Chapter 2

Jiangxi's Rural Christians
And Congregations

M ost studies of Christianity in China, preoccupied with the diplomatic
ramifications of various incidents or the cultural gap revealed by
certain cases of conflict, have not looked closely at Christianity at the
local level. It was, after all, in city or town neighborhoods or in village or
rural districts, where actual contact between missionaries, Christians, and
non-Christians occurred. In China's tightly knit communities people
typically lived and worked close together, constrained mainly by Confucian
standards of behavior and the need for social harmony. Christians were
concurrently members of a family, a kinship group, and a local community.
Although religion may have affected some relationships, Christians and
non-Christians still had to deal with everyday matters of personal and
mutual concern. This chapter will explore the shape and role of the
Catholic Church in Jiangxi's rural communities. Besides examining the
respective activities of priests and catechists in their areas of ministry, we
will look at individual Catholics and their socioeconomic backgrounds.
From the cases under consideration, it will become clear that friction
between Catholics and non-Catholic neighbors in the countryside usually
had little to do with religion.

Background on the Church in Jiangxi

Father Matteo Ricci and a small group of travelers left Guangdong
Province in 1594 with the goal of establishing the Society of Jesus in
Beijing. However, Ming officials at Nanjing prohibited them from proceeding further. Forced back along the route he came, Father Ricci
arrived at Nanchang. Feeling welcome there, he stayed and began Jiangxi's
first mission station on June 28, 1595.[1] Although Ricci departed four
years later, other Jesuit priests followed to proselytize in the province. In

1616 Father João da Rocha established Jiangxi's second mission at Jianchang (Nancheng), a joint prefectural-county seat in the province's eastern section. Some four decades later another Jesuit priest opened a church in southern Jiangxi at Ganzhou (Gan, also a joint prefectural-county seat). By the 1680s the Jesuits had erected at least seven churches, mostly in the north, and four or five priests ministered to the province's several thousand Catholics.[2]

Too few Jesuit priests in a large area with many people amounted to a call for assistance. Over time and in small numbers, missionaries from the Society of Foreign Missions in Paris (Société des Missions Etrangères) and the mendicant orders, that is, Augustinians, Dominicans, and Franciscans, arrived to help. Of these, the Franciscans were the most important. The first Franciscan friars crossed over the Meiling Pass from Guangdong into southern Jiangxi in 1685. Within two years they had purchased property and established a church and residence at Nan'an (Dayu), a joint prefectural-county seat and convenient first rest stop for missionaries traveling north. Over the next decade friars made fourteen hundred converts in the area. By the end of the 1690s the Franciscans had established six missions in southern Jiangxi; their work at these and other locations continued into the eighteenth century.[3] Catholicism had bright moments elsewhere in the province, too. In 1712, for instance, a missionary baptized fifty adults in just one month at Jingdezhen, the famous center for fine porcelain production.[4]

The Yongzheng emperor's 1724 proscription of Christianity, however, deeply affected continued growth. Throughout China, officials implemented the edict by expelling missionaries and confiscating Church property. The priests who remained moved about with extreme caution. In Jiangxi the personal safety of missionaries depended upon moving only among Catholics whom they trusted and by avoiding the cities. One Franciscan lived with devout Catholics for extended periods during the 1770s while proselytizing in southern Jiangxi.[5] Through the years additional imperial edicts and government actions brought further pressure against Christianity. In 1784–1785 officials arrested priests in different provinces, including Jiangxi, and sent them to Beijing to be imprisoned.[6] The Qing's efforts to proscribe Christianity varied from area to area, yet the net effect was to severely curtail open Church activities and hinder growth of Catholic congregations.

Missionaries from the Congregation of the Mission arrived in Macao during this dark time. The Vincentians came to replace the Jesuits, whose society the pope dissolved in 1773. After assuming control of Jesuit affairs in Beijing in 1785, the Vincentians, who came predominately from France, gradually assumed responsibility for other formerly Jesuit areas, including Jiangxi. Father Jean-François-Régis Clet passed through Jiangxi in 1792 on his way to Hubei Province. He spent almost a year in Jiangxi drawing new converts to the Church. He commented:

> I have baptized over a hundred adults who were sufficiently well instructed. I could have baptized a much greater number who asked for this favour, but I thought they had not sufficient knowledge of the doctrine; and we have noticed that catechumens who are easily baptized also easily fall away under persecution.[7]

Over forty years passed before the next Vincentian priest from Europe arrived in Jiangxi. During this long interregnum, the mission made adjustments. By necessity and default, the Church entrusted the faithful to the care of Chinese clergy.[8] The few remaining Chinese priests in turn had to use catechists to watch over and maintain the faith of the scattered rural congregations. The proscription of Christianity forced priests to keep a low profile and to avoid trouble. Priests sometimes traveled at night and steered clear of administrative centers to avoid contact with officials.

Given the Qing government's position, Catholicism had went underground to survive, operating in a manner similar to that of other "religious sects."[9] However, the rapid expansion of Western interests and a Western presence in China during the early nineteenth century revitalized Church activities. In 1833 Father Bernard-Vincent Laribe arrived in Jiangxi, establishing himself in a village located near the province's second-oldest site of Christian activity, Jianchang, where he worked openly and successfully. According to Father Laribe, about six thousand Catholics lived in Jiangxi's far-flung congregations. He tried to visit each congregation once a year and lay a foundation for more growth.[10] The return of European priests, increasing numbers of Chinese clergy, and changing times made it possible for Catholics to establish new churches such as the one built in 1834 at Meijia Lane just outside Wucheng, an important commercial center on the shores of Poyang Lake north of Nanchang.[11] Throughout the province, Christian congregations openly and steadily expanded.

Following the first Opium War, the French obtained concessions for Christian missions in imperial edicts of 1844 and 1846. The Qing now officially permitted the construction of churches, but only in the five treaty ports. Under certain conditions old church buildings in the interior could be returned to the Catholic Church, and Chinese who sincerely believed in Christianity could now practice their faith without fear of punishment.[12] Chinese law still prohibited missionaries from entering the hinterland, yet many did so surreptitiously. Wearing disguises to hide their nationality and occupation, some priests entered Jiangxi via the overland route from Guangdong, while others went by boat to Fujian, then by foot to Jiangxi.

Church growth soon warranted the creation of a separate vicariate apostolic for Jiangxi, which the Holy See placed under the control of the Congregation of the Mission in 1845.[13] The first vicar apostolic (a titular bishop) appointed from the Congregation was Father François-Alexis Rameaux. Bishop Rameaux admired the accomplishments of Father Laribe and other priests and supported their efforts to establish Church schools while nurturing the faith among Catholics. Just three years later, Catholics succeeded in building a new church at Wucheng.[14]

There are not many early numerical summaries for Jiangxi, but one made in 1841 counted 6,998 Catholics in the province.[15] Only one bishop and six Vincentian confreres watched over all of them, although one Dominican priest also remained active in Jiangxi.[16] Such numbers appear to be accurate and are consistent with tallies made by other priests over the next decade.[17] In 1849 ten priests cared for 8,536 Catholics; altogether there were twenty-five churches or chapels, one seminary, and eight schools.[18] When the Taiping Rebellion erupted in Guangxi and then spread northward, there were around nine thousand Catholics in scattered congregations all across Jiangxi.[19]

The rebellion's intense, prolonged fighting and the chaos it generated meant terrible suffering for Catholics. Initially at least, the Taipings kept friction with Catholics and missionaries to a minimum because the rebels saw them as brethren if not allies. One missionary reported that in some areas the Taipings burned down temples but not chapels.[20] During the mid-1850s rebels occupied most of Jianchang Prefecture and maintained friendly relations with the missionaries in the village of Jiudu. The Taipings for the most part respected the Catholics of this village and did not destroy the extensive Church property there. A friendly Taiping leader stationed in Jianchang issued missionaries seven travel-security passes so they could freely visit Catholic congregations in other parts of rebel-occupied Jiangxi.[21]

With time Taiping-Catholic relations deteriorated, partly because of Anglo-French military assistance to the Qing.[22] As imperial forces mounted successful counteroffensives, trouble developed between Taipings and Catholics. As rebel forces became more desperate and less disciplined, they fought and looted to survive, unconcerned whether their victims were Christian or not. Taipings destroyed Catholic homes and shops, as well as Church property all over Jiangxi. During the rebellion period, especially its last half, some three thousand Chinese Catholics—one third of the total number in Jiangxi—died. Most of these deaths were a consequence of the general rebellion, but a number of them resulted directly from Taiping depredation.[23]

Catholics suffered not only at the hands of the Taipings, but also at the hands of imperial forces fighting the rebels. The dynasty had long suspected missionaries and Catholics of disloyalty. The imperial edict of 1724 made these suspicions public and probably contributed to the general association of Christians with the proscribed White Lotus sect.[24] Over the rest of the eighteenth century officials periodically arrested priests on the charge of participating in this sect.[25] In the nineteenth century local officials, gentry, and common people in various parts of Jiangxi linked Catholics with the rebellious religious sect known to officials as the "Vegetarians" or "Vegetarian bandits" (*zhaifei*).[26] According to the French priest Father Anot, in the mid-1840s an official visiting Sanqiao, a rural locality in Gao'an County that was home to many Catholics, called it a village of "fasters" (from eating meat), that is, Vegetarians.[27] Later, the Taiping leader Hong Xiuquan's modified Christian theology would lead many to link Catholics with the Taipings. With the imperial armies regarding Catholics as rebels,[28] it is not surprising that in 1857 a Qing military officer in Wucheng ordered his soldiers to kill the church caretaker, destroy the church, and demolish all shops owned by Catholics because of his doubts about their loyalty.[29] Wucheng's Catholics soon rebuilt at Dagou Lane but that church, under circumstances not disclosed in official reports, was also destroyed by fire in the same year.[30]

While political distrust of Christians apparently knew no geographical or "class" bounds,[31] letters from missionaries who served in Jiangxi contain only one report of converting a Vegetarian sect leader and his family.[32]

Even though the association of Catholics with sectarians is unjustified by the facts, the mere perception that even small Catholic congregations posed a threat to local order must have affected them, unnecessarily making them targets of government control measures and general suspicion.[33] When Catholics came under suspicion for collaboration or sympathy with rebels, there were grave political consequences for them and diplomatic complications for the Qing, who were bound by foreign-relations concerns to protect Christians from undue harassment and harm.

The Shape of Church Congregations

Details about Church personnel and congregations are quite sketchy in most studies of Christianity in China. Missionaries had many duties and responsibilities, and information about their role in the various congregations under their care helps bring into focus the extent of their influence locally, the regular activities of Chinese priests, and the critical importance of the local lay leaders. Records on the process of conversion point to the central role played by catechists and indicate that day-to-day Church activities were in their hands. From the *jiao'an* materials we also gain insight into the personal importance of conversion to local Catholics, and the Chinese perspective on the point at which one became a Catholic. These details flesh out in an important way our understanding of the experience of Christians in rural China.

Missionaries and Chinese Priests

Except for their names and brief biographical data, we do not have much information on the individual missionaries and indigenous priests who served in Jiangxi; we know little about their respective backgrounds, personalities, abilities, or work habits.[34] To go to China from Europe for lifelong service with no expectation of returning home on furlough or for retirement meant that missionaries were men of high devotion to their faith and their work. Once in-country, most priests, and especially those in the interior, lived in isolation from the treaty-port world. Catholic missionaries of one order or congregation seldom had contact with those of another and usually had limited knowledge of common problems or achievements. For many years at a time, missionaries operated exclusively within their own organization's provincial jurisdiction or vicariate.[35] Often alone or isolated from confreres, struggling with the Chinese language, lacking the comforts of home, and sometimes lacking physical security, missionaries had a hard life, one compounded by constant travel. Of course, Chinese priests also endured hardships. Although they usually came from long-time Catholic families and probably took some solace in their families' support for their endeavors, they still spent most of their time away from home and on the road.[36] One veteran Chinese priest went so far as to suggest that priests *should* minimize contact with relatives to become accustomed to the demands of "detachment and disinterestedness."[37]

Catholic clergy traveled constantly in Jiangxi because so few of them had to serve such a large and densely populated area. We can make a reasonably precise count of Vincentian missionaries and Chinese priests who worked in the province during the nineteenth century. In 1832 we find one French and six Chinese priests; by 1849 the number had increased to four French and six Chinese priests; in 1871 the Church stationed six European and thirteen Chinese clergy in Jiangxi; in 1884 the count stood at twenty-one European priests and six sisters, along with twenty-three Chinese priests; and in 1898–1899 there were thirty-six European priests and twenty sisters, together with eighteen Chinese priests.[38] The Church spread its personnel thinly and gave them large jurisdictions to supervise. During the late 1860s, for example, the vicar apostolic—or bishop—of Jiangxi assigned Father Fu Ruhan to go to Ji'an, Ruizhou, and Linjiang prefectures as well as other undisclosed places to propagate Catholicism.[39] In 1870 Chinese officials noted that a single missionary working in Fuzhou Prefecture traveled constantly.[40] Again in 1889 officials commented that a missionary assigned to preach in Ji'an, Fuzhou, and other prefectures moved about unpredictably.[41]

Consequently, in Jiangxi, as elsewhere in China, few Catholic congregations had the benefit of a resident priest.[42] Western and Chinese clergy could at best assume only a supervisory role over the faithful. Depending upon the size of the congregation, a priest might visit it once or twice a year for a stay of one day to two weeks. In this brief stay the priest had to make time to celebrate Mass, administer the sacraments, hear confessions, catechize the young, check on the congregation's morals, and, if necessary, settle local Catholic quarrels or expel the wayward.[43]

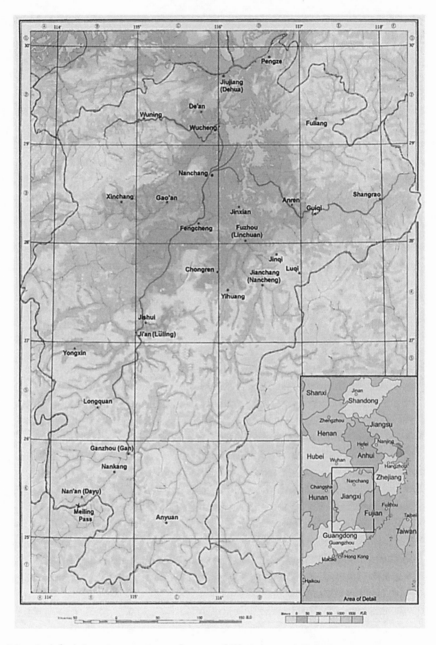

Map 1: Administrative centers and areas of Christian activity

Special circumstances in a locality could draw the attention or call for the presence of a priest. For example, a Catholic dispute with local officials over ownership of vacant land led one missionary to go to Ganzhou City in 1873.[44] Missionaries might also go to an area to initiate the construction of a new church or to supervise some other building project.[45]

Few missionaries tolerated Chinese government-imposed restrictions on their freedom to travel or, for that matter, on their actions. To be sure, missionaries enjoyed rights guaranteed by treaty, and this encouraged certain expectations. Missionaries commonly sought and often gained direct access to a range of provincial and local officials, even though this access was not provided for by treaty.[46] Missionaries saw themselves as the official equals of government office holders and the social equals of local gentry. At times, missionaries traveled by palanquin, with pennants and an entourage—a manner befitting a Chinese official. This gave them a certain prestige and minimized inconvenience, especially in the countryside. Not unlike the treatment villagers afforded officials, Catholics sometimes greeted missionaries by setting off firecrackers and by prostrating themselves. Bishop François-Adrien Rouger received this welcome in 1884 when he arrived in the Langqi area. In other provinces Catholics even greeted the arrival of priests this way.[47]

Vincentian missionaries who spent most of their adult lives in Jiangxi sometimes encountered serious health problems. When illness or injury warranted and circumstances permitted, the missionary went to Jiujiang (Dehua, a joint prefectural-county seat and open treaty port after 1861), Ningbo, and sometimes to Shanghai for medical treatment.[48] If the missionary died in Jiangxi, his confreres buried him at the local church cemetery or in the cemetery at one of the larger churches in places such as Nanchang and Fuzhou (Linchuan, a joint prefectural-county seat in eastern Jiangxi). When Laribe, then a bishop, died in Wucheng in 1850, he received a burial ceremony befitting his rank. Likewise, when Joseph-Martial Mouly, the Vincentian vicar apostolic of Zhili, died in Beijing in 1868 he was buried with all the pomp and ritual due his station, in an ancient cemetery to the west of the city that included the graves of Ricci, Schall, and other famous early missionaries.[49]

Missionaries have generally been castigated for their high-handed and biased efforts to protect all Catholics from anything they thought smacked of harassment.[50] One explanation for this approach is that due to their large ecclesiastical circuits and heavy work burdens, missionaries in

Jiangxi often had to work with less than complete information about the problems Catholics were involved in.[51] Some priests, sharply aware of this deficiency, enlisted Chinese Catholics to investigate for them.[52] Others assertively urged Chinese officials to pursue all Catholic-generated griev-ances, some of which led to court and detailed testimony from those summoned. Regardless of their resources and methods, missionaries genuinely tried to support Catholics embroiled in legal cases or community problems. And sometimes, as noted by one Chinese scholar, their assertiveness and intervention in the legal system promoted fair treatment for Catholics who had been wronged.[53]

Catechists and Other Lay Leaders

Whether located in an urban area or in the countryside, a Catholic congregation usually did not have a resident priest. How did the congre-gation maintain itself during the priest's absence? Who played prominent roles in leading it, and what were their responsibilities? Depending upon the locality, a congregation might have included several categories of members: adorers, catechumens, and lay people, along with their catechists, lay leaders, elders, and headmen. Each of these, of course, constituted an important element within the congregation.

Once a person expressed interest in learning about the Catholic faith, a priest or catechist would first enroll him or her as an adorer. According to Father Antoine Anot, this did not constitute conversion but was rather a "first grace," whereby the person's heart opened and made possible the receiving of Christian teachings. At this moment it was crucial that the priest arrive and begin explaining and exhorting lest the "semi-convert" turn away.[54] If the adorer, usually under the care and direction of a catechist since the missionary traveled so much, mastered the rudiments of Catholic doctrine and if he disavowed belief in idols and discontinued ancestor veneration, enrollment as a catechumen came next, followed by baptism and confirmation. This at least was the ideal situation; in fact there was much variation.

From each congregation, depending on its numerical size, the priest selected one or more Catholics to serve as catechists.[55] Catechists were congregation members who had already received baptism and confir-mation; they tended to be adult males. Normally the priest selected the catechist, but sometimes the catechist seems to have emerged from the membership, distinguished by age, knowledge, or preexisting position in the congregation. One missionary in Jiangxi characterized catechists as "the most distinguished among Christians."[56] However catechists came to their position, and whatever their motivation to serve, they in fact assumed critical responsibilities and often led their congregations.

The presence and key role of catechists in Jiangxi is evident as early as 1700,[57] and missionary accounts from different times and places in China during the eighteenth century confirm their importance.[58] Not surprisingly, missionaries arriving in China during the early nineteenth century also relied heavily on them. According to spokesmen for the Catholic Church writing about missions in China and Asia in 1839 in *Annals of the Propagation of the Faith*, there were two types of catechists: "travellers" and "settled." The former often accompanied priests, serving as guides and assistants. The Church required them to be celibate, partly because of their priest-like duties and partly because priests sometimes sent them to visit congregations on their own. The latter type, usually married or widowed men, remained in their home villages. Both had similar duties: They presided over prayer meetings and read religious lessons; they catechized and taught; they exhorted, consoled, and supported Catholics in need of care; they baptized the infants of Catholics as well as non-Catholic children and adults on the verge of death; they conducted funeral services; they solved problems and kept the congregation together. Catechists also made the first all-important overture to interest non-Catholics in Christianity. In sum, catechists nurtured and protected the flock until the priest's next visit. Upon the priest's arrival the catechist then reported, as a sort of group confessor, on the congregation's religious health.[59]

The Church expected much from its catechists. How did priests train and prepare these pivotal figures for their demanding and extensive duties? At first, there seems to have been no systematic, organized approach; in Jiangxi the Church left much to the discretion of individual priests. Consequently, the quality and dedication of catechists varied. One missionary had two catechists swear on the bible during church services that "they would teach in all its purity the doctrine of Christ and discharge to the best of their power the other duties of their office."[60] How they actually performed is unknown. Another priest, Father Joseph Li, commented on the inadequacies of six catechists he encountered in the Nanchang area. He noted that they had received little training and needed to be molded in order to support him.[61] During visits to nearly all his congregations in the early 1840s, Bishop Rameaux appointed many catechists and charged them with instructing "neophytes," initiating Christian practices, and baptizing children in danger of death.[62] In 1846 the new bishop of Jiangxi, Bernard-Vincent Laribe, established a plan for the training of *catechistes-prêcheurs* and put a specific priest in charge of implementing it. An important objective for the bishop was the refutation of "superstitious books."[63] Much later, Bishop Jules-Auguste Coqset noted in 1892 that the Vicariate of Southern Jiangxi needed a school in which to train "good catechists."[64] Unfortunately, details on just what constituted a "good" catechist and glimpses of catechists in action in the nineteenth century are rare.

Catholic elders and headmen were also important. Kenneth Scott Latourette finds these types of leaders prevalent in west China in congregations lacking resident priests or catechists.[65] Local Catholics themselves evidently selected the headmen and the bishop approved them. Although Catholic elders and headmen may not have had special religious training or perhaps only training comparable to that given catechists, they still played an important role in their congregations. Their duties included supervision of the Catholic community; care for the sick and dying; conduct of religious services, including public prayers as well as baptisms, wedding and funeral rites; and the introduction of non-believers to Christianity.[66] The strong functional similarity between Catholic elders or headmen and catechists in different regions makes the distinction between them nominal.[67] Any similar role played by women goes unmentioned in the primary sources.

Likewise, I find no specific mention of elders or headmen among the letters written by missionaries and priests in Jiangxi. The *jiao'an* materials for Jiangxi, however, present a fully Chinese perspective and regularly mention adult male converts identified as *jiaotou*. Literally meaning "religious headman," this seems to have been the local term for catechist.[68] *Jiaotou* was the term such leaders themselves used. Catholics knew them by this title, and men who were *jiaotou* freely disclosed their position to local officials. In the Chinese view, *jiaotou* were the crucial link in the conversion process. One man recalled, "On April 1, 1874, I took Zou Yaya [a *jiaotou*] as my teacher [*shi*] and studied Catholicism."[69] Since other new converts claimed to have this teacher-student relationship to several other men in the same locale, it can be inferred that they served as *jiaotou*, too.[70] *Jiaotou* also assumed the prerogative of rejecting converts if they acted wrongly. "On February 27, 1873, I became a Catholic," stated one man. "Later, because I was not friendly with [other] Catholics, the *jiaotou* expelled me."[71]

With the exception of one *jiansheng* degree holder, Wang Jiarui, who acted as a *jiaotou* and who may have become a priest, all other lay leaders seen in Jiangxi's *jiao'an* came from the ranks of the common people. As *jiaotou*, they commanded some prestige and power, rendering assistance to Catholics whenever possible. For instance, when in 1872 a *gongsheng* degree holder publicly upbraided a Catholic for refusing to contribute money for a local theatrical performance and then attending anyway, the insulted Catholic immediately turned to a *jiaotou* and together they planned to redress the affront. After they physically attacked the degree holder, officials arrested them, but later released them on bond to another *jiaotou*.[72]

In Yihuang County in 1874 officials arrested nine Catholics and one *jiaotou* for their part in a series of crimes. Another *jiaotou* immediately stepped forward and presented a petition to local officials in which he defended the law-abiding record of the area's long-time Catholics. He declared that the men arrested had only recently converted, a fact corroborated by the criminals' own depositions. He also admitted that no one had first checked on the character of the men. Rather than defending them as fellow Catholics, the *jiaotou* hoped officials would punish the men quickly and sternly to clear the record of local Church members.[73]

One further example helps illustrate the range of activities engaged in by *jiaotou*. In Qiposhan, a rural area about eighteen miles from the Jinxian county seat, Catholics refused in 1891 to contribute any money towards the expenses of a local festival. Word about trouble between Catholics and local people in nearby Xiebu, a rural marketplace, added to the tension. Violence seemed imminent. A *jiaotou* of one village began to prepare the Catholics for self-defense. According to a deputy who investigated the situation, the *jiaotou* "slaughtered pigs and gathered [the Catholic] people together, preparing knives and spears with which to resist [attack]."[74] This *jiaotou* displayed real talent as an organizer.

Clearly, *jiaotou* acted not only as catechists but also as leaders of their congregations. Other prominent positions in local Jiangxi congregations included congregational headmen (*huizhang*, *jiaozhang*), church managers (*jiaodongshi*, *dongshi*, *guanshiren*, *guanshi*, and *sishi*), and church caretakers (*kanjiaotang*). The latter usually had living quarters provided at the church, as did some church managers.[75] These men probably had some influence over other Catholics who resided at or near the church.[76] Unfortunately, *jiao'an* materials say nothing specific about either their roles or functions. Nor is there evidence to support Prince Gong's 1875 condemnation of chapel keepers as local bullies, troublemakers, and obstacles to justice.[77] To be sure, the *jiaotou* cited above who was arrested in Yihuang County qualified on two of these counts. However, most catechists and other lay leaders seem to have been honest, law-abiding subjects of the Qing dynasty.

Conversion to Catholicism

Missionaries and Chinese priests used various means to attract new adherents to the faith. Potential converts were exposed to the Church through sermons, medical work, aid to the poor; through the establishment of schools, orphanages, and opium refuges; and through intervention in lawsuits. The course of religious instruction, according to one scholar, seems to have been the same for the various Catholic orders and congregations. In 1864 the vicar apostolic for Guizhou, Louis Faurie, described clearly and at length the ceremony by which one became an adorer, the first step toward the faith:

> When a pagan has been told what he is to understand by the true religion and . . . declares his belief in one God and his desire to become a Christian, he is . . . taught the sign of the cross. As soon as he can do this without being prompted two candles are lighted on the altar and he is placed on his knees. He holds in his hands a paper on which is printed all that he has to repeat. An old Christian kneels near him, so as to be able to direct him how to answer. The ceremony commences by making the sign of the cross: then five prostrations while reciting the following words:
>
> First prostration. "I believe in God. I abjure all my past errors."
>
> Second prostration. "I hope that God in His infinite goodness, will forgive all my sins."
>
> Third prostration. "I love and adore God, beautiful, almighty, more than anything else in this world."
>
> Fourth prostration. "I detest with all my heart the sins of my past life and I firmly resolve never to commit them again."
>
> Fifth prostration. "I pray the Blessed Virgin Mary, my mother, to obtain for me from God, by her powerful intercession, the grace of final perseverance."
>
> After this the Apostles' Creed is recited, also Our Father, Hail Mary, and the Ten Commandments. Then is added this declaration:

"The commandments of God that I have just recited are contained in these two: To love God above all things and one's neighbor as oneself. These ten commandments have been dictated by God that all nations might observe them. Those who keep them faithfully will be recompensed with eternal glory in heaven. Those who disobey them will be condemned by Him to the eternal torments of hell."[78]

The applicant "then concluded with five thanksgivings—for the creation, nourishment, and preservation of his life, for redemption, for pardon for sins, for having been brought to a knowledge of the true religion, and for all other blessings."[79] The ceremony thus ended, and the priest enrolled the applicant as an adorer. The priest expected the adorer to go to Mass and to follow Catholic precepts. Significantly, the adorer now considered himself a Catholic.[80]

The next step was enrollment as a catechumen. The Catholic Church decreed that before admittance to baptism one must not only study devoutly, but also observe Church doctrine. In other words, the Church put the catechumen on probation. When the catechumen demonstrated through knowledge of "his catechism, the chief mysteries of the Faith, the more important Catholic symbols, the Lord's prayer, the Ten Commandments, the precepts of the Church, and the effect of baptism," and through his actions that he had no involvement with opium, concubines, or other behavior the church considered immoral, then he could be baptized.[81] In Guizhou the process of moving from adorer to baptism, that is, of learning Church doctrine and rites and demonstrating sincerity via the approved moral life style took about two years. After a priest had baptized the catechumen, bishops had responsibility for the final step, confirmation. But because of the size of their jurisdictions, many bishops had no choice but to let priests handle that process, too.[82] From the perspective of the Church, the confirmed person was now a bona fide Catholic.

A general description of the process of attracting and converting non-believers to Christianity in Jiangxi during the nineteenth century can be pieced together only from miscellaneous statements of different priests. One of them felt that this work benefited from the good example set by those who had already converted.[83] In 1842 another priest mentioned the good results achieved by converting merchants and artisans. Honest, sensible, affable, and frequently in contact with many others, these men made the spread of the faith easier.[84] The character and business success of these Catholics impressed others and attracted them to Christianity. Priests found converts of quality and means not only in Jiangxi, but elsewhere as well. In Sichuan during the eighteenth century, Catholics came from different strata of society and a missionary visitor to that province in the 1840s observed that the majority of them came from the "middle ranks of society."[85]

In Jiangxi in 1860 Father Rouger wrote of a first encounter with a man who came to him expressing interest in Christianity. The priest spoke with him at length and gave him books in Chinese on the catechism, prayers, and two volumes written by Chinese colleagues. Father Rouger suggested that the man pray and the man replied that he did not know how. The priest then told him to recite in his language, according to the practice of local Catholics the following prayer: "By the sign of this saintly cross, O' Lord our God, deliver us from our enemies, in the name of the Father, the Son, and the Holy Spirit."[86] The man did so, taking the first and most difficult step towards Christianity.

Instruction in Christian doctrine and catechism were critical to advancing an adorer to baptism. In 1852 a missionary in Jiangxi wrote that his work was difficult because of the basic ignorance of doctrine on the part of prospective Catholics who had never received religious instruction as children. With this in mind, he set out to catechize children each Sunday.[87] Another priest stated that he required four catechisms of all children.[88] The course of instruction or probation in Jiangxi lasted various lengths of time. Father Anot reported in 1872 that some catechumens requested baptism after a few months and others after five years.[89] Father Rouger, like most priests, delegated to catechists the task of educating the catechumens.[90] Clearly, the Catholic clergy intended to emphasize religious instruction and maintain standards. Letters written by priests convey a strong sense of concern for fostering sincere and good Catholics. Moreover, missionaries often distinguished in their reports between catechumens and lay people, noting how many of their congregation were preparing for baptism. For the priests, conversion to Christianity could not formally occur until one had passed through a process of religious training.

Information from Jiangxi's *jiao'an* helps us understand conversion from the Chinese side. For example, we can see that people treated conversion to Christianity as a noteworthy event in terms of family history. The Xiaos, proprietors of a beancurd shop in Potou, a marketplace in Lüling County, proudly stated that "since the Ming dynasty [their family] had been Catholic (*rujiao*) for ten generations."[91] A man living in the same county stated that "I [and my family] have been Catholic for five generations (*xiaode chile wudai jiao*)."[92] Another man said "[my family] has been Catholic (*rujiao*) for three generations."[93] Some newcomers to Christianity remembered the exact day of their conversion. One man stated that on "the eleventh day of the second month of the thirteenth year of Tongzhi [March 28, 1874], I became a Catholic (*tourujiao*)."[94] Clearly, making the commitment to Catholicism was memorable for individuals and significant for families.

The Chinese words used to signify "conversion" also help clarify the view of Catholicism held by ordinary people. The most commonly used terms in the *jiao'an* documents are *rujiao* and *jinjiao* (literally, to enter the faith), but *fengjiao* (to receive or accept the faith), and *xijiao* (to practice the faith) are also used to indicate that one followed Christian beliefs.[95] From the contexts in which these terms were used, it is clear that individuals actually made a commitment to enter into or receive religious instruction, to study and practice Catholicism, rather than receive the rite of baptism. I believe that these new adherents were technically either adorers or catechumens, and according to Church canon they were not yet Catholic. From the Chinese perspective, however, people felt that they had "entered the religion" or converted.

The examples of conversion cited in the sources primarily involve men. Given the male domination of traditional China, it is not surprising that the conversion of adult men had considerable impact on other family members. Hailing from the joint prefectural-county seat Ji'an (Lüling), in 1869 Wu Aiyao explained it this way, "When I was young I followed my father in converting (*rujiao*) to Catholicism."[96] Another man revealed even stronger paternal influence: "Since my father converted so did the rest of the family."[97] In rural Xinchang County in February of 1868 one Yan Bingyi and his entire family converted at the same time.[98] Another father did not oppose the conversion of an adult son because he saw it as an act of self-improvement. The son's wife and concubine converted, too.[99] The Church did not permit concubinage, and how it handled this situation passes without mention. Nor do we know how the wife and concubine felt about becoming Catholic. In another instance, we learn of a widowed mother led to Christianity by her adult son.[100]

There is some evidence of women exercising a parallel influence. Priests certainly saw Christian women as having a positive effect on members of their families and on neighbors. Devout women lived

Christian lives when married and resolutely kept the faith as widows.[101] There are also records dating at least to the 1840s in Jiangxi, and even earlier in Sichuan, of unmarried Catholic women, so-called "consecrated virgins," who devoted themselves to a religious life.[102] Since the Church in Jiangxi had no convents for women, they continued to live with their families or independently. Father Joseph Li mentions, for example, sixty virgins who lived in poverty and survived by either farming, gathering herbs, collecting firewood, or weaving. He notes that they were all good and pious women.[103]

Missionaries also had high hopes that the girls of Catholic families, as well as orphaned and abandoned girls raised by the Church, if married to non-Catholics, would have a beneficial impact on their husbands and their in-laws. Father Rouger wrote in 1879 of a "brave" Catholic woman who after marrying a non-believer helped bring about his conversion and the baptism of their children.[104] Examples such as this encouraged missionaries, who knew that the children of some Catholic families might be lost to the Church. In Jianchang Prefecture during the latter decades of the nineteenth century, poor Catholic families sold more than two hundred young daughters to non-Catholic families.[105] This situation decreased the possibility of creating new and all-Catholic families from the marriage of these girls to Catholic men.

If the Church's ideal was an all-Catholic family, how many families converted together or eventually became entirely Catholic? Aside from recording the number of marriages, data provided by priests does not give details that would clarify who came to Christ as an individual or as part of a family group. Indirectly, through priests' comments about particular people and events, some relevant information comes to light, however. For example, one Catholic woman married a non-Catholic who never converted. Nonetheless, ten of their eleven children received baptism.[106] In another village, Father Wang Renhao (Joseph Wang) noted that in 1890 "fourteen entire families renounced their superstitions" and became catechumens. Over a period of a few years, forty people from these families received baptism.[107] The commitment of so many families at one time was unusual; the gradual conversion of individuals over time probably was more the norm. Although priests certainly wanted the conversion of whole family units and made it one of their goals, with so many variables involved in family life, the baptism of all members of a family at the same time was difficult to achieve.

Given this difficulty it would be surprising to find evidence of villages or lineages converting en masse. Rather than all at once, the conversion of a village would have come over time. Even so, I have not come across any villages in Jiangxi that I can verify as completely Catholic.[108] There are, however, accounts of the "conversion" of entire, probably single-lineage, villages in neighboring Guangdong during the 1860s and after.[109] These villages evidently became Catholic, as did some in southern Shandong in the 1890s, to gain the protection of missionaries.[110] I believe that the difference between Jiangxi and these two other provinces lies in the fact that Vincentian priests knew from experience and accepted that real converts were made little by little, that is, individuals and sometimes families converted, rather than large groups. In any case, priests in Jiangxi do not mention being approached by lineage groups or by villages seeking protection through collective conversion. Such group conversions would surely have attracted official attention, and yet Chinese records do not contain reports of this phenomenon in Jiangxi either.

Congregation Size and Distribution

From data available for Jiangxi it appears that Catholics comprised only a small numerical part of the villages in which they lived. The statistics priests compiled for Jiangxi for the period from 1840 to 1900 allows for estimates regarding the size range as well as the average size of Catholic congregations.[111] Following his tour of the province in 1842, Bishop Rameaux reported in detail on the many places he visited. He counted altogether 7,110 Catholics and 160 congregations.[112] The locations for these congregations were mostly villages and rural towns, though a few were within county seats and joint prefectural-county seats and their "suburbs." At this time the village of Jiudu appeared to have the largest congregation, with about four hundred Catholics; the next largest had around two hundred. The smallest had only one family, that is, four or five persons, but the bishop did not indicate how many congregations consisted of only a single family.[113] Based on raw numbers alone, the average congregation would have been about forty-four people. Using the figures from 1842, if we remove the two largest and the smallest congregations from the calculation, the average drops to forty-one.[114] In 1881 in northern Jiangxi the average was about forty-nine per congregation.[115] By the end of the nineteenth century there were 23,338 Catholics living in 548, mostly rural, congregations: the average size of each congregation was around forty-three persons. If we add the 15,333 catechumens listed separately to this total, then the average congregation size increases to about seventy-one.[116] Over the nineteenth century, assuming a family size of five people, we thus have on average eight Catholic families and six families of catechumens per congregation, that is, per village with a congregation.[117]

Jiangxi's fertile fields and large population made for densely populated villages, but the size range varied as greatly there as elsewhere in China.[118] When we look at the percentage of Catholics in rural Jiangxi, we find that priests and Chinese officials alike sometimes provided approximate figures. For example, Sanqiao in Gao'an County, where about three hundred Catholics lived in 1884, was mostly Catholic.[119] At other times, priests noted that the Catholic population in three unidentified villages was 80, 67, and 50 percent of the total.[120] The Catholic population of Jiudu seems to have been around 33 percent in the 1840s and may have increased during the 1880s to between 60 and 80 percent.[121] Catholics numbered 50 percent or more in only three or four villages. Where villages included Catholics among the residents, they almost always constituted a minority. Throughout the century different missionaries remarked at how small and scattered the Catholic congregations were in Jiangxi.[122] Clearly, Catholics lacked the numerical strength to be independent communities or the enclaves that some scholars have seen as typical of Catholics.

Furthermore, the Catholics of Jiangxi do not appear to have dominated any village through the control of lineages or as the majority in single-lineage villages. Although lineage organizations were a common feature of rural society in this province, where a kinship group was involved in *jiao'an*, Catholics were always in the minority. Information on one lineage in Longquan County shows that it had more than 180 adult men (*dingkou*), of whom only six headed convert families.[123]

Neither Chinese officials nor priests who worked in Jiangxi mention the conversion of entire lineages. While lineages in Jiangxi sometimes behaved like those in neighboring Guangdong—growing and splitting along socioeconomic axes, resulting in rich-strong and poor-weak branches that generated intralineage tension[124]—there is no evidence that Jiangxi's Catholics came only from disadvantaged branches, or that some kinsmen turned to Christianity due to lineage divisions or related problems.

The Socioeconomic Background of Catholics

Catholics in Jiangxi came from all walks of life. Converts included virtual outcasts, namely "mean people" (*jianmin*) at one end of the social spectrum, and a few lower degree holders (*jiansheng* and *shengyuan*) at the other.[125] Not one Catholic of higher degree status appears in any Jiangxi *jiao'an*.[126] Among the occupations of Catholics we find agricultural laborers and both property-owning and tenant farmers. Carpenters, smiths, masons, and varnish workers became Catholic as well. Some Catholics worked as barbers and tanners (mean professions), and some came from the ranks of the unemployed and the very poor.[127] A few Catholics became highly successful merchants while others ran small shops and sold everything from jewelry to clothing, from beancurd to pork. All these people remained part of the communities in which they lived and had ongoing contact with non-Catholics.[128] The contention that Catholics were "separated from too intimate contact with non-Christian neighbors" is simply not appropriate for Jiangxi.[129]

Certainly the vast majority of Catholics were poor common people, yet so were most Chinese. Catholics did get involved in lawsuits and sometimes broke the law, but this does not mean they tended to be troublemakers or habitual criminals. The social and occupational diversity found among Catholics in Jiangxi makes it difficult to conclude, as others have for Catholics in general, that they were particularly disreputable or disloyal. In fact, there were signs that Catholics actively supported the Qing. One of Nankang County's militia directors who had converted to Catholicism fought against Vegetarian sect bandits threatening the area during the 1850s.[130] Even Western missionaries were known to cooperate with the authorities. In 1874 a French bishop set an example for local Catholics by voluntarily furnishing information that led to the arrest of men planning an uprising in Wuning County.[131]

The Church admittedly did sometimes attract men susceptible to illegal activity, but they were usually from a relatively disenfranchised population already prone to troublemaking. One group of Catholic "converts" was responsible for incidents of assault, robbery, and extortion perpetrated against the well-to-do of Yihuang County in the 1870s. But their social profile and the weakness of their affiliation to the Church suggest that a Catholic identity was at most incidental to their criminal activities. Of the ten men arrested, two were laborers while the rest were without professions and unemployed. None of the men had heavy family obligations or restraints; only one man was married and most of his cohorts indicated that one or both of their parents were deceased. Nine of the ten men had "converted" only two months before their illegal activities began, and one man had been expelled by a *jiaotou* from the ranks of local congregation but remained part of the band.[132] I would venture that this profile is more revealing about patterns of local discontent than conversion patterns. To be sure, Catholicism somehow initially drew these men together, but their exposure to it seems to have been minimal, and their religious belief appears incidental to how and why they acted out their dissatisfaction. This case was certainly atypical of conflict that arose between Catholics and non-Catholics and does not prove that Catholics were less committed to the established order than any other segment of the population.

*   *   *   *   *

Catholic missionaries first began work in Jiangxi in 1594. Although they faced many difficulties, including imperial proscription from 1724 to 1844, missionaries and Chinese priests still made slow but ongoing progress. After 1844, with their presence in China guaranteed by Sino-Western treaty agreements, Catholic efforts intensified. Priests of the Congregation of the Mission in Jiangxi worked in the province's capital city, as well in its remotest villages.

Since missionaries and priests were few in number, their actual presence in the Catholic congregations was restricted to periodic visits. Consequently, they relied heavily on catechists and other lay leaders. Catechists especially played a crucial role in sustaining and preserving Catholic congregations. They conducted services and in general tended to the religious needs of local Catholics. Most significantly, catechists frequently initiated contact with non-believers; their key role in the conversion process cannot be overstated.

Priests and catechists found converts among Chinese of all walks of life. Catholics were mostly common people, but this is to be expected in a society where they were the overwhelming majority. Otherwise, Catholics defy categorization: We find some who were beggars and some who were yeoman farmers, people of the mean professions and those engaged in handicraft work, men and women, old and young, married and single. I can find no justification for sustaining the negative image of Catholics as the dregs, miscreants, outcasts, or disloyal members of Chinese society.

Chapter 3

The Rural Church Presence and Sources of Local Conflict

With the faithful scattered throughout the province, missionaries had to improvise to meet their spiritual needs. Rural Catholics attended religious services in oratories and temporary chapels until sufficient numbers of believers and funds permitted establishment of a formal church. Many Catholics furnished their homes for church use or later donated funds or materials for church construction. But sometimes church construction and the expansion of Catholic activities generated tension and even violence when they engaged local sensitivities.

The Establishment of Churches and Places of Worship

Where priests and congregations built churches and held religious services was certainly a factor in relations between Christians and non-Christians in rural communities. This topic is complex because it involved not only the treaty rights accorded Christian missions but also the socio-cultural changes that resulted from the practice of Catholicism in Jiangxi's towns and villages. A look at the establishment of churches and chapels in Jiangxi brings into sharper focus issues that concerned missionaries in their work and shaped the reception of Christianity in local communities.

The Jiangxi Countryside: Different Locations, Different Needs

The Sino-Western treaties of 1858 and 1860 permitted missionaries to enter China's interior and to recover Catholic Church property confiscated a century earlier. Consequently, after 1860 Catholic missionaries hoped to establish themselves within or close to many principal government administrative centers.[1] Priests had several reasons for doing so: Some former Church properties were located there; major land and water routes provided convenient access to these places; contact with officials and communications to consular officials also proved easier from these locations than elsewhere; and, of course, there remained the symbolic importance of proselytizing in centers of gentry-official authority. Furthermore, after years of ministering to small and often isolated rural congregations, the concentrated populations of the cities were especially attractive. Mission headquarters were often located in or near large cities.

Nanchang, Jiangxi's largest city and provincial capital, combined several of the favorable attributes listed above. Father Ricci had established the first Catholic church inside the Nanchang city walls, and over the years several other churches were build in the immediate vicinity of the city. By the mid-1830s priests began returning to congregations near Nanchang. In 1861 the French chargé d'affaires asked Father Antoine Anot to convey copies of the treaties of 1858 and 1860 to the governor at Nanchang. On that occasion Father Anot acquired property within the city walls for a new church.[2] After the destruction of three church buildings in and near Nanchang in 1862, Father Anot fled the area. Diplomatic negotiations over the return of missionaries to the Nanchang area dragged on for over a decade. To Catholic missionaries, their physical presence in the provincial capital signified their right to proselytize across the entire province, although their absence there did not actually affect operations elsewhere. Not until the very last years of the century did Catholic missionaries again establish themselves within the Nanchang city walls.[3]

Catholic priests were attracted to almost all administrative centers in Jiangxi. Most prefectural cities were sites for churches and in the late nineteenth century vicars apostolic established headquarters in three cities—Jiujiang, Fuzhou, and Ji'an—that gradually developed into large mission compounds. Priests built churches at or near many of the county seats and sometimes made these locations their principal residence. In addition, where large central market towns such as Wucheng and Jingdezhen had numerous Catholics, priests built churches for them. Further down the list, intermediate or standard market towns like Dengjia (Anren County) had a chapel, while Catholics in country villages usually worshipped in a temporary chapel or simply held services in a Catholic's home. Cangliaoqian in rural Gan County illustrates the church-residential configuration of one congregation. An official noted in 1896 that the vicinity of the Church's property was mostly occupied by residents surnamed Xie who had been Catholic for a long time.[4]

Periodically, missionaries reported on the numbers of Catholic churches and chapels established in Jiangxi.[5] In the early 1840s Jiangxi had eighteen chapels, and by the late 1890s, the Church presence had grown to 105 churches and chapels.[6] From the time missionaries legally returned to Jiangxi through the remainder of the nineteenth century, formal Catholic churches and chapels were widely scattered, their locations dictated by local circumstances. The number of believers at a certain locale, the availability of funds for construction or remodeling, and access to suitable property determined how and where Catholics built churches and chapels or established large mission compounds. Chinese sources confirm this. According to the 1870 report of the Jianchang prefect, only a few churches existed in two of the five counties under his jurisdiction. The prefect mentions "one large church within which there were ten or more vocational students of different ages" in rural Nancheng County, at the seventh *du* of the north *xiang* (that is, at the village of Qidu); at the ninth *du* (at the village of Jiudu) stood "one large church and also one orphanage." The prefect notes two other small rural churches in Nancheng County and one he found at a site outside the prefectural city's north gate. In rural Nanfeng County Catholics built two large churches, one situated near the county seat. The prefect states that he found no churches in the other three counties.[7]

The physical style and size of church buildings in Jiangxi varied greatly. In the early years most were small and modest. Some were identified as Catholic churches (*Tianzhu tang*) by Chinese characters written on the outside, and some were unmarked. Chapels were usually inconspicuously located in existing structures. In 1859 one Jiangxi missionary reported that one could expect to find in villages where Catholics resided a common building that might be called a church. The building was no different from those around it. With a poorly kept exterior, an interior with a dirt floor, no arches, an old cross, and a few deteriorating religious images, it amounted to a kind of rough shelter.[8] A few early churches were large and imposing new masonry structures probably with a European flair.[9] With time more and more buildings were conceived large and built solidly of brick and stone. Of these just a few, for example a church located in the county seat of Guiqi during the

1890s, were in a Chinese architectural style. In Guiqi Catholics also established an orphanage, school, and hospital in addition to the church.[10]

Most rural congregations, however, lacked even a chapel or oratory, and priests out of necessity celebrated Mass in people's homes.[11] But this became impractical when the number of Catholics in an area grew too large. In 1894 Bishop Casimir Vic, finally recognizing the needs of eight hundred Catholics who lived within a three to five miles radius of each other in a rural locale in Fuzhou Prefecture, proceeded to plan out the mission in this order: first a good chapel, then a residence for the priest, school buildings, and a hospital.[12]

Regardless of a church's size, style, and location, missionaries faced certain difficulties in obtaining a suitable building site (see also chapter 5). Chinese claims of geomantic problems had to be dealt with, and sometimes real estate was fraudulently sold to missionaries without the knowledge of the actual owners.[13] At other times, missionaries encountered local boycotts. Residents of one area in Anren County in 1883, for instance, prohibited the sale of property to outsiders.[14] Having local Catholics purchase land for use as a church site might circumvent this, but local people could still respond with threats or attempts to ban the sale of building materials or the use of local labor for church construction.[15]

A highly complicated matter for missionaries was the land-purchase procedure. By treaty agreement and through an evolving set of arrangements, missionaries could buy and rent property anywhere. Chinese authorities required that transactions be reported to them so they could verify rightful ownership, clear the deed, and determine if any other obstacles prevented the use of the site for construction of a church. Once Chinese officials had approved it, the transaction could be completed with the deed put in the name of the "Catholic mission," that is, the congregation of that place, and held as its "collective property."[16] Even though this procedure was said to protect missionaries, they objected to it because it encouraged the introduction of obstacles to church construction and often forced them to select other, less desirable sites.

The purchase of property for a church, its construction, and its operation all required money. Missionaries had some funds available and frequently assisted local congregations with church construction and upkeep. Father Antoine Anot, for example, loaned money to Catholics in Anren County to refurbish their church.[17] In cases of damage or destruction to church buildings, officials sometimes collected an indemnity from people living in the surrounding area and earmarked it for rebuilding.[18] During the 1850s Catholics used profits from two Catholic-operated stores that sat next to the church at Wucheng to purchase religious appurtenances and meet all worship expenses.[19] Four Church-operated shops in Jiujiang generated a considerable amount of revenue during the mid-1860s, which Catholics used to fund orphanages.[20] Missionaries never seemed to have enough money for their work, so successful, albeit small commercial activities like this continued. In 1877 Father Anot reported that the shops in Jiujiang made money that helped support Church activities there.[21] Catholics operated these shops openly. In one instance Chinese authorities reported that a priest had purchased a shop outside Jiujiang in the mid-1890s, and the business made profits that went for Church use.[22]

The most important source of church funding came in the form of donations from the Catholics themselves. They helped by providing room and board to visiting priests, by giving their time, money, and property, and supported their churches in many other ways. In 1868 outside the city of Ji'an, the local congregation donated money to remodel and expand one Catholic's house for use as a church.[23] At rural Jiudu Catholics built a new church in 1872 with funds provided mainly by one local patron. This man, a successful tea merchant and the brother of a priest, generously donated a large sum—around 6,660 taels—or two-thirds of the money needed. Missionaries felt they could rely on him for assistance at any time.[24] In Jiujiang two wealthy Catholic families donated a considerable sum towards the construction of a hospital.[25] In the 1880s the Huangs, a successful tea trading family in Jianchang Prefecture, regularly gave 2 percent of their profits to the Church. On one occasion, the amount came to three thousand taels, and the bishop used the money to construct a church in another prefecture.[26] Extremely poor Catholics in a rural area of Fuzhou Prefecture desperately wanted to have a church building and in 1894 offered to bring one stone each for its construction. Bishop Casimir Vic estimated that this and other donations would amount to 10 percent of the total cost.[27] One does not need to cite more examples to conclude that Chinese Catholics have not been given enough recognition for their varied and generous contributions to the Church, contradicting the common view of them as takers rather than givers.

Religious Services in Rural Areas

Catholics built churches and chapels of various sizes in the market towns and villages of rural Jiangxi. According to a Catholic from a market town in Anren County, "A church was established at Dengjia and the [local] people who converted (*rujiao de ren*) all came there to worship. Sometimes they stayed and rested at the church."[28] The size of this congregation is not clear, but worshippers at the Dengjia church must have come from all over the surrounding countryside and spent some time in town before returning home. It is logical to assume that they came from the standard market area for Dengjia and had commercial reasons for coming to town, too. Shrewd missionaries may have deliberately selected market towns as convenient places to hold religious services and build churches.[29] Such locations would have allowed easy contact with a periodic but regular group of religious "customers." For the unwary priest, certain risks also came with working or living in a market town. In 1891 a market-day crowd at Xiebu, Nanchang County, destroyed a missionary's house. When the crowd dispersed for home in many different directions, local officials were at a complete loss to identify and trace those responsible.[30]

Missionaries, of course, had basic practical reasons for the selection of certain locations as church sites. When Father Antoine Anot wanted a particular site in Dongqi, a rural area of Anren County, for construction of a church, Chinese officials asked him to select another location from several they offered. Those places, the priest objected, "are out of the way [and since] there are no Catholics in the vicinity there is no need for a church to be built [there]. Moreover, the market town is distant and purchasing food would be difficult."[31]

Catholics in the countryside considered themselves fortunate if they had a formal, separate place of worship. Only 66 congregations out of 247 in the Vicariate of Northern Jiangxi, which encompassed ten prefectures, had even a "small church or chapel" in 1882. The remainder had only a "poor shelter" or a "dirty house" in which to hear Mass.[32] Similarly, in southern Jiangxi priests said Mass in a Catholic's home 75 percent of the time.[33] Chinese authorities noted that in one village in Jinxian County, "There was no church, just a house [where] scriptures were recited."[34] Unfortunately for Catholics, such gatherings for prayers and scripture reading sometimes aroused suspicions. In 1866 Catholics who met to worship in a house in a Nanchang County village were mistaken for members of the Vegetarian sect.[35] This occurred shortly after the close of the Taiping Rebellion, when people remained on edge. As the decades rolled by, however, this sort of accusation eventually ceased.

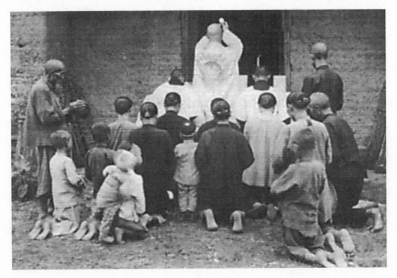

Fig. 1. Celebrating Mass in rural Jiangxi. *Source:* "Kanchow Jubilee, 1921–1946"

Catholics really had little choice about meeting in their homes until a church could be built for their congregation. It is impossible to say at what size a congregation required or could support a church or chapel of its own. One rural area with more than thirty Catholic families had no special structure for worship.[36] Certainly, a typical villager's house could not seat a congregation of that size. In another case, a missionary sought to have a church constructed in rural Longquan County where between six and twenty-odd Catholic families lived.[37] Bishop Géraud Bray wrote in 1882 that he said Mass in the dirtiest chapel he had ever encountered in one village in rural Guiqi County. He promised the approximately 150 Catholics there that he would help them build a new chapel, provided they contribute toward the expenses. They did, and the bishop ordered a new one constructed. Bishop Bray commented that elsewhere in Guiqi catechists from each congregation had besieged him to evaluate the need to build a chapel in their villages. In the end, he was faced with too many requests and because of his always limited cash reserves could only act on the most urgent of them.[38] Just what constituted urgency is hard to say and the bishop does not reveal his thinking. Clearly it was not necessarily a matter of numbers because, as mentioned above, some eight hundred rural Catholics within a few miles of each other in the Fuzhou area had to worship in various homes because they did not even have a chapel.

A View From Inside the *Jiao'an* Materials: Two Cases

Mistrust leads to the burning of a church, Ji'an 1869. Religious services held in Catholics' homes might have led to suspicions about sectarian activities, but closed church doors caused other misunderstandings. Although in less formal settings non-Catholics could easily observe Church ceremonies, priests sometimes restricted access due to a lack of space or even fear of disruption by curious and sometimes hostile visitors, particularly in towns and cities.[39] To some non-Catholics, churches were off limits and seemed dark, perilous places. Church liturgy also took on an aura of mystery. Rumors about immoral and even personally dangerous practices that took place inside churches added to their negative image. Hostile gentry creatively embellished such rumors in anti-Christian literature that circulated widely in many regions of China.

These perceptions aside, what do we really know about local Catholic churches and the services held there? In 1869 gentry and other local residents destroyed a church located outside the west gate of Ji'an. The official investigation that followed provides details about the church building, its interior, the mechanics of worship, and the concerns of non-Catholics. In the case at hand, depositions were taken from several locals who worshipped at that church. Nowhere else in the Jiangxi section of the *Jiaowu jiao'an dang* materials for 1860–1900 are similar details preserved.

Here is a description of the church and the situation that led to its destruction given by Wu Aiyao, a jeweler of thirty *sui*.[40] I quote him at length, and where minor gaps exist, I have parenthetically inserted information from the depositions of other local Catholics.

Last year [1868], [Father] Fu Ruhan came to Ji'an to preach[41] [and] rebuild Chen's [a local Catholic] residence, which is located in front of the people's granary [for Church use]. Altogether there were three buildings: the main building was forty-two feet long and had three rooms. Across from it was another building with three small rooms and to the left of the main building another [structure] with two rooms, including a kitchen. (There was also a small thatched shed occupied by the church caretaker.) All of the tiles and lumber needed [to build] (plus, the money for roofers, carpenters, and workmen) had been donated, based on our [the Catholics'] ability to do so.

[We] did not erect a votive tablet outside the gate [to identify the compound] as a Catholic church. In the main hall [of the church] hung a scroll with a picture of Jesus on it, four red gauze lanterns, and four small hexagonal glass lanterns. In the center [of these] hung an opaque glass lantern. To each side [of the scroll] were posted [religious] proclamations. On top of the [altar] table were flower vases, pewter candleholders, incense burners, and other items. Pennants and banners were not used when we worshipped, nor were vegetable or fruit [sacrifices] offered.

In the three small rooms, [we] stored the pewter lanterns, the vases, the table curtain, and the wooden items ordinarily used [in services]. When [Father] Fu Ruhan came and when it was time to worship, then and only then did we set up the [worship] vessels [and appurtenances]. There were no vessels made of gold or silver, or any other vessel [not already mentioned].[42]

Although Wu Aiyao was not present in 1869 when the church was destroyed, the account of another Catholic eyewitness provides some details of that event. During the prefecture-level civil service examination in Ji'an, several examination candidates came to the church on three occasions. On their second visit, they gained entry to the church and complained about a couplet displayed inside. On the next visit, they and a number of other people pushed their way into the church, tore down the offending couplet and set the building on fire.[43]

Prevailing attitudes toward Christianity must have helped the candidates succeed in stirring up local people on what seem to have been fairly slim pretenses. However, a number of Catholic practices were suspect, such as men and women worshipping together.[44] This violated social norms and led some people to see the church as an immoral, filthy place. And other things Catholics did were considered improper. According to a report by the Ji'an prefect and Lüling County's acting magistrate, "When trifling incidents accidentally occur in the countryside, they [Catholics] claim that religion is involved. They then try to intimidate others and depend on the influence [of the Catholic priests to help them]. Therefore,

. . . all are filled with hatred [for them]." These officials reported that although the local gentry and common people (*shimin*) tried to prohibit their children and juniors from converting to Catholicism, some "ignorant [common] people" could not be stopped.[45]

This report thus expresses a strong anti-Catholic bias and partially explains why the Ji'an church was destroyed. In Wu Aiyao's statement, however, there is also a suggestion that the Catholics blundered. First, allowing ready access to the church would have showed the general public that there was nothing strange or mysterious inside. In fact, the church's interior decorations bear a striking resemblance to those used in family shrines and temples.[46] Second, it was customary to hang votive tablets outside temples and ancestral halls. By neglecting to do this, the congregation missed the opportunity to give the compound an appealing and positive name, which could have enhanced the Church's image socially or psychologically.[47] Third, even though the local Catholics financially supported the church and its expansion, the priest seems to have initiated the building project. I believe it was the priest's presence and efforts to expand the church that drew the attention of the examination candidates and locals. It gave them the opportunity to play on existing negative attitudes and led to the church's destruction.

Such were the difficulties encountered by Catholics near Ji'an. Another case centering on the construction of a church about fifteen years later in Longquan County illustrates how the Church as a power outside the community proper could create problems even within kinship groups.

Lineage opposition to construction of a church, Longquan County, 1884. In early May of 1884 Bishop François-Adrien Rouger and a Chinese priest left Ji'an for the county seat of Longquan, which was part of Ji'an Prefecture but on its periphery near the border with Hunan Province. They then continued to Langqi, a village twelve miles away. According to Chinese officials, the villagers in Langqi were all surnamed Hu, but in fact a few other families lived among the village's several hundred Hu lineage members, among whom some were practicing Catholics.[48] Evidently, Catholics of neighboring villages looked to Langqi as the center for local religious activities, probably because of an old but small chapel located there.[49] The congregation hoped to expand its facilities, so Luo Yuanhui, Gou Yifou, and Hu Jingxi requested that the bishop visit and oversee the construction of a church.[50] Catholics also wanted an orphanage building to house the girls already taken in by priests under the auspices of the Association of the Holy Childhood.[51] Since Longquan County lacked even one formal church building, the bishop assented. But the building project and the bishop's arrival in Langqi stimulated local opposition.

That opposition took two main forms: a written and word-of-mouth campaign to quash the project and direct action. Scathing notices were posted anonymously and rumors circulated. One placard called attention to the presence of a Frenchman who in his determination to build a Catholic church would cause great harm to the locality. The author of this text did not disclose how the locality would be harmed, but stressed that somehow the construction must be blocked. The same notices warned that local people should sell neither building materials nor food supplies to the bishop. "Those discovered doing business [with him] will be sentenced to heavy punishment with no leniency."[52] In addition, rumors circulated to the effect that the bishop planned to construct a fort, not a church, and would bring in foreign weapons and foreign soldiers to defend it.[53] The message of the written notices and the rumors was clear—the bishop was dangerous and the construction project was not in the best interest of the community. Eventually, locals stopped the project by destroying the building and forcing the bishop to flee, possibly with injuries.

Given the seriousness of the disturbance, Chinese officials stepped in quickly to investigate. Their report reveals significant information on how the presence and activities of a missionary could contribute to discord in rural areas. Officials acknowledged that there had been postings and rumors that made advance of the project difficult. The Longquan magistrate stated that when a crowd gathered in Langqi to stop construction of the church, the bishop had left in haste, but was unharmed. The crowd subsequently destroyed the church foundation and building materials. In addition, the report stated that people took personal items the bishop and his party had left behind; they even ripped the windows and doors from the house where the bishop had stayed and stole personal items and two animals from the home of one Catholic, Hu Zuxuan.[54]

Although it cannot be determined exactly when the first residents of Longquan converted to Catholicism, they initially worshipped at a church or chapel in a neighboring county. Among them were members of the

Hu lineage of Langqi who traced their ties to Catholicism back one hundred years and through several generations.[55] Within the village everyone knew the names, numbers, and religious status of all the families. Moreover, according to the Catholics themselves, there had been no previous trouble or incidents.[56] By the 1880s about forty Catholics, counting men, women, and children, came from six families bearing the Hu surname. They and other local Catholics attended religious services in a house originally belonging to Hu Zuhui that had been purchased by a priest more than forty years earlier. This dwelling served as the local chapel and as a lodge for visiting priests. The bishop referred to it as "the old church," but no one else labeled it a formal Church structure.[57]

The combination chapel-lodge evidently could not comfortably handle either the local congregation or the clergy's hopes for expansion. During the spring of 1882, then again in 1884, Bishop Rouger secretly ordered two Catholics, Hu Zuxuan and Hu Jingxi, to lend their names to contracts for the purchase of contiguous field parcels in Langqi. The land was purchased from one Catholic with the surname Hu, two non-Catholics surnamed Hu, and one villager of a different surname. The deeds all specified that the Hu Wenshan tang, probably the name of a lineage branch hall, would manage the newly purchased land. The buyers did not mention that the Catholic Church was behind the purchase and would actually control the property. Nor did anyone inform the Longquan magistrate that the county's first formal church and first orphanage would be built on the site.[58] Bishop Rouger, a veteran missionary with thirty years experience in China, ignored the property purchase procedures stipulated by the Sino-French Berthemy Convention of 1865 and secretly took possession of the deeds.[59]

On May 14, 1884, the bishop arrived by boat near Langqi accompanied by a priest, attendants, masons, and carpenters. The bishop's party displayed a large French flag, and the bishop traveled in a palanquin with a red parasol. Guo Yixing and Hu Jingxi, two local Catholics, sounded a gong and set off firecrackers to announce the bishop's arrival and to clear a path for him. Other Catholics, men and women alike, bowed as the procession passed by them on its way to Langqi, treating the bishop as if he were an official visiting the countryside. Upon arriving at Langqi the bishop and his immediate retinue stayed at the chapel-lodge and the forty workmen stayed with various Catholic families.[60]

The grand procession and large entourage attracted much attention locally and evoked various reactions. Some local residents expressed surprise while others displayed indignation and fear via the anonymous placards and rumors. Still others now saw clearly the deceitfulness of the earlier property transactions. Bishop Rouger, observing the commotion and opposition that his presence in Langqi had produced, feared that if he delayed the start of construction even slightly residents would find a pretext to stop the project for good. The bishop therefore ordered Guo Yixing to supervise the workmen and begin construction immediately, using the bricks and mortar already purchased by Luo Yuanhui.[61]

For non-Catholics of the Hu lineage, work on the church foundation progressed too quickly. Soon the exterior walls were two to three feet high outlining a rectangular building about ninety-six feet long by eighty-four feet wide.[62] Members of the Hu lineage felt that a building at this site would impair the local geomancy. Hu Zutang, Hu Jiawen, and others representing the lineage went directly to old Hu Zuxuan (aged seventy *sui*) and his fellow Catholics to express their opposition to the location and size of the church and to point out that the building would disturb the geomancy of the Hu ancestral hall.[63] The lineage representatives also stated that they regarded the Catholic Hus' support for the church to be "assisting heterodoxy," an assertion not subsequently emphazised.[64] The Catholics rejected all such arguments and quarreled with their kinsmen. Jiao Mingfeng, a *shengyuan* degree holder from a nearby village, went to Langqi and tried unsuccessfully to mediate the dispute.[65] Meanwhile more and more residents of other villages were attracted to Lanqi because of the commotion.

On the morning of May 20, 1884, people gathered at the new church site to prevent further construction. Bishop Rouger saw the volatility of the crowd and recognized the danger of the moment. According to the official report, he ordered his bags packed and then hurriedly departed unharmed along with the workmen. After their departure, the crowd destroyed the church foundation and remaining building materials, damaged the chapel-lodge where the bishop had stayed, and stole various items of personal property. The bishop went about two miles to the village of Shangyuan where he stopped to catch his breath and reassess the situation. Once again, a crowd of people gathered around him, some of whom had followed him from Langqi.

When the situation became too threatening, the bishop decided to return to the safety of Ji'an.[66]

According to the version of the incident submitted by the bishop to Chinese officials, gentry-led militia brought together over one thousand people who descended on Langqi. Besides assaulting and nearly killing him, the militia also stole money, valuables, and religious objects from him and his party; they then destroyed the old and new church buildings, and robbed more than twenty Catholic families of personal property, including domestic animals.[67] Only with the assistance of an old non-Catholic who sheltered him, loaned him shoes to wear, and personally escorted him under the cover of darkness did the bishop escape the area. The bishop walked for almost three days before arriving exhausted at his residence in Ji'an.[68] In a report to the Vincentians' superior general in Paris, another priest with knowledge of the incident stated that between 120 and 130 Catholics in the area had suffered great losses.[69] The bishop himself estimated the vicariate's total losses to be as high as 12,000 francs, a heavy financial blow.[70]

The reports produced after investigations by several Chinese officials indicate that they believed the bishop to have exaggerated the conflict that occurred at Langqi as well as his injuries.[71] Officials determined that no organized militia or gentry had been involved, only local villagers.[72] To find out exactly who had taken part the magistrate ordered "upright gentry" (*zhengshen*) and the *baojia* headmen of the various villages to investigate and report to him.[73]

The destruction of the church building at Langqi village highlights for us local sensitivities. Catholics had purchased property under the pretext of ownership by a lineage hall. Clearly, as part of the village community Catholics could easily buy property and make false but believable claims. And, as the Catholics themselves pointed out, their religious beliefs were nothing new, and they had long peacefully coexisted with their non-Catholic kinsmen. Friction developed only when the bishop suddenly arrived amidst great fanfare and when the land-purchase scheme surfaced.[74] Naturally, non-Catholic Hus felt deceived and angry. They nonetheless first attempted to reason and negotiate with the Catholics, a significant sign again of old habits and customary relations. Why the Catholics took an inflexible stance and refused to negotiate is difficult to understand unless we consider the presence of the bishop. With the failure of their overture, the lineage evidently decided they had no recourse except direct action. There is no evidence that lineage members participated in the destruction and thefts, however. People from other villages stepped in, we must assume, with the tacit approval if not encouragement of the Hu lineage group.

In their subsequent negotiations with the French, Chinese officials countered French claims of local government prejudice against Catholics by insisting that the bishop had ignored proper property purchase procedures at Langqi.[75] The Chinese felt that the bishop should have notified the magistrate in advance of the purchase. Moreover, had the bishop announced his travel plans in advance, Longquan authorities could have taken the measures needed to protect him.[76] Although the bishop had blundered in more ways than one, the Chinese government still agreed to compensate him for the Catholics' property losses. Officials and missionaries did not settle on the amount of the compensation until 1896.[77]

Community-level Problems and Cases of Litigation

The Zongli Yamen's efforts to regulate missionaries' and Chinese Catholics' activities and the treaty powers' responses to these efforts are adequately delineated elsewhere for the 1860s.[78] Although other studies provide bits of the story for the remainder of the nineteenth century, a full account of Christian cases in a diplomatic context has not yet been written.[79] Likewise, we still await a comprehensive analysis of the import of *jiao'an* in a domestic setting, with stress on the sociocultural issues.[80] In Jiangxi certain types of local conflict between Catholics and non-Catholics resulted in litigation. These small and mostly rural cases help us understand the often personal nature of such conflict and provide another perspective on Christianity in the community setting.

A Priest Claims Religious Persecution, Chongren and Anren Counties, 1872–1875

In 1872 the Chongren magistrate ordered the gentry leader Wang Po and other gentry to carry out *baojia* registration in Qiuqi, a market town. This was part of a general effort by authorities to reinvigorate security efforts and reestablish ties with local communities. The numerous Catholics of Qiuqi, however, refused the household registration cards; they

further rejected requests that they contribute to the theatrical performances scheduled in conjunction with an upcoming festival. Subsequently,
when Wang Po spotted a Catholic at a performance, he scolded him
publicly for freeloading. The Catholic and a catechist later avenged the
insult by physically attacking Wang. Community concord soon evaporated
and county authorities had to intervene to reestablish order (for details on
this case, see chapter 6).

To Father Antoine Anot the trouble in Qiuqi smacked of persecution.
In a March 1873 letter to Chinese officials, Father Anot reported that
since January of that year Catholics had been repeatedly targeted for
beatings, robbery, and extortion; there had been numerous incidents.[81]
Chongren's acting magistrate retrieved from the county files thirty-four
complaints made by Catholics. No trial had been possible in twenty-six of
the instances because plaintiffs and witnesses could not be found or because
insufficient information precluded further investigation.[82] Three of the
eight cases tried, however, offer an idea of the real nature of the tensions in
Chongren.

A local quarrel. Wang Faxing, a Catholic, quarreled with an intoxi-
cated man who had been publicly discussing Catholicism—evidently in
uncomplimentary terms. Wang took the man to the local church where
Catholics forced him to apologize. Later a relative of the man, who was
active in the local *baojia* bureau, sought out Wang to discuss the matter.
Outside Wang's carpentry shop the two men argued and a crowd gathered
to listen. In the course of the argument, someone slipped into the shop
and stole some tools. Wang thought the whole incident had been staged
and filed suit. The acting magistrate disagreed, but still ordered compensation for Wang's loss.[83]

An unpaid loan. Mrs. Hu née Huang formally complained that Zou
Jiaxiang and others wanted to arrest her husband because he was Catholic.
After her husband fled, without leaving a clue as to his whereabouts, Zou
and others extorted money from her. The acting magistrate ascertained
that the Hus had borrowed money from Zou. While Hu was gone on
business Zou came to collect. Mrs. Hu delayed and Zou made threats
until she repaid the money. Because Mrs. Hu felt both threatened and

insulted, she accused Zou of extortion. The acting magistrate ruled the complaint unwarranted and took no further action.[84]

Harassment of a Catholic beggar. Mrs. Huang née Liao, a Catholic, filed a complaint stating that the directors of the local *baojia* bureau had tried to arrest her husband because he was Catholic. As a result of his flight to avoid arrest he left his family. A young son then died of starvation and exposure. The acting magistrate discovered that Huang had indeed left his family because he feared repercussions for the attack by Catholics on Wang Po, but that Mrs. Huang had not complained immediately. Moreover, in court she could not identify the *baojia* bureau defendants. The acting magistrate determined that the Huangs were beggars and that after the father left a son had indeed died. The acting magistrate made no mention of whether or not the *baojia* directors had actually attempted to arrest Huang. Instead, he ruled that the *baojia* directors were not responsible for Huang's son's death, and so the case ended.[85]

These three brief cases, and others as well, point to multiple causes behind local conflict and litigation between Catholics and non-Catholics. Religion was one element, yet the facts do not support Father Anot's claim of persecution. The situation was more complex, as this incisive comment by Li Xucheng, a local gentry, reveals.

This is the home area of common people and Catholics. Is there ordinarily contact [between them] or not? [Of course,] for debts are owed, rents are due, and there are IOUs. These are the endless affairs . . . [of any community. Because of the rift caused by Catholics who would not register for the *baojia* or contribute money for the theatrical performances, relations between] the people and Catholics were not friendly. Here and there, payments of rents and debts were sought. [There were] arguments and quarrels and [some] desired to have people arrested and prosecuted by officials in order to recover [money] or because of various things that were taken in lieu of the debts. Subsequently, the real situation was obliterated and complaints were made of extortion, assault, and robbery. There were many inaccuracies, and it was feared [by some] that a judicial settlement would come from these lies. Therefore, many hid and would not be questioned [in court]. Now both sides recognize that there were misunderstandings. The people and Catholics are once again [on] amicable [terms].[86]

But in 1875 Father Anot again contended that over the previous two years there had been nearly one hundred instances of harassment against Catholics in Anren County. He charged that "villainous gentry" (*bishen*) sought to eradicate Catholics from the Dengjia market town area, and to that end had formed a "united gang" (*liandang*) from the local Wang lineage and yamen runners. They had extorted money and robbed or destroyed the property of numerous Catholic families.[87] Bishop Géraud Bray also contended that the trouble arose because the Wang lineage head had organized a "society" to force Catholics to apostatize.[88]

The Zongli Yamen asked Jiangxi provincial officials to inquire into these accusations. After the Anren magistrate had reexamined each of the recent Catholic complaints in the county files, he reported to the acting governor, Liu Bingzhang, that fifty-two of the cases were groundless. Except for one that the magistrate had settled, all the other cases had been dismissed.[89] For thirty-seven other Catholic complaints, not one plaintiff could be located (one man was deceased) where the supposed persecution had taken place.[90] Lacking plaintiffs, the magistrate could hold no trials.

Acting Governor Liu Bingzhang commented, "In most litigation between common people and Catholics, if the latter's facts are lacking [they then] hide and will not come [to court] in order to get the missionary to appear and argue [on their behalf]."[91] When officials presented Father Anot with the results of their investigation, he could only say that the Catholic plaintiffs must have gone elsewhere or become sick, or that difficulties must have prevented them from appearing at court. The priest subsequently dropped his charges and requested that the Anren magistrate close the files.[92]

For a time real tensions existed between the common people and Catholics of Chongren and Anren counties. Catholic complaints, mostly false, centered on minor disputes involving mundane matters, which the Catholics apparently had no intention of seeing through in court. That this was the thrust of the conflict suggests three things: First, rural society was or could be very litigious; second, Catholics drew on problems typical of their rural context as the basis for their complaints; and third, it is clear that Christianity per se was not a consuming issue. When matters involving Catholics are removed from the community context it is easy to accord unwarranted prominence to religion—as did Father Anot. Although the priest's charges may have been made sincerely, he pursued them in error. A clearer view of the situation comes from Li Xucheng, the gentry who pointed out that problems between Catholics and their neighbors were in fact nothing special—and that normal relations among people in the community had been restored.

Problems between Catholics and Non-Catholics, Shangrao and Lüqi Counties, 1884–1899

Throughout the nineteenth century in Jiangxi, we find situations comparable to those described for Chongren and Anren counties.[93] When, on February 27, 1899, the French minister complained to the Zongli Yamen about Chinese mistreatment of a missionary in Chongren County, the Zongli Yamen ordered provincial officials to investigate the complaint at hand and the overall situation.[94] This led to an official inquiry into the *jiao'an* of several counties. The magistrates of Shangrao and Lüqi counties reviewed their respective yamen files and reported case summaries of litigation involving Catholics.[95] Significantly, these cases had already been settled; the magistrates had not previously reported them to their superiors nor had missionaries previously complained about them to French authorities. These cases again point clearly to local, secular problems as the main causes of conflict.

A soured business relationship. In early 1894 Gui Bogao moved from Linchuan County to Tashui in rural Shangrao County. He became partners with one Xu Yunjin in making and selling grasscloth. Gui lived and worked at Xu's home and continued to do so after Xu ended the partnership two months later. Gui, who was a Catholic, continued the business alone while living with Xu, whom he paid room and board. When Gui took a short trip sometime in late 1897 or early 1898 Xu confiscated his grasscloth and bedding as security for his unpaid rent.

Gui Bogao took the dispute to court. The magistrate questioned both sides and then ruled that Gui should pay the rent-money owed to Xu and that Xu should return Gui's property to him. On February 23, 1899, the magistrate closed the file on this case.[96]

A widow and her false complaint. Mrs. Xu née Xia, a widow and mother of Xu Yunjin (from the case above), complained to the magistrate that her son lacked a proper profession and had sold land belonging to her without her permission. To redeem the property and clear the title she had had to pay the buyer two hundred *yuan*. Secondly, she complained that her nephew, Xu Yunzhang, who was Catholic, had purchased land from her in 1889, but had not paid her all the money due. He now refused to make further payments. The widow claimed that because of her advanced age she needed the money for the purchase of a coffin and other items.

According to Xu Yunzhang, however, his cousin, Xu Yunjin, actually owed *him* money, but to avoid repayment had instigated his mother's false complaints. On March 15, 1899, the Shangrao magistrate stated there was no evidence to support the widow's complaint against her nephew. The magistrate granted leniency to the widow because of her age and ordered Xu Yunjin punished for his misdeeds.[97]

The illegal purchase of grain stored at the Shangrao county seat. In 1899 Yan Huaxing, a commoner and a Catholic, went to the Shangrao county seat. There he arranged with two gentry to purchase a small amount of grain held in storage. As Yan and a helper carried the grain in shoulder-pole baskets out of the county seat via the south gate, Fang Defu, another gentry, stopped them and confiscated the grain. Yan filed a complaint with the magistrate.

The magistrate investigated and determined that Yan Huaxing and his family were materially well-off. In attempting to purchase grain held in reserve, Yan had broken the law. This was not unusual, according to the magistrate, because commoners frequently worried about grain shortages before the new harvests were ready. "The little people compare trifling amounts constantly and the circumstances [of this case] originated in this. Since not much grain was purchased [we] should forego further deliberations." The magistrate closed the case by ordering Fang Defu to compensate Yan for his confiscated grain.[98]

A farmland and irrigation dispute. The Catholic Wang Fuheng complained to the magistrate that a neighbor had ignored an earlier judicial decision by excavating a new irrigation embankment that when filled with water would prove dangerous to Wang's property. Wang also disputed the location of another neighbor's lime storage and adjacent cesspool. This neighbor, surnamed Huang, countercharged that Wang, while constructing a new home near their joint property line, had disturbed a grave located on Huang's land, necessitating that he relocate it.

The documents on this dispute are sketchy, but it appears that the farmers involved did not want to pursue it and refused various summons to appear in court. Nonetheless, the Shangrao magistrate ruled that, based on the information gathered, Wang's fields had actually benefited from the new irrigation embankment. Wang, moreover, was indeed responsible for having disturbed a gravesite and had to pay his neighbor six *yuan* to cover the reburial expenses. Since no one petitioned to continue the litigation, the magistrate noted the case closed on June 20, 1899.[99]

A village school property dispute. Fu Jingxing, a *juren* degree holder, and others made a formal complaint to the Lüqi magistrate sometime during June-July 1884. Thirty years earlier they had, on behalf of the village school, purchased a dilapidated building and land from Lin Xiaozou and his wife, Lin née Fu. The building served as the school's office. In 1889 several side rooms of the repaired building were rented out to one Lin Junfa, Lin Xiaozou's grandnephew, who made regular rent payments to the school. When his father, Lin Xi'en, his mother, Lin née Chen, and his brother, Lin Ruijin (a Catholic), moved in with him two years later, they refused to pay rent. They claimed that this section of the building had not been sold to the school. Lin née Chen protested to the magistrate that Fu Jingxing had in fact usurped their property and was now simply trying to use the school's possession of the building as a way to swindle them.

The magistrate looked into the complaints of both sides and tried to piece together the property's ownership history. He discovered that during the Taiping Rebellion, at the time of Lin Xiaozou's sale, Lin Xi'en and his family had fled to Fujian. Before they returned to Lüqi County, Lin Xiaozou had died. Meanwhile the village school had taken possession of the purchased building. When Lin Xi'en and his family returned they moved back into their old house. They refused to pay rent to the school and wanted the school to vacate Lin Xiaozou's property. Upon Lin Xi'en's death, Lin née Chen found stored in a wooden chest an old deed that she supposed was proof that the building sold to the school was in fact the common property of the Lin lineage, thus her countersuit.

The Lüqi magistrate determined that the deed of sale held by the school was the valid one, since it had been signed by Lin Xiaozou. Lin née Chen and her son Lin Ruijin realized their wrongdoing and pleaded for leniency. The magistrate documented their plea for the records and ended the trial.[100]

Marital problems between a husband, wife, and concubine. Throughout China it was common practice for the Catholic Church to take care of orphans and waifs. A church in Lüqi County reared a girl with the surname Zhang. She converted to Catholicism and when she was grown the Church assisted in her marriage to one Deng Tuanpeng, a non-Catholic. She and Deng had no children and because of this Deng lineage elders worried. Not only was Deng Tuanpeng without offspring but so too were all of his brothers. The lineage wanted blood heirs and instructed Deng Runji to order Deng Tuanpeng to take another wife. If the two then succeeded in producing a boy, the lineage hoped that this "one son could take the place of two for the ancestral hall."

At that time, one Lu Sanyuan was married to a woman with the surname Rao. Lu, however, was too poor to support a wife and sold her to Deng Tuanpeng. The woman became Deng's concubine in order to bear him sons. In the beginning Deng née Zhang, the legal wife, and Deng née Rao were on good terms. Later the two women came to have frequent problems centering on trifling domestic matters, and Deng Tuanpeng often had to intervene in these disputes. Deng née Zhang thought her husband took the concubine's side, which made her more quarrelsome than ever. After the wife began to hear community gossip regarding the household's problems, she pressed her husband to get rid of the other woman. When he refused Deng née Zhang left him, returning to the church where she grew up.

Sometime in May or June of 1897 Deng née Zhang filed a formal complaint with local officials claiming that her husband had mistreated her and had favored the concubine. The Lüqi magistrate ordered runners to summon those involved. Once in court Deng née Zhang stated that she now regretted having listened to gossip about her marital situation. She feared that her complaint might cause her husband to "suffer a loss" (*shoukui*). For her husband's sake she begged the magistrate for leniency. Spokesmen for the Deng lineage appeared in court stating that Deng Tuanpeng was willing to divorce Deng née Rao. Given the turn of events, the lineage apparently supported this decision. Deng Tuanpeng later stated that "Deng née Rao has been divorced and can remarry. Deng née Zhang has returned and [we] live together. All is well." He requested that the magistrate forego further deliberations. The magistrate agreed to close the files because this was simply a case of suspicions and not one of adultery or favoritism.[101]

Hard feelings over a Church loan. In mid-1897 a small disturbance occurred at a church in Songshi, a rural area market town about twenty miles northwest of the Lüqi county seat. Yang Xing, the church manager, formally requested that the magistrate arrest Liu Wanzu and other non-Catholics he held responsible. The magistrate responded by ordering an investigation and sending runners to summon those involved to court for questioning.

From the depositions taken in court, the magistrate learned that Liu Wanzu had earlier mortgaged agricultural land he owned to the local church. He had repaid the loan except for four *yuan*. When Liu decided to move from the Songshi area he went to the church to settle the debt and retrieve his deed to the land. Although the documents on this case do not provide details, someone—probably Yang Xing—stipulated that to clear the mortgage Liu not only had to make the final payment but also he had to express thanks to the Church for extending the loan. This angered Liu and he refused. Later, according to Yang Xing, Liu and other men returned to the church looking for trouble and spoke of destroying the church building. A worker at the church took exception to these threats and argued with the men. Since Liu and the others could not make the worker verbally back down, they beat and injured him. They did not harm anyone else or damage the church.

With the investigation and inquiry concluded, the Lüqi magistrate found Liu Wanzu completely to blame. The magistrate ordered him to pay the Church the four *yuan* still owed on the mortgage and to reimburse the Church worker for his medical expenses. This settlement apparently satisfied everyone and the case ended.[102]

The above cases all involved Catholics and non-Catholics. The frequently mundane nature of the disputes points to the fact that religious affiliation was no barrier to various day-to-day dealings. The same appears true of contact between Catholics and Protestants, as illustrated in the following case.

An Overdue Loan Leads to Murder in Jiaokeng, Fengcheng County, 1898

On March 14, 1898, Fan Yuqi reported to the Fengcheng magistrate that his nephew, Fan Zhewu, had been murdered by Li Jingzheng and Cai Mingliu.[103] The subsequent official investigations reveal how a seemingly trivial matter could suddenly explode into a major criminal case. Although the victim and the two defendants were all Christians, religion played no part in this case. Instead, the facts of the case center on the personal matter of a loan.

According to his deposition, Li Jingzheng was a native of Fengcheng County and lived in a village near an area called Jiaokeng. His age was sixty-six *sui*, and he had no close family members alive at the time. In addition, he was a *jiansheng* degree holder and a Protestant. In early 1898 Li loaned fifty copper cash to Fan Zhewu, a man with whom he was well acquainted and who wanted the money to purchase salt.[104] Fan was thirty-six *sui* and either a farmer or a laborer. He was Catholic and lived in a neighboring village. Li and Fan had had no previous conflict or hard feelings toward one another.[105]

The two men agreed on a deadline for repayment of the loan. The deadline passed, however, and on March 10 Li encountered Fan on a local roadway and took the opportunity to demand repayment. When he did so, Li stated,

> Fan Zhewu cursed me and said I should not block his path and demand repayment. Subsequently, we cursed each other and quarreled. I would not submit [to him]. We quarreled [more but] I feared that he was a violent [man], so I departed for home. [My] heart was filled with hatred so [I] conceived the idea of getting help to beat [Fan and thus] vent my anger.[106]

Later that same day Cai Mingliu, who was also a Protestant and a friend of Li, came to visit at Li's home. Li told him of the confrontation with Fan. At Li's request Cai agreed to help beat up Fan Zhewu. They then went out in search of Fan. Sometime in the afternoon, they found him. Fan was on his way home, carrying a sharp tree-pruning knife. Li again cursed Fan for repudiating the loan. According to Li, Fan then swung his knife at them. Cai Mingliu reacted quickly, grabbing Fan to take away the knife. In doing so Cai accidentally wounded Fan on the forehead. Fan continued to be aggressive and fought more with Cai. Li did not intervene, but stood to the side cursing Fan. Fan got the worse of it—he suffered another knife wound to the forehead and fell to the ground. The wounds were unexpectedly serious and a short time later Fan died. Li Jingzheng and Cai Mingliu both fled the scene.[107]

Deng Renjiu witnessed the fight and informed the deceased's uncle, Fan Yuqi.[108] Since the *dibao* position for that locality was at the time vacant, no other report of the murder had been made when Fan Yuqi contacted the Fengcheng magistrate.[109] Magistrate Tang Dingxuan sent runners to arrest the accused and to summon witnesses. Following standard procedure, the magistrate also ordered an autopsy. The coroner (*wuzuo*) examined Fan Zhewu's body and determined that he had died from a knife wound to the head.[110]

Magistrate Tang's successor, Wen Jugui, continued the investigation. On November 4, 1898, Wen obtained the removal of Li Jingzheng's purchased *jiansheng* degree and ordered runners to arrest him.[111] Cai Mingliu remained at large and officials never succeeded in arresting him. The only witness to the murder, Deng Renjiu, did not appear in court because he had left the county on business. In judging the case, Magistrate Wen depended on evidence he gathered, relying heavily on Fan Yuqi's testimony and Li Jingzheng's deposition.

Wen Jugui's replacement as magistrate, along with the Nanchang prefect, each repeated the investigation and trial. The acting judicial commissioner of Jiangxi also investigated and personally questioned Li Jingzheng. None of these officials found any discrepancies in the original trial report or in the description of the case as presented above. The officials ruled that although Li did not act in the assault and homicide, he was still the original conspirator. According to Qing legal statutes, officials sentenced Li to one hundred blows with the heavy bamboo and permanent banishment to a distance of one thousand miles.[112]

It is significant that while the three principal men involved in this case were Christians, religion was not at issue even though officials mention in a February 1898 report that there had been boasting, quarreling and fighting between Catholics and Protestants at another rural locale in Fengcheng County.[113] This case, however, boiled down to conflict over a small, unpaid loan. The amount of the loan did not financially make or break Li Jingzheng, but Fan Zhewu's repudiation of it and aggressive attitude could and did engage Li's temper and notion of face. The loan then became a matter of principle. Given the age, physical, and status differences between Li and Fan, it is not surprising that Li called on a third party for assistance. Cai Mingliu wanted to help a friend and fellow believer, not commit murder. Yet, the affair ended in Fan's death because anger and issues of face overruled rational behavior.

The next case also turns on a face issue, when Church authorities used the death of a missionary at a county yamen to gain advantage over local officials and expand Church operations. Although the case reached the Zongli Yamen and the French minister, it was not Christianity that was at issue. Rather, at stake was just what constituted proper Chinese respect for a deceased Western priest.

Removal of a Missionary's Casket from the Guiqi County Yamen, 1895–1897

In early March 1895 Father Jean-Marie Bresson purchased a house at the county seat of Guiqi. This experienced French missionary quickly occupied the house because he anticipated opposition once his presence became known. He had two reasons for going to Guiqi: First, it provided a central and convenient location for the care of nearby country missions; second, Bishop Casimir Vic wanted Father Bresson to establish for the first time a church and residence there in preparation for expanding Church operations. Both men believed that some of the local gentry, with the consent of the magistrate, would incite people to act against the priest, and on consecutive days a crowd came to Father Bresson's house— first damaging the building, then assaulting him. Instead of abandoning Guiqi, the priest went directly to the county yamen to complain to the magistrate. Since it was getting late, and due to the circumstances, the magistrate allowed him to spend the night at the yamen as an official guest.[114] The next day Father Bresson told the magistrate that he would not leave the yamen until the magistrate repaired his house. A standoff developed and three months passed with Father Bresson ensconced at the yamen. When a new magistrate took office hopes of a settlement rose, but the priest contracted smallpox and died on June 19, 1895, with Father Alexandre Dellieux in attendance. After Father Bresson's body was prepared for burial and placed in a sealed casket it remained in the room he had used at the yamen.[115]

Bishop Vic quickly decided upon a course of action. He blamed Chinese officials for opposing Father Bresson's purchase of property, for failing to compensate him for damage to it, and for the priest's death. He contacted French diplomats for assistance against the Chinese. The bishop intended to use this affair to help settle other matters. He wrote, "I desire, at least, to profit by existing trials, to settle questions bearing upon the Vicariate. When we shall have been granted the satisfaction we demand, we shall attend to the obsequies of our dear Confrère."[116]

Of course, the bishop never revealed his strategy to the Chinese. He informed Guiqi officials that when the time came Father Bresson's casket should be removed from the yamen via the main entry. The magistrate, according to Bishop Casimir Vic, would not permit this because only a magistrate who died in office received the honor of having his casket depart through the yamen's principal gate. The magistrate countered that the priest's body could be removed at a spot where part of the yamen wall was broken down. The bishop thought that this demand showed deliberate contempt for Catholicism, and he interpreted it as an insult.[117]

The French minister, whom the bishop had contacted for help, agreed that there could very well be "hidden meaning" in the magistrate's insistence that the priest's body be removed through a broken wall.[118] The minister petitioned the Zongli Yamen. He demanded that officials there instruct the Jiangxi governor to order the Guiqi magistrate to accord the priest's body proper respect and permit the coffin to exit through the main gate.[119] The Zongli Yamen responded with another solution. The magistrate could open another section of the wall and construct a new middle-sized gate specifically for the removal of the coffin.[120] Both sides attached much importance to this issue, and the bishop deftly used it as a delaying tactic while he acquired the leverage he needed to settle other unrelated matters. The bishop left Father Bresson's remains at the yamen for nearly two years while he worked to establish a local church and Catholic school, as well as planning for an orphanage. All of this quickly occurred in an administrative center previously without any Church buildings. Although one anonymous placard advocated stopping the foreigners' purchase of property for Church use, nothing happened.[121]

On the Chinese side, there are no further communications or information on the matter. According to Catholic accounts, resolution did not come until March 1897 when the bishop finally removed Father Bresson's casket via the main gate. The funeral procession included the bishop, six priests, and five hundred Catholics; they escorted the coffin to the house Father Bresson had purchased two years earlier. Bishop Vic boasted that "it was rather a triumphal march than a funeral."[122] They planned to bury the priest there once they completed construction of the church.[123]

There is no way of knowing decisively whether the magistrate intended his position on the removal of the priest's coffin to be an insult, but it is hard to avoid this conclusion. The reactions of the bishop and the French minister certainly show how sensitive the French were about face and their treatment by the Chinese. On one level, this case reveals how perceptions and attitudes—French and Chinese—could lead to disagreements and conflict quite apart from matters of religion. On another level, this case demonstrates Catholic perseverance and willingness to link unrelated problems in the pursuit of overall operational goals. The gravity of this symbolic dispute put the Chinese on the defensive, allowing the Catholic presence in Guiqi to become firmly entrenched.

Fortunately for the Catholics, the events of 1895-1897 did not result in hard feelings. The new magistrate helped by treating them favorably. He told Father Dellieux, "If I say nothing [against you], the people will do nothing against you."[124] The magistrate also posted orders that the people should not harass Catholics.

★   ★   ★   ★   ★

Chinese officials sometimes noted in the *jiao'an* documents that Catholics were still to be considered Chinese.[125] This meant that adherence to Catholicism or Protestantism did not remove one from the Chinese context, either legally or socially. The findings presented above indicate that Chinese Catholics in Jiangxi indeed remained in close contact with non-Catholic kith and kin. Such contact on occasion led to conflict and sometimes resulted in adjudication in the magistrate's court, but this probably happened no more often than in the general population.

From the cases that did go to court, we may conclude that some, if not all, conflicts must be viewed as having multiple causes, with religion sometimes being a factor, but not necessarily a cause. Missionaries were of course sensitive to the religious identity of parties to a conflict and certainly may have tried to emphasize that to their own and their believers' advantage. But in fact we have seen that many of the disputes involving Catholics pivoted on issues strikingly nonreligious—unpaid debts, land ownership, marital problems, and claims (both true and false) of extortion, robbery, and even wrongful death. Whether in the countryside or in the towns and cities, *both* Catholics and non-Catholics precipitated these problems. Although missionaries may have later become involved, they were not themselves the source of the original disputes.

Chapter 4

Catholics in Lineage and Family Affairs: The Personal Dimension

At present, scholarship on Christianity in China provides the stereotyped view of Chinese converting for whatever sociolegal advantage or economic benefit they could get from conversion or from zealous priests. The expectation has been that Catholics tended to isolate, even segregate, themselves. And when conflict occurred in the countryside, they either initiated it or became the proper targets of non-Catholics fed up with their gaining, solely because of religious affiliation, an unfair edge in daily affairs and litigation. Certain *jiao'an* materials do substantiate this view. In the 1869 joint report cited in chapter 3, the Ji'an prefect and the Lüling acting magistrate made the highly critical assertion that "after conversion Catholics break off contact with relatives and neighbors," and the local people hated them.[1]

We may presume that these two officials had good reasons for their opinion, but in fact, what do we really know about their sources of information and about Catholics' daily lives and contact with other Chinese? From the case studies presented in the preceding chapter, it is clear that Catholics remained part of the communities in which they lived. Although they may not have registered for the *baojia* or helped finance local theatrical performances, Catholics still borrowed money, purchased grain, bought and sold property, and in general had business and personal dealings with non-Catholics.

If Catholics retained their day-to-day contacts in the community and were not segregated from non-Catholics, perhaps claims of their separation should be taken only figuratively. Maybe Christianity offered rural common people, whose physical horizon extended only as far as the next market town and whose intellectual world was bounded by illiteracy and village society's traditions, new approaches to life and relief from certain cultural practices.[2] For example, many Chinese Catholics stopped venerating their ancestors, a move that could generate tensions for new converts. An official report about the Li family, commoners who lived in Lüling County in 1861, noted:

> [Mother and son] were enticed to convert [to Catholicism] by [Father] Yuan Dao'an. Unexpectedly, [they] broke the ancestral tablets and would not permit [family] support of Buddhism. The [local] people did not intend to accept this and repeatedly urged them to relent. . . . People wanted to beat [the son] because his mother had taken up [the Catholic] religion under his lead.[3]

Squabbles within lineages over ancestor veneration could also be complicated, since they involved vested benefits and privileges associated with membership. Take the case of Zeng Loufa, a Catholic from Anren County, who filed a legal complaint in 1874 against kinsmen after they denied him a share of free pastries (*pubing*) customarily distributed by the lineage to its members. The acting magistrate determined that once Zeng (and others) had become Catholics, they not only stopped making sacrifices to their ancestors, but also discontinued financial support for these sacrifices as well as expenses the lineage incurred for very pastries under contention. The lineage decided that because Zeng Loufa refused to contribute, he should forfeit those benefits. The acting magistrate decided that within the lineage no distinction should be made between Catholics and non-Catholics—everyone would contribute grain and everyone would receive pastries. The Zengs agreed to comply.[4] Presumably they did so and resolved the matter.

Elsewhere in the same county other people also developed restrictions about sharing lineage benefits. During Qingming of 1874 the Wangs provided free pastries to kinsmen, as was customary. When a Catholic, Wang Kaixiu, arrived at the lineage hall to receive his presumed share, the lineage head refused him on the grounds that as a Catholic he no longer venerated their ancestors.[5] Similarly, in Fengcheng County in 1892 kinsmen prohibited a Catholic from joining a lineage celebration that involved drinking wine.[6] Clearly, Catholics' expectations of continued membership in their kin groups created complications and sometimes conflicts for them and their relatives; they had to work out some resolution to these problems in their daily lives. How did they do this?

This is a difficult question to answer because much of our current knowledge of late Qing society comes from the observations of nineteenth century Western visitors, studies of the literature and documents of the gentry, and extrapolations drawn from later field work. A serious information gap exists regarding the attitudes, opinions, and lives of the common people, especially regarding those relative few who followed Christianity.[7] The uniqueness of the *Jiaowu jiao'an dang* materials lies in its accounts of ordinary and often illiterate Catholic and non-Catholic Chinese, who left no other records except their transcribed oral depositions. From these people's accounts it is sometimes possible to ascertain what various individuals—men and women, young and old— thought about tensions between Catholics and non-Catholics generated by specific problems. We may observe how they behaved in situations in which they had a personal stake and how they dealt with issues important to them, their families, and their lineages. Their actions and reactions thus provide a window onto the values and priorities of ordinary people and permit us to see how Catholics remained integral to their local communities.

Catholics as Members of Lineages: Settling Disputes

In south China's rural society, lineages were pervasive and typically dominant social organizations. Lineages helped stabilize village life by providing group rules and requiring that they be observed by all kinsmen. There was little room for behavioral or moral deviation. The cases below provide a perspective on intralineage contact between Catholics and non-Catholics, what caused tensions between them, different views of those tensions, and how the parties involved handled them. In the first case we observe how a large lineage and its strong leaders dealt with a troublesome relative who had converted to Catholicism. In contrast, the second case shows a weak lineage struggling to deal with an unruly Catholic kinsman. Case number three reveals how the hesitancy of some lineages to take matters to court made them vulnerable and how a Catholic might take advantage of the absence of lineage or village constraints. The last case, occurring late in the nineteenth century, concerns a property dispute between Catholic and non-Catholic kinsmen that turned violent.

A Catholic Challenges Lineage Authority: The Yans of Xinchang County, 1868–1869

Some four hundred households of the Yan lineage dotted the Xin'an area of Xinchang County. Besides the minor disputes common to any large lineage, the Yans had one special problem: a prominent local figure and Catholic named Yan Bingyi. Because of specific complaints against Yan, the lineage took formal and collective action against him. Yan Bingyi responded by repeatedly requesting that the Xinchang magistrate and Ruizhou prefect investigate his situation and hold a trial.[8] Local officials did neither, so Yan appealed to Father Antoine Anot.[9] With the French missionary's assistance, Yan Bingyi succeeded in presenting his case, supported by twenty-one documents, directly to the Zongli Yamen in March of 1869. The Zongli Yamen quickly requested that the Jiangxi governor order an investigation.[10] The subsequent report of the Nanchang acting prefect, together with Yan's and other local-level materials, provide an unusually close view of intralineage conflict.

Although it is not clear that Yan Bingyi ever tilled the soil, his wealth was closely tied to agricultural land holdings.[11] He was financially successful and in 1857 purchased an honorary government position with the Beijing mint and bureaucratic rank (*zhiyuan*, ninth of nine). This status gave Yan local prestige, influence, and minor privileges. The Taiping Rebellion, which disrupted most of Jiangxi from 1852 to 1864, evidently had little effect on his rising fortunes. During the late 1860s, he was an elderly but active landlord, moneylender, and businessman-trader—a man of means and status, and part of the local elite, albeit at the lower end. Yan and his entire family were also Catholics, having converted in February 1868.[12] The timing of their conversion would later become an important issue in this case.

From testimony given by three degree holders of the Yan lineage, we learn about Yan Bingyi's periodic involvement in trouble. In 1836, for example, Yan Bingyi paid a fine to the lineage for harboring a thief and receiving stolen property. Again in 1859 he was linked to a similar incident.[13] Of more interest, however, are the problems that occurred in early 1868. On January 15 Wang Zhaofeng, a neighbor of Yan Bingyi, discovered that Yan's son had butchered one of his pigs. When Wang asked for compensation, Yan refused. Wang then took the matter directly to the Yan lineage head, Yan Yuanshe, who ordered Yan Bingyi to pay four strings of cash in recompense. Yan ignored the order.[14]

Next, a relative and former worker for Yan Bingyi complained. Yan Jiaodun had planned to marry in 1867, so he borrowed twenty-five strings of cash at 30 percent interest from Yan Bingyi. Yan Jiaodun provided his property deed as collateral, but after he repaid the loan during January and February of 1868, Yan Bingyi kept the deed and tried to extract more money. "I was very worried," stated Yan Jiaodun, "so I brought [the matter] to the lineage for settlement."[15]

Finally, Yan Bingyi's own household generated problems. After the death of a son, his widowed daughter-in-law remained with Yan's family. Ignoring the Confucian ideal of widow chastity, Yan Bingyi attempted to force the widow to remarry. Because the woman refused, he cursed and beat her. The widow's mother decided in early 1868 to take the matter before the Yan lineage for resolution.[16]

On March 18 the Yan ancestral hall was opened for public deliberations (*gongyi*) about these various complaints.[17] Yan Jiaodun stated that while he was present to settle his property deed problem "All of a sudden I became angry and spoke of Yan Bingyi's improper behavior, thievery, and various other ordinary affairs."[18] Yan Jiaodun revealed that at various times Yan Bingyi had stolen kindling, lime, and poppy plants from local residents. On the basis of this, and information from Wang Zhaofeng and the widow's mother, the Yan lineage decided that Yan Bingyi should: (1) return the deed to Yan Jiaodun; (2) pay compensation to Wang Zhaofeng; and (3) provide land for the widow's support and allow the widow to return with all her personal belongings to her mother's home to live.[19] The Yans also discussed the use of family discipline (*jiafa*), that is, corporal punishment.[20] However, they did not physically punish Yan Bingyi in deference to his age and because he pleaded for pardon. The lineage released Yan only after he agreed to pay a fine of one hundred strings of cash and to write a statement promising to refrain from future illegal activities.[21]

The Yan lineage had settled several matters but continued to deal with Yan Bingyi-related affairs. Gentry from the county seat contacted the lineage regarding his delinquent payment of "worship" money for his grandfather's tablet housed at the Xingxian Temple.[22] The Yans again opened their ancestral hall for deliberations and decided that the next time the lineage sold grain from its warehouse, they would also sell grain stored there by Yan Bingyi to settle the debt with the temple. On June 28 the Yans sold eighty-two piculs (one picul was approximately 133 pounds) of Yan Bingyi's grain for sixty-four strings of cash, the exact amount needed to clear his account with the temple.[23] Later, because the Yans remained concerned about the widow's settlement, ten or so kinsmen went to Yan Bingyi's house on August 7 to ensure the safe and complete transfer of all her possessions back to her natal home.[24]

Yan Bingyi's version of these same events stood in contradiction. Yan stated that the lineage resented his conversion to Catholicism on February 28, 1868, because it meant he would now neglect ancestor veneration. Moreover, he claimed that the lineage considered it improper for a man with bureaucratic rank to become Catholic: other kinsmen might mistakenly follow his example.[25] Yan Shanqing, a prominent lineage member and *gongsheng* degree holder, and others presumed upon their influence as gentry to oppose and fine those who had converted.[26] They directed kinsmen to bring Yan Bingyi to the ancestral hall on March 18. Yan stated that they forced him to confess in writing that he and his descendants were "heterodox bandits agitating [the people] to convert unwittingly to heresy. . . . If I dare do this again, I will readily give all my property to the public [i.e., the lineage]."[27] The lineage then fined Yan the one hundred strings of cash. After he promised to pay it within two months, they released him.

Why Yan Bingyi waited more than two months before lodging a complaint with the Xinchang magistrate is unknown. In his complaint of June 8, and in later ones as well, he stressed that armed kinsmen persecuted him because of his conversion to Catholicism. To Yan Bingyi the solution was simple: the magistrate should arrest the ringleader, Yan Shanqing, and hold a trial.[28] Although the magistrate responded to Yan's first complaint by sending runners to investigate, he made no arrests and held no trial.[29] With his petitions to the magistrate unanswered, Yan Bingyi appealed to the Ruizhou prefect on June 19.[30] The magistrate ignored the prefect's orders to investigate, Yan claimed, and such official laxness allowed the Yan "lineage thugs" to do as they pleased. Thus, on June 28 the Yans sold eighty-two piculs of his grain, stole money, and posted signs declaring his fields off limits; on August 7 they damaged his home and stole personal belongings; and on October 28 they seized his rice and bean harvests.[31]

"The magistrate is corrupt and his runners also take bribes, so there have been robberies without cessation," Yan Bingyi alleged.[32] He also believed that his lineage had bought off the county bureaucracy to prevent the investigation ordered by the prefect. Yan said he refused to play this game, "to scatter money" to yamen underlings. He claimed the magistrate told him face to face: "First, you are not the Yan lineage head and second, you are not cultivated [i.e., educated]. . . . If one thousand taels [of silver] are not given [to me] then it is not possible [for me] to be reasonable. There is a capital in the north and one in the south, so let a person go make his accusations. [Yet really] what recourse is there but the magistrate?"[33]

After the acting prefect of Nanchang investigated the various allegations and held trial, he ruled that the Yan lineage had neither persecuted Yan for his Catholicism nor robbed him. Only because various people complained to the lineage about Yan Bingyi's behavior and activities did the lineage act. "The [lineage] hall was opened for public deliberations, which was proper given that rural hall's regulations," stated the acting prefect. "It was done with the purpose of restricting lineage sons and brothers from acting as bandits." The lineage's extraction of Yan Bingyi's written promise to reform and its fine against him were therefore proper means of control.[34]

However, the acting prefect clearly wanted to see amicable relations reestablished among the Yans. The acting prefect nullified Yan Bingyi's fine and, in recognition of Catholic religious practices, ruled that he need not make monetary contributions for veneration of his ancestors. Yan Bingyi could seek a refund from the Xingxian Temple, but on the condition that if he did so his grandfather's tablet would be removed. Finally, the acting prefect noted that one's religion must not be used as a pretext for making complaints. He explicitly ordered Yan Bingyi not to take advantage of his conversion to Catholicism to start trouble or as an excuse to act arbitrarily.[35]

This case allows us to see how one lineage's adjudication process actually worked. According to local gentry,

In Xinchang [County], no matter whether [a person is] gentry or commoner, as soon as someone lodges a complaint and brings it before [their] lineage, it is then necessary to open the [lineage] hall, sound the drum [to alert kinsmen], and gather [the lineage] for public deliberations to distinguish the trivial and the serious. Before the ancestors [the lineage levies] a punishment or fine. This is to warn [other] lineage members not to act like bandits."[36]

The way the lineage dealt with their kinsman Yan Bingyi supports this description of the lineage's role in local affairs. That Wang Zhaofeng took his complaint against Yan Bingyi not to the Wang lineage or to the magistrate but to those with presumed authority over Yan is noteworthy as well. The Yan lineage held deliberations for complaints lodged by local commoners Wang Zhaofeng, Yan Jiaodun, and the widow's mother, as well as for those made by gentry from the county seat. The social status of the plaintiffs and the defendant apparently did not affect this stage of the settlement process.

Enforcement of lineage decisions was another matter, one dependent upon social status and power. Yan Bingyi, for example, initially ignored his lineage head's decision regarding compensation for Wang Zhaofeng's pig. It could very well have been that Yan Bingyi's age, wealth, and *zhiyuan* status permitted him to take such a stance against the lineage head and influential degree holding members of the lineage. However, the collective lineage action against him quickly altered the power equation. Yan Bingyi converted to Catholicism in order "to scheme to resist" the action his lineage was about to take against him.[37] Yan's strategy—using Catholicism as leverage against his kinsmen—seems transparent given the timing of his conversion, his subsequent claims of religious persecution, and his use of a missionary to circumvent local officials. The Yans noted this and observed that Yan Bingyi was not the only Catholic in the area, but he was the only one complaining of harassment.[38]

This last point warrants emphasis. Indeed, the *Jiaowu jiao'an dang* collection contains no other concurrent cases for this area, suggesting that other Catholics in Xinchang County were peacefully coexisting with their non-Catholic neighbors. This is significant and leads to the conclusion that Yan's conflict with his lineage and with his neighbors came not because of his conversion to Catholicism, but because he conducted himself improperly in business, family, and personal matters. His case again indicates that Catholics such as Yan Bingyi remained part of and answerable to their lineages.

Catholics and Conflict over a Votive Tablet in Huzhai Village, Fuliang County, 1873–1876

The world-famous kilns of Jingdezhen, located near the Fuliang county seat, produced porcelain used by the emperor himself.[39] This area had long been a site of Catholic missionary activity.[40] At various times, Catholics constructed churches and chapels in the county, including one in Huzhai, not far from Jingdezhen. Although this village was not a single-lineage community as the name might imply, the Hu lineage appears to have been the dominant cognate group and its lineage branches still held common property. However, the process of segmentation had weakened Hu lineage power.[41] This is apparent from the conflict that began in 1873.

Hu Bayi, an influential Catholic and leader of one branch, decided to sell a building, part of which the lineage apparently once used as a hall, to members of another branch in July of 1872.[42] The purchasers later sold the property to Hu Wenpin, a *jiansheng* degree holder of their branch.[43] Early in February 1873 Hu Wenpin removed from his newly purchased building a votive tablet placed there by a distant ancestor important to Hu Bayi. Belief in Christianity evidently had not affected the importance of ancestors to Hu Baiyi, because he considered the action arbitrary and insulting, and demanded recompense of one hundred strings of cash. After a month passed, Hu Bayi and five other Catholics wanted the matter settled. They cajoled and pressured Hu Wenpin for several days until he finally agreed to pay a "fine" of three hundred odd strings of cash.[44]

On April 20, 1873, Hu Bayi encountered Hu Wenpin on the street and angrily accused him of now wanting the magistrate to intervene in the matter; he then tried to drag him by the arm to the church to be punished. Hu Wenpin pulled free and fled with Hu Bayi in hot pursuit. Hu Bayi caught up and wounded him with a knife. Hu Wenpin again escaped, but by the time he returned home he was absolutely livid.[45] A short while later Hu Wenpin and a nephew went to Hu Bayi's house. Hu Wenpin was screaming insults and curses outside the gate when suddenly Hu Bayi rushed from the house with a knife. During the cat-and-dog fight that ensued Hu Wenpin wrestled the knife away from Hu Bayi and stabbed him repeatedly with it. Although a bystander stopped the fight, his actions came too late. Hu Bayi lay dead.[46]

Cousins of Hu Bayi quickly found Hu Yuanji, a local functionary of the county yamen (*dibao*), who verified that the corpse was covered with knife wounds.[47] On the way to report the homicide to the magistrate the *dibao* and Hu Bayi's cousins were stopped by Huang Wanqing, a Catholic and Hu Bayi's former medicinal herbs instructor. Huang demanded hush money instead of Hu Wenpin's prosecution, threatening that local Catholics would harass anyone who dared report the murder.[48] The *dibao* and company reluctantly agreed. Through the mediation of two Hu kinsmen (both *jiansheng*), Hu Wenpin gave Huang 130 strings of cash and signed a promissory note to pay 380 strings more.[49] In addition, Hu Wenpin agreed to pay a sum as Hu Bayi's patrimony.[50]

There the matter rested—temporarily. Unknown to all, He Pengfei, a Catholic and eyewitness to the above events, went to Jiujiang, where he told Father Li Yuqing what had traspired. Father Li, together with two Catholic congregational headmen and several others from the church at Jingdezhen, returned with He Pengfei to Huzhai.[51] On May 15, according to the deposition of the *dibao*, Father Li summoned him, a cousin of Hu Bayi, and the two *jiansheng* mediators. Father Li told them that Huang Wanqing had no authority to demand hush money and that Huang had agreed to return both the unspent money and the promissory note.[52] The priest then allegedly insisted that Hu Wenpin pay three hundred taels of silver as hush money directly to him. Bargaining reduced the amount and Hu Wenpin agreed to furnish the village church with an annuity.[53] If this account is true, Father Li, like Huang Wanqing, successfully played on local disdain for litigation. Hu Wenpin must have decided that paying the priest a set amount was better than the alternative of going to court and giving yamen functionaries an unknown amount over the course of a trial.

The hundred-odd Chinese pages of official reports and depositions for this case do not disclose how the matter finally came to the attention of local officials. Oddly, the French were unusually closemouthed about the affair. The Fuliang magistrate, several deputies, the Raozhou prefect, and officials in Nanchang, one after the other, all examined the case files. They conducted efficient and thorough investigations from beginning to end. By October 1873 runners had arrested all the actors in this drama, save for Father Li Yuqing and several minor characters. The county magistrate took depositions from Hu Wenpin, Huang Wanqing, the two *jiansheng*, a man holding unspecified official rank, and others. Their statements provided the details of the case. Those involved and arrested were severely punished as officials closed the case files in 1876.[54]

Although some matters remain clouded, this much is clear—the Hu lineage was not a single entity under unified and strong leadership. Instead, we see two major branches in close contact: one was dominated by the Catholic Hu Bayi, the other by the non-Catholic Hu Wenpin. The real estate transaction certainly was not central to this case and could not have constituted the only interaction between the two branches. There must have been other business or social relations not disclosed in the documents. The removal of Hu Bayi's ancestral votive tablet alone could not have generated the amount of emotion and violence that ensued; other problems between the branches surely simmered. The importance of the votive tablet to Hu Bayi, however, probably does indicate that he continued to honor his ancestors and so remained engaged in certain important cultural traditions. In this sense, and in terms of contact with kinsmen, he clearly remained part of the village community. It is also noteworthy that while Catholicism per se did not trigger the conflict, the Catholic participants certainly complicated it.

Aversion to Litigation Allows a Catholic Extortionist To Operate in Rural Fengcheng County, 1878–1879

Xiucai, a rural marketplace in Fengcheng County, had a small Catholic congregation and a church. Gong Gaozi, a married commoner in his mid-forties with two children, lived in a nearby village. Gong was a bit of an operator and gave the following account of himself, "I have been a convert for many years (*xiaode rujiao duonian*). I have constantly made mischief [but] no one has dared find fault [with me]."[55] This comment suggests that Gong thought his Catholic status protected him, but whether it directly motivated him to make trouble is not clear. Gong's case, which centered on his involvement in two separate incidents of extortion, allows comment on his perception of certain people's vulnerability to extortion and leads us into the realm of rural attitudes regarding litigation and, indirectly, religious status.

Local people considered the mountain land situated behind the village of Niexing to be public property. The Nies maintained their

family cemetery on one slope. They planted pine trees on three sides of
the cemetery and posted a sign prohibiting the felling of these trees.
During the night of January 27, 1878, Hu Yougui cut down four of the
pines and transported them down the mountain. The next morning Nie
Jianba happened along and spotted the logs. Nie, realizing that Hu had
taken trees from the cemetery, seized him so that the Nie lineage could
punish him. By chance, Gong Gaozi encountered the pair. Seeing Hu, his
neighbor and friend, in a difficult position, Gong persuaded Nie to release
him. Nie left but stated that he would ask his kinsmen to settle the
matter.[56]

From Gong's testimony, we learn that he thought Nie Jianba was
wealthy but weak.[57] Motivated by greed, Gong decided to turn the tables
on Nie. He and Hu Yougui went to Nie's house. Gong started a squabble,
falsely stating that Nie had felled some trees and had been discovered by
Hu. With the lie told, Gong threatened Nie: "If money is not paid in
compensation, then officials will definitely be informed so they can make
arrests and prosecute." Badly frightened, Nie Jianba handed over eighty-
nine strings of cash to Gong. Gong in turn gave nineteen of the strings to
Hu and kept the rest.[58]

Another chance for extortion presented itself during February 1878.
Gong Lisi, a third cousin to Gong Gaozi, gave a local man, Gong Yousan,
a monetary surety for the temporary use of a firewood ax. Gong Yousan
tried to recover his ax without repaying the surety and the two men
argued repeatedly. Eventually, Gong Yousan returned the money to
Gong Lisi and the latter returned the ax.[59]

On March 6 Gong Lisi died of an illness and his older brother buried
him. Gong Gaozi approached the brother with a plan because "Gong
Yousan was wealthy and afraid of trouble."[60] The brother refused to
cooperate, so Gong Gaozi went alone to Gong Yousan's home. Gong
Gaozi accused Gong Yousan of having angered Gong Lisi, precipitating
the man's sudden death. He also accused him of having bribed the
brother to bury Gong Lisi secretly to prevent county authorities from
knowing about it. Gong Gaozi had set the scene properly for delivery of
the essential point: "If money is not given to me," declared Gong, "[the
death] will be reported to officials for prosecution." The scheme worked.
Gong Yousan, "fearing implication," paid forty-six strings of cash to end
the matter.[61]

Somehow, the Fengcheng magistrate learned of these acts.[62] He dispatched runners and Green Standard soldiers to arrest Gong, who quickly left town. Nie Jianba then went to the county seat to report the crime directly to the magistrate. Gong remained at large until arrested by runners and soldiers on July 13, 1879. Hu Yougui, however, avoided apprehension. Local officials held five trials.[63] They finally sentenced Gong Gaozi to one hundred blows of the heavy bamboo and three years of penal servitude. Officials dismissed from service (*geyi*) local *baojia* headmen because they had neither deterred Gong nor reported his deeds.[64] Although Nie Jianba and Gong Yousan failed to report the crimes committed against them, officials did not punish them. Officials ordered the return of any valuables recovered to the two men, according to ownership.[65]

Gong Gaozi considered his two victims to be wealthy but spineless. Let us consider their options. First, we presume that complaints initially went to lineage or village elders. In fact, Nie Jianba stated that he intended to take the tree matter to his lineage for settlement, though he apparently never did. Nor did the Gongs attempt to use their lineage to deal with Gong Gaozi. Unless the local lineages' leaders were also afraid of Gong, too powerless to do anything, or unaware of the extortion, there is no ready explanation for their failure to act.

Second, no one seemed willing to go to the magistrate to complain or test Gong's threat to go to the magistrate, which was another option.[66] Gong intimidated people because he acted like a bully, not because of his religious status, which no one mentioned as a factor. Moreover, no missionary intervened to pressure local officials or rescue Gong from punishment. The case reflects on religion only because it shows Gong Gaozi, a Catholic, remained an active, if less than honorable, part of the local scene. Indeed, Gong understood, and I would venture shared, his victims' general aversion to litigation. To pursue problems in the magistrate's court meant contact with rapacious yamen runners and the payment of supralegal fees.[67] This worked in Gong Gaozi's favor because paying extortion was cheaper and simpler than going to court. While Nie Jianba and Gong Yousan had not done anything wrong, they could afford to pay the blackmail and chose to do so. Lastly, authorities' harsh punishment of Gong Gaozi also demonstrates that everyone, Catholics included, remained part of the community and could not act with impunity.

Indemnification for Destruction of Property in Yangjiang Village, Yongxin County, 1897

This rural case illustrates further that while regular contact between Catholics and non-Catholics could lead to problems, these were often resolved through kinship and shared interests in village harmony. In early 1897 Liu Lüjie, a Catholic, took possession of a piece of land in the village of Yangjiang owned by the Liu lineage and located near the front gate of the lineage hall. The Liu lineage believed he occupied the property without rightful title, but exactly how the Lius attempted to resolve the dispute was not disclosed in the documents preserved on this case. Negotiations evidently broke down and led to hard feelings, with lineage members very angry at Liu Lüjie. They subsequently destroyed his house and various items of personal property. Liu Lüjie then took the matter outside his lineage and appealed to Bishop Jules-Auguste Coqset and Church authorities in Ji'an for help.[68]

The bishop intervened on Liu Lüjie's behalf and complained in writing to Chinese officials. The Yongxin magistrate investigated and summoned Liu Runjiu, a lineage elder, and others to court for questioning. From their depositions the magistrate concluded that the conflict was not serious or irreconcilable. He therefore left it to the Liu lineage to decide the ownership of the property. The magistrate did soothe the bishop and Liu Lüjie by indemnifying the latter for his losses and by punishing with the cangue one lineage member for his role in the destruction of Liu Lüjie's property. Liu and the lineage agreed to obey local gentry and elders and restore amicable relations.[69]

The Yongxin magistrate recognized this case for what it was: an internal problem of the lineage. Land ownership and possession were at issue, precipitated by Liu Lüjie in direct challenge to lineage authority. To be sure, Liu Lüjie was a Catholic and knew he had recourse to the Church for possible protection from, and advantage against, his lineage. Yet, he did this only *after* the conflict turned violent. Also, to his credit, when Liu sought assistance from the bishop he made no claim of religious discrimination or conflict. This is significant. First, it indicates that he and other Catholics had generally lived in the community without strife. Second, by not making false accusations Liu Lüjie kept the investigations and the involvement of outsiders—the bishop and the magistrate—to a minimum. This was important if the community wanted to return easily to some semblance of accord, a goal that all parties seemed to desire, given their willingness to work together to restore good relations.

Cases Involving Women: Did Christianity Make a Difference?

The Yan Bingyi vignette above highlighted the difficulties facing one widow when her Catholic father-in-law wanted her to remarry. In the countryside, the insecurity of women in general and widows in particular was part of an empirewide, dynasty-long story that usually involved economic factors. For instance, in one poor backwater county of Shandong Province in the early Qing, widows regularly remarried under pressure from their deceased husband's relatives, who stood to take their property and the dowry, while being relieved of sustenance expenses.[70] Another factor may have been that women with property became too independent as widows, leading men to pressure them to remarry so they would again come under full male control. The *jiao'an* materials reveal how rural women in Jiangxi during the late Qing reacted to this situation, their choices, and whether a Christian presence made any difference in their experiences or thinking.

The cases presented below all began with problems involving women and provide insight into whether or to what degree Catholics were affected by the sociomoral discourse that affected non-Catholics. In the first case a Catholic laborer became sexually involved with a non-Catholic widow and created great difficulties for her and her family. Adultery is at the center of the second case, where we observe a married Catholic enamored with a relative's wife. The third case also involves sexual conduct. A single man, who later became Catholic, attempted to rape his widowed sister-in-law and brought grief to his family. The village setting for the fourth case brings to the fore two Catholics who tried to force a local widow to remarry into the lineage of one of them. The last case focuses, in a different way, on the independence of certain Catholic businesswomen, probably widows, and the expectations of the community in which they lived.

Widow Wu's Romance Leads to Murder in
Pengze County, 1872–1878

In Pengze County's twenty-fifth *du* (a rural administrative area), someone committed a murder on the evening of October 15, 1876.[71] Shortly afterwards, the county magistrate ordered runners to investigate and make arrests. Ten days after the murder the magistrate received a report from a *dibao*, Gao Xianxi, which outlined the important facts of the case. Gao's information came mostly from the man who discovered the homicide, the victim's brother. Based on this crucial report, which included all the names of those involved, officials made arrests and held a trial.[72] The testimony of six people, the main participants, allows the retelling of what was virtually a rustic soap opera.

In 1872 Mrs. Wu née Luo, a widow, hired Zhang Chunxing, a Catholic of forty *sui* to help her and her son Wu Leixia (twenty-four *sui*) do farm work. In the Wu household, social codes involving formality and distinction were set aside: employer and employee ate at one table and addressed one another in familiar terms. By September 1872 Zhang's flirtatious advances towards Mrs. Wu led to sexual intercourse.[73] Wu Leixia and his wife's discovery of the intimate nature of the relationship between mother and hired laborer complicated the housing arrangements. Soon the lovers forced the son and his family to move out and work elsewhere for a living. Wu Leixia stated, "Because Zhang Chunxing was a violent man, I was afraid that my strength was not sufficient to oppose him. I dared not seize the adulterers because I was also afraid of broadcasting my mother's dishonor."[74] It was mainly the last reason that stopped Wu from lodging a complaint at the county yamen.

In the compact agricultural communities of China, few actions went unnoticed by neighbors. Not surprisingly, by March of 1873 talk circulating among the villagers regarding Wu Leixia's curious treatment by his mother. According to Zhang's brother, Zhang became sensitive to local gossip and concerned that the local *dibao* would get wind of the illicit love affair and expel him from the village.[75] The clever Zhang quickly found a solution. Before the magistrate Mrs. Wu explained that "Zhang Chunxing said if I did not agree [to marry him], he would definitely expose our adulterous affair and cause me to be without the face [needed] to go on as a human being. He thus intimidated me. I was compelled to consent reluctantly for lack of an alternative."[76] Zhang formally employed a go-between to make the nuptial arrangements and became her uxorilocal husband. He thus legitimized the love affair.

Mrs. Wu, however, did not thereby regain peace of mind. Zhang Chunxing forcibly took charge of the house and all the fields, and Wu Leixia remained helpless to prevent it. In an emotional deposition, Mrs. Wu cried out that she could no longer stand the beatings and curses of her new husband. Zhang wanted to sell the land for cash and to take his wife, against her will, to his native Anhui. She, on the other hand, wanted to protect the Wu family property. Tearfully, and because she saw it as her only option, she surreptitiously turned over the property deed to her son for safekeeping.[77]

A sort of stalemate existed until October 15, 1876, when Zhang finally forced his wife to disclose the whereabouts of the deed. Zhang grabbed a metal rake and rushed to Wu Leixia's hovel. He angrily demanded the deed while banging on the cooking stove with the rake. Then he slapped Wu's wife. Wu Leixia, who was at a neighbor's house at the time, heard the commotion and called friends to help him. Wu returned home armed with a small knife and two of the three men with him carried sticks. Zhang tried to flee but the men beat him severely.[78] With Zhang stunned and weakened, Wu Leixia launched a savage knife attack. Wounded numerous times about the neck Zhang collapsed in a heap and died.

The four men immediately realized that they had committed a serious crime. Their only option, reasoned Wu Leixia, was to hide the body. Late that same night the four men carried the corpse to a small hillside cave behind the village where they unceremoniously left it. Each of the men, of course, swore to be silent about the incident. The sole witness, a laborer hired by Zhang to dig taro root, feared implication in the murder and promised to keep quiet, too.[79]

Zhang Chunxing's brother noted his obvious absence and searched vainly for nine days before locating the body. Someone tipped him off, for he sought out the laborer who had witnessed the fight and the hiding of the body. With information obtained from that laborer, the Zhang brother notified Gao Xianxi, who as *dibao* reported the murder to the Pengze County magistrate.[80] The magistrate, accompanied by a coroner, went to the cave, where they examined the putrid corpse, determining only that it was covered with knife wounds.[81]

Officials brought the leading characters to court, save the marriage go-between and one of the four assailants. The Pengze magistrate, the Nanchang prefect, and the judicial commissioner each tried the case in succession. Each of these three trials and reinvestigations substantiated the facts presented above. No one made Christianity an issue in the case and no missionary intervened except for one missionary's request for information on how the Catholic Zhang had died. Hence, Jiangxi officials forwarded the county records to Beijing.

In September 1877 Wu Leixia died of an illness while under runner escort from one county seat to another. Officials had found Wu guilty of homicide provoked by a vicious scoundrel. According to one Qing code, the punishment for such a crime was one hundred blows of the heavy bamboo and three years' penal servitude.[82] Each of the accomplices received eighty blows of the heavy bamboo as punishment. Officials recognized the extenuating circumstances and judged Mrs. Wu an adulteress; for illicit intercourse with Zhang Chunxing they sentenced her to one hundred blows of the heavy bamboo and the cangue for a period of one month. However, they reduced the severity of the sentence by allowing her to commute the latter punishment to a cash payment.[83]

Initially, Mrs. Wu's relative independence as a widow seems to have led to her predicament. In contrast to "the three obediences" (*sancong*) expected of women, Mrs. Wu from the time of her husband's death in 1864 had never been subordinate to her son.[84] She took charge of the farm, hired labor, and controlled the property. For the widow, possession of the property deed symbolized more than family wealth. It also represented her independence and security. However, the autonomy that had come with Mrs. Wu's widowhood collapsed once Zhang compromised her sexually. Because she valued her moral standing and because the village community esteemed widow chastity, Mrs. Wu became a hostage to Zhang. Although Zhang was a Catholic, his religious beliefs seem to have had no bearing on his actions. Like most Chinese males, he sought to use traditional moral standards to his advantage. While Zhang could force marriage, wrestle management of the fields from his wife, and beat her, in the end Mrs. Wu thwarted him by withholding the property deed. Out of these circumstances grew a dilemma for Mrs. Wu; she could either retain the deed and risk losing it and everything to Zhang, or she could relinquish the deed to her son, a man less likely to take advantage of her. She reluctantly chose the second option.

Mrs. Wu clearly deemed a widow's morality to be important, if not in practice, at least in theory. Wu Leixia agreed. Even though Wu Leixia was the legal heir to the Wu property, Zhang still kicked him out of his natal home and forced him from his father's fields. Wu did not file a complaint because his filial desire to preserve his mother's honor took precedence. Ironically, the rural currency of an elite ideal, widow chastity, in a village community made it possible for a common laborer to control, to a degree, an otherwise independent-minded, propertied woman.

The villagers' acceptance of this ideal affected Zhang's actions, too. Since his religious status did not provide immunity or advantage in his situation, he feared expulsion from the village should the *dibao* learn of his affair with Mrs. Wu.[85] And for Mrs. Wu, marriage to a Catholic made no difference either; she still stood to lose her property and the independence that came with its ownership.

A Love Affair and A Double Homicide in Gao'an County, 1873–1876

A large branch of the Chen lineage made their home in the village of Zhongfang, Gao'an County, where they also had an ancestral hall. Although some of the Chens were Catholics, they lived side-by-side and were in close contact with their non-Catholic relatives.[86] One Catholic, Chen Zongxiang, in March 1873 during the absence of a "lineage uncle" (a relative outside his mourning circle but one generation older) on a trading trip, became enamored with the uncle's wife, Mrs. Chen née Hu. By November or December of 1874 an illicit sexual affair developed. Chen Zongxiang, aged thirty-eight *sui* and a married man himself, brazenly visited the lone Mrs. Chen (one *sui* his junior) at her home. She lived in a house shared with Chen Zhonghe, her husband's uncle. One day late in 1874 this uncle accidentally overheard the two lovers chatting. When Chen Zhonghe called out for people to come help him apprehend the visiting paramour, Chen Zongxiang saw the wisdom of a speedy departure. The uncle severely upbraided Mrs. Chen and sternly warned her against further contact with Chen Zongxiang, now her admitted lover.[87]

When Mrs. Chen's husband returned home, Chen Zhonghe informed him of all the details. The husband, after verifying the story with his wife, beat her. According to Qing law, adultery was grounds for divorce; it was also within the rights of the husband to seize and turn in the adulterer to the county magistrate.[88] The husband followed the second course only and repeatedly sought Chen Zongxiang in order to take him to the magistrate for prosecution. Since the cuckolded husband's efforts failed, he requested that his uncle, Chen Zhonghe, capture and transfer Chen Zongxiang to the county seat for trial should he return.

On March 13, 1875, under the veil of nightfall, Chen Zongxiang slipped back to Mrs. Chen's bedroom. Again Chen Zhonghe discovered them and, with the aid of nine kinsmen, confronted the nocturnal visitor. Chen Zongxiang pulled a knife and resisted violently. In the struggle to disarm him, the Chens wounded Chen Zongxiang with his own knife. With his hands tightly bound together, and with Mrs. Chen treated likewise, the Chens marched them off to the county seat. Soon after starting the pair sat on the ground and refused to budge. They insulted their captors. According to a kinsman and witness, "Chen Zongxiang lay on the ground cursing wildly and said that even if they were taken to the magistrate, they would not be found to have committed a serious crime. In the future [he swore] they would definitely seek revenge by murder."[89] Chen Zhonghe testified that at this point "I became momentarily very angry because Chen Zongxiang and the woman had committed adultery and corrupted our family's morals. Yet they cursed and reviled us and planned revenge against us."[90] Seeing a shallow pit nearby Chen Zhonghe ordered the pair placed in it and buried alive.

A witness notified Chen Zongxiang's wife and she reported the incident to the *dibao* for verification. The *dibao*, Zhang Weixiu, then reported the murders to the Gao'an County magistrate.[91] Armed with the names and information provided by the *dibao*, the magistrate sent runners to investigate and locate those implicated. Later, the magistrate and a coroner set out to Zhongfang for a first-hand inquiry. They found the deceased lying in a pit, their hands bound together with rope. The coroner noted several knife wounds on the body of the man, but concluded that he and the woman had died of suffocation. The magistrate then ordered them reburied elsewhere.[92]

Runners had not yet made any arrests when, on March 24, 1875, Chen Zhonghe and three of the nine wanted kinsmen surrendered to authorities for trial. Before the Gao'an magistrate concluded the trial, he left office. An acting magistrate reinvestigated and tried the men again. The Ruizhou prefect repeated the process and found no factual discrepancy in the evidence. Officials forwarded the materials to the Zongli Yamen in compliance with a missionary's request for information regarding the Catholic's death. Officials sentenced Chen Zhonghe to execution after the autumn assizes and sentenced each of the three accomplices to one hundred blows of the heavy bamboo. Authorities still wanted the other six men apprehended for trial at another date.[93]

No one mentioned the involvement of any lineage or branch leader in this case. Nor had anyone taken the problem to the lineage hall for adjudication while it remained a case of adultery. Contrary to the usual practice of the lineage resolving disputes and problems to stifle neighborhood gossip and minimize damage to the group's prestige, the Chens looked to the magistrate for formal prosecution, even though Chen Zhonghe was of the older generation and Chen Zongxiang his "lineage grandson."[94] Chen Zhonghe was a man of action, though apparently without formal authority. Twice he had discovered his nephew's wife engaged in an illicit affair with a man and twice he had summoned kinsmen to seize them. And in the end it was Chen Zhonghe who ordered the murders.

Since Chen Zhonghe stated that the love affair "had corrupted our family's morals" and implied that their standing in the community would be affected, and since his explicit orders to stop the affair had been ignored, the issue was clear. The sit-down ploy by the two lovers and their defiant attitude, if unpunished, might have caused irreversible damage to the credibility of lineage authority, especially among those of the younger generation at the scene.[95] Moreover, although the tryst was a serious legal matter,[96] the lovers claimed that it was inconsequential. Whether this position was indicative of a real difference of opinion on mores, or simply a bluff, is not clear from the record. I would venture that the lovers were caught up in the highly charged emotions of their romance—first excitement, then perhaps love, and finally indignation at being apprehended.

As for Chen Zhonghe, while venting his own emotions, mostly anger, on the two lovers, he lost sight of the fact that committing a double murder would jeopardize the general welfare of the lineage branch. When his head cleared, his voluntary surrender to county authorities was no doubt intended to protect his lineage from unnecessary or prolonged harassment by runners seeking his arrest. The love affair of 1875 cost the Chens three lives and had involved a large number of kinsmen. The murders and the trial must have left a deep imprint on the lineage itself. Community moral standards applied to everyone, including Catholics, and were of deadly seriousness in rural Gao'an County.

A Catholic Attempts to Rape a Widow: Revenge and Suicide in Jinqi County, 1877–1880

According to the Jinqi magistrate's report, after the death of Xu Shouxiang in 1876, Xu Yuxiang, the deceased man's elder brother, sought his widow, Xu née Yu, for marriage.[97] For a time, the widow just fended off her brother-in-law's advances, but eventually she went to her mother-in-law Xu née Li (hereafter, Mrs. Xu) in hope of controlling the situation. Although the mother rebuked Xu Yuxiang, slowly his ardor turned into obsession. One day during May–June of 1877, Xu Yuxiang found the widow alone in her room. He entered uninvited and unsuccessfully tried to rape her. The widow screamed for help and Mrs. Xu soon arrived to stop the struggle. Xu Yuxiang returned to his own room followed by his mother. He replied to her reprimands with offensive language and an unrepentant attitude. Xu then tied up his mother with a rope, evidently to prevent her further interference. Xu née Yu had quietly slipped away to seek assistance from Xu Ruilong, her uncle by marriage. Xu Ruilong immediately went to untie Mrs. Xu.[98]

By now the entire neighborhood knew of the ruckus and that Mrs. Xu wanted her son prosecuted by the magistrate. Hearing this, Xu Yuxiang quickly left home. Mrs. Xu did not in the end make formal charges, most likely because Xu Ruilong removed the recalcitrant son's name from the Xu lineage's genealogical record.[99] The Xus had now disinherited and ostracized Xu Yuxiang, but how long this solution worked is unclear.[100] From the official report, we know that soon after this Xu Yuxiang converted to Catholicism and had Catholic friends to depend on. He later returned home and began to cause trouble. Xu Ruilong then filed a complaint with the magistrate. The magistrate sent runners to investigate and Xu Yuxiang fled the area to avoid arrest.[101]

Xu Yuxiang now carried a grudge against his uncle and on April 2, 1880, boldly returned home to confront him. Xu Ruilong reprimanded his nephew, but the latter grew surly, cursed, and drew a knife to attack. As Xu Ruilong dodged his nephew, two kinsmen appeared on the scene. They physically subdued Xu Yuxiang and bound his hands. The three men marched the family rebel off towards the county seat. At a rest stop, Xu Yuxiang managed to free himself. Apparently fearing punishment for his various wrongful deeds, he jumped into a pond and drowned. All efforts to save him went for naught.[102]

Xu Ruilong now feared prosecution and punishment. Through another kinsman, he beseeched Mrs. Xu not to report the suicide to county officials. She agreed, partly because Xu Ruilong promised to buy her land and take care of her family, and partly because Xu Yuxiang had been a disobedient and unfilial son anyway.[103] The local *dibao* did not report the death either, yet somehow the magistrate learned of the case and dispatched runners to investigate.[104] Mrs. Xu decided to cooperate fully, went to the magistrate, and lodged a complaint that told everything.

Clearly, Xu Yuxiang's aggressive behavior was not tempered by his conversion to Catholicism. Although he evidently found some solace among Catholic friends, when Xu returned home and challenged his uncle, he acted without the physical presence and support of other Catholics. After kinsmen seized him, Xu feared humiliation and punishment at the magistrate's court, a fate that even his status as a Catholic could not prevent. We will never know whether Xu realized the Catholic Church did not condone suicide. Obviously, religion was not the issue, rather it was the trouble that had grown out of Xu's obsession and violence.

When sentencing Xu Ruilong, the trial officials considered it impossible for him to have foreseen the suicide. The officials stressed the necessity of reporting deaths for verification of circumstances. They decided his punishment by analogy to (*bizhao*) a substatute on the cover-up of a death through bribery.[105] However, officials considered the amount of the bribe relevant only in cases not involving a mourning-circle relationship between the principals. Since this case involved an uncle–nephew relationship, officials sentenced Xu Ruilong to one hundred blows of the heavy bamboo with a one-degree reduction (to ninety blows) because Xu Yuxiang had not died at his hands. Furthermore, authorities decided that Xu Ruilong need not keep his promise to support Mrs. Xu.[106] Of the three other Xu kinsmen involved, only the one who helped arrange the cover-up received punishment.

Officials absolved Mrs. Xu of blame, noting her son had been recalcitrant and that she and the Xu lineage had handled a difficult matter.[107]

We know nothing about Xu Yuxiang's motivation for converting to Catholicism, save the likely propulsion toward it that his disinheritance may have provided. Conversion certainly neither changed him nor helped him. His new religious beliefs clearly did not moderate his anger toward his uncle. Last but not least, his activities and death did not lead to Church intervention, so Catholicism seems at best incidental to this case.

Catholics Try to Force a Widow to Remarry in Baishui Village, Jishui County, 1899

In August 1899 the Zongli Yamen learned that on July 5 people in the village of Baishui had assaulted and kidnapped a priest, Father Dong Fuda.[108] Bishop Coqset blamed the Jishui County magistrate for failing to protect the missionary and not helping him after he suffered serious injuries.[109] At about this time, the Ji'an prefect also received a letter from the Catholic Church, probably written by the bishop. The letter stated that Father Dong left neighboring Yongfeng County to inquire into quarrels involving litigation between common people and Catholics of Baishui and other rural localities in Jishui County. People surnamed Huang, who lived in the countryside at Datangkou, believed the priest had come to instigate litigation and consequently had seized him.[110]

Local officials investigated and found at the center of the trouble two Catholics, Feng Yugui and Huang Bangyi. These men had attempted to force a widow, Zhou née Ye, to remarry with a man who belonged to the local Huang lineage.[111] When their efforts failed, they robbed the widow and sought to have her punished by the Huang lineage under family law.[112] At that moment, the Catholic priest arrived on the scene. Several Huangs went to the church school to personally invite him to come with them to the lineage hall to discuss the matter. Father Dong sensed trouble and exited via a rear window. On the way out, the priest scraped his arm—the full extent of his injuries.[113] A local Catholic congregational headman exhorted everyone to remain calm and stopped any potential trouble.[114] Father Dong then returned to Yongfeng County.[115]

To settle this case, Expectant Magistrate Zhang Pengcheng went to Ji'an to discuss it face to face with Bishop Coqset.[116] In their discussions the bishop stated that Feng and Huang had been falsely accused of robbery. Zhang showed the bishop depositions taken from the widow and her father whereupon the bishop admitted that Huang, a poor commoner, often did not mind his own business. Zhang then readily agreed not to punish them in order to help calm the Catholics and local people.[117] As a gesture of conciliation, the Jishui magistrate provided a sum of money for Father Dong's medical expenses, which Zhang Peng-cheng conveyed to the bishop. The two men from the Huang lineage who had caused the commotion were to be punished with the cangue.[118] The bishop seemed appeased and wrote a letter stating that he considered the case closed.[119]

Details of this case went all the way to both the French legation and the Zongli Yamen in Beijing, though it had been a relatively minor and easily resolved matter. Although the lineage's motivation remained hidden, some local country people thought the Huangs had financial reasons for pressing the remarriage.[120] Besides this possibility, we should note the lineage's position regarding the widow had nothing to do with religion. It was simply that local men who happened to be Catholics became embroiled in a situation common among many families and lineages. Catholics were not immune from the various pressures that compelled men to want widows remarried. Once the problem with the widow arose, the Catholics were as eager as anyone to see it resolved. They went to the priest in hope that he would help. This is another case where Catholics still looked primarily to the lineage for assistance. In this very important sense, Catholics clearly remained closely identified with their kinsmen and invested in rural mores.

Catholic Businesswomen Refuse to Contribute Money to Local Theatrical Performances, Nancheng County, 1899

In December 1899 Father Antoine Tamet, a French missionary stationed in Nancheng County, reported to the French minister that a man named Li Yusheng had harassed Catholic women and the magistrate had punished Catholics because they would not contribute money to support local theatrical performances. The minister requested that the Zongli Yamen order Jiangxi officials to investigate.[121] Since the reply by the governor of Jiangxi is not available, we must rely on information provided by the French.

Father Tamet stated that four Catholic women moved from neighboring Linchuan County to Xiaoshi Street in Nancheng County's thirty-seventh *du*. The women all had two surnames, indicating their marital status, but the involvement or presence of their husbands went without comment. They appeared to be completely on their own and without any male support—most likely they were all widows. These women had jointly established and operated a retail business of some sort, and had done so for many years.[122]

Shopkeepers in the area all contributed money to support theatrical performances presented as part of periodic local festivals. Accordingly, the *du* headman, Li Yusheng, expected money from the businesswomen, too. When they refused to contribute, Li had several local ruffians knock down their shop's door and steal items. While doing so, they started a fire—perhaps intentionally, perhaps accidentally—which spread to some twenty shops and houses in the area. The fire destroyed much property and caused the loss of one life.[123]

One of the Catholic women, Yang Yongtai, then filed a complaint with the magistrate, forcing him to hold a formal inquiry into her allegations of harassment. According to Father Tamet, Li Yusheng responded by bribing yamen functionaries to get the magistrate to arrest the women and four other Catholics. Yamen underlings beat the Catholics in an attempt to force them to make the expected monetary contributions. The Catholics still refused, so the magistrate had them punished and kept in detention at the county jail.[124] Although Father Tamet intervened on their behalf, his efforts had no impact on the magistrate. Thus, the priest appealed directly to the French minister in Beijing.

The minister stated in his communication to the Zongli Yamen that he wanted the Nancheng magistrate to release the Catholics from jail. In addition, the minister pointed out that the Chinese could not require Catholics to contribute money to certain community activities such as theatrical performances and rites devoted to entertaining local temple deities. Indeed, the Zongli Yamen had made this concession in the early 1860s, yet in many localities people continued to expect Catholics to contribute.[125] With the Catholics' business located among other shops and the homes of non-Catholics, the *du* headman evidently found it difficult to see them as anything but part of the rural community.

Particularly noteworthy is that this case involved Catholic women, who, apparently independent of any male assistance, ran a business and supported themselves with income from it. Their financial success and a sympathetic missionary may explain the self-confidence needed to stand up—not just as Catholics, but also as women—to the *du* headman and his bullies. In this case, we see that women in rural China may have had more options for getting by than are usually expected and more moxie than they are generally given credit for.

★　　　★　　　★　　　★　　　★

The cases presented in this chapter provide a sharp picture of local Chinese society, with lineages, families, and individuals—both Catholic and non-Catholic—in the foreground. Several common issues stand out. In the case of Yan Bingyi we noted his failure to support his grandfather's tablet at the local temple. Although we can easily identify ancestor veneration as a pivotal point of tension between Catholics and their relatives, we must remember that other issues were involved, too. Yan Bingyi's case and others given here illustrate how pecuniary motivations were significant on both sides. During the periodic division of common lineage property, income, or benefits, the exclusion of Catholics increased the proportionate share for non-Catholics. Thus, non-Catholics stood to gain by excluding them. However, Catholics who were still involved in other group affairs expected a share of certain lineage benefits. Catholics did not see their religion as relevant to their status as continuing members of their kinship groups or as part of the local community

The cases here also allow us to see how people handled disputes and the workings of justice through, as one scholar terms it, the informal (kinship and community) mediation and formal (county magistrate) adjudication systems.[126] On the informal side, families and lineages not only served as mutual support systems, they also regulated rural life by maintaining and enforcing proper behavior on the part of all members. Families and lineages were the first line of defense in preserving social order. On the formal side, the magistrate's ability to perform his stabilizing role at the local level depended to a great degree on the reportorial work of subcounty personnel such as the *dibao*. When such personnel did not report community problems to the county yamen, magistrates were denied the crucial information needed to maintain public security. Whenever Christians were implicated in the breakdown of local security, government officials went on alert. This is an important topic that I will pursue in depth in chapter 6.

Formal government actions supported family and lineage methods of control and reinforced traditions regarding widow chastity, marital fidelity, and male and elder generation dominance. The world of the common people—both Catholics and non-Catholics—reflected the values behind such traditions. Catholicism seems to have had little impact on the currency of local Chinese values in Jiangxi's rural congregations. One explanation for this is the limited Church involvement in cases centered on customary rules. And Yan Bingyi's use of the Church to forward his complaint all the way to Beijing did not become standard practice.

It appears then that no simple characterization fits Catholic or non-Catholic interests and behaviors in rural Jiangxi. What are we to make of the range of standards and actions seen among rural people? I believe that among the varied and complex factors that affected everyday life were not only the tangled strands of human emotions, but also the underlying insecurity of life in the late Qing. Regardless of religious beliefs, security for men and women, married and widowed, families and lineages, was tied to local stability and a steady livelihood that in turn depended on the ownership or control of property. These issues were of common concern for everyone.

Chapter 5

Settling Property Disputes Involving Christians and Missionaries

Rural property transactions generated "a substantial number of disputes and lawsuits" in the late Qing.[1] Since Christians remained a part of the communities in which they lived, it is not surprising to find them also entangled in these problems or participating in this larger sphere of rural interaction. Proposed purchases and actual transactions, usually for the purpose of establishing a formal church in the community, enmeshed not only the buyers and sellers, but also other local residents with vested interests. Thus, cases involving rural resource use and geomantic concerns in various times and at different locales reveal the social dynamics at the heart of property disputes and give further cues that bolster our understanding of Christianity at the local level. These disputes were often resolved because Catholics and non-Catholics found mutual accommodation preferable to any alternative.

But when missionaries got involved, the Catholic Church hierarchy and the Chinese bureaucracy stepped in to wrangle over legal and technical issues. The Church usually pointed to its treaty-based right to own property in China. Qing officials, on the other hand, wanted to oversee how missionaries or Christians acquired their property and monitor their compliance with standard purchase procedures established by treaty and supplemented by bilateral agreements between France and China. To better understand the complexities of local land disputes in Jiangxi, we must first delve into the historical background of Church-owned property in China and the treaty provisions governing real estate transactions.

The Early Period and Treaty Agreements

From the very beginning, missionaries in China sought to purchase real estate to establish residences, mission stations, and churches. Matteo

Ricci obtained the Catholic Church's first property in Jiangxi when Ming officials permitted him to buy a building in Nanchang in 1595 for use as a residence.[2] Unfortunately, there is a dearth of information on how and where other properties were acquired by the Jesuit, Franciscan, Dominican, and Vincentian missionaries who came to Jiangxi over the next three centuries. We do know, however, that imperial efforts to curb Catholic activities during the eighteenth century affected the public operation and maintenance of existing churches. From 1724 through the early nineteenth century, missionaries either abandoned various Church properties in the cities and large towns or saw them confiscated by Chinese officials. Only a handful of missionaries remained in China, and they moved away from provincial and county administrative centers and operated clandestinely in order to avoid trouble.[3]

Beginning in the 1810s Catholic missionaries returned to China with renewed zeal and in ever-increasing numbers. Disregarding both personal safety and imperial proscription, Catholic priests ministered to the faithful who remained attached to the surviving rural chapels or oratories and, at the same time, began to establish new churches. As noted in chapter 2, during the early Daoguang reign (1821–1850) a Franciscan missionary bought property in a rural area of Gan County in southern Jiangxi and built a church there.[4] In northern Jiangxi near Wucheng, a central marketplace and active commercial center, Vincentian missionaries opened a new church in 1834.[5] Such initiatives portended further Catholic Church expansion that would follow the forcible opening of China by Western powers. The Opium War and the treaties that followed reflected, in part, the growing presence and influence of the mission enterprise. In the treaties of 1842 and 1844 missionaries acquired the right to reside and build churches in the five newly opened treaty ports. These treaties implicitly prohibited missionaries from traveling, residing, or proselytizing in the interior.[6] Under pressure from the French, the emperor issued an edict in 1844 ending the 1724 proscription of Christianity. The Qing now officially tolerated its practice by Chinese as long as Christians did not "excite trouble by improper conduct."[7] The edict, however, explicitly restricted missionaries to the treaty ports. In 1846 the emperor ordered Church property built during the reign of the Kangxi emperor (1662–1722) and still preserved to be restored to Chinese Catholics except "those churches which have been converted into temples and dwelling houses for the people." The emperor reiterated the prohibition against missionaries being in the interior of China.[8]

It goes without saying that some missionaries ignored the emperor's travel limitations and thereby created a need for further treaty clarifications of their position and rights in China. Thus, when the Western powers and China negotiated new treaties from 1858 to 1860, missionaries obtained by treaty the right to proselytize anywhere in China, while Chinese were granted the right to practice Christianity without harassment or interference if they so chose.[9]

The most significant treaty change for missionaries came in Article VI of the Sino-French Convention of 1860. This article confirmed the emperor's 1846 restoration of Church property while also broadening the wording. The Chinese government now agreed to compensate Chinese Christians for "churches, schools, cemeteries, lands, and buildings" confiscated from them earlier. The article did not specifically limit compensation to losses that occurred during Kangxi's reign period. Missionaries considered the restoration of previously owned properties important, but not as crucial as the establishment of new bases anywhere in China from which they could expand. Their presence, which they wanted to be permanent, required the acquisition of new Church properties. Since the treaty negotiators had not specifically addressed this issue, extraordinary measures were taken to correct the lapse: a Catholic missionary serving as translator for the French government surreptitiously added to the Chinese text of Article VI a sentence not included in the authoritative French version. This additional sentence granted French missionaries the right "to rent and purchase land in all the provinces, and to erect buildings thereupon at pleasure."[10]

French missionaries quickly began to rent or purchase various properties and construct new churches, and Qing authorities permitted it. Missionaries of other nationalities assumed the same rights and benefits as the French via treaties that accorded most-favored-nation treatment to the signatories. Chinese officials did not realize until 1869 that these words were present only in the Chinese version of the treaty and were, technically, spurious.[11] By that time, the expanded property gains brought about by the language added to the Chinese version of the treaty, became a fait accompli.

The Berthemy Convention, 1865

The efforts of French missionaries to recover previously confiscated properties and to purchase new sites soon opened questions regarding implementation of the treaty articles and the establishment of acquisition procedures. Matters came to a head in early 1865 when Li Hongzhang, the governor of Jiangsu, refused to permit missionaries to purchase property located outside the treaty ports of his province.[12] The French minister in Beijing, Jules Berthemy, wrote to the Zongli Yamen to protest this contravention of Article VI. After discussions with the French, the Zongli Yamen formally agreed on February 20, 1865, to the following:

> Hereafter, if French missionaries enter the interior to purchase land and buildings, the seller (insert the name) shall specify in the deed of sale that he sold the property to become part of the collective property of the Catholic church of that place. It will be unnecessary to record the names of the missionary and the [Chinese] Christians."[13]

This short statement constitutes the entirety of the Berthemy Convention.

Although the French did not officially publish the Berthemy Convention until sometime later, they clearly considered it part of the treaty corpus.[14] On the Chinese side, the Zongli Yamen put its weight behind the agreement and brought into line provincial authorities like Governor Li Hongzhang. The Berthemy Convention did help clarify the mechanics of property purchases by French missionaries: the seller was to note on the deed that he sold the property to members of the local Catholic Church, collectively. By excluding any non-Chinese individual or missionary organization from the deed, the Chinese, in essence, tried to establish that the property remained under Chinese jurisdiction rather than becoming part of treaty port enclaves or leased areas.[15] The Zongli Yamen reiterated this principle in a letter to Li Hongzhang, accompanied by a transcript of the Berthemy Convention. The Zongli Yamen emphasized that if Church properties always belonged to Chinese Christians collectively then China certainly would not be harmed by the practice.[16]

In their implementation of the Berthemy Convention Zongli Yamen officials either assumed or intended that a property owner contemplating a sale to the Church would first inform local authorities and obtain their approval before proceeding. Thus, no one would make direct sales of private property; all sales would be channeled through Chinese official-dom.[17] The earliest case testing this point that I have found in the *Jiaowu jiao'an dang* occurred in 1868. On December 19, in a communication to the French minister over a property purchase dispute in the city of Shengjing (Shenyang), officials of the Zongli Yamen stated that, according to their understanding of the Berthemy Convention, Catholic missionaries should first find suitable property, discuss the purchase and terms with the owner, then report the proposed purchase to local officials for handling.[18]

The Shengjing property dispute and many others that followed revealed the limitations of the Berthemy Convention. Although the text of the agreement spelled out the details for listing the new property owners, it did not specify the steps that led to completion of a sale. Since local officials frequently had to deal with problems arising from property transactions, the Zongli Yamen took the position that if local officials approved all the transactions, such potential problems could be avoided. Recurring problems included outright fraudulent sale by people who did not own a property or property sold by people who possessed only a clouded title; other problems involved the location of a property, its intended use, and the conformity of that use to community beliefs about local geomantic forces.

To missionaries, however, official involvement meant at the very least obstacles and delays to the purchase of property, and often automatic denial of approval. Catholic priests suspected that Chinese officials simply did not want churches established in their jurisdictions and thus sought to make purchases difficult. Local officials seemed all too ready to point, for example, to community concerns about local geomancy or to the validity of a deed as reason for blocking a sale.

Since property sales to the Church occurred in all parts of China, Chinese officials needed to find a general way to prevent these accompanying problems. In 1876 the governor-general of the Liangguang provinces reported that property owners contracting to sell property to the Catholic Church must first inform local officials. They then would investigate the transaction, verifying the property's location, its boundaries, and the validity of the owner's deed. They would also determine that the property owner indeed wanted to sell the property to the Church. If local officials encountered no problems or obstacles, they would approve the sale. However, should a property owner sell privately to the Church without first reporting the sale to local officials, that seller would be punished severely.[19]

This formal Chinese position and the continuing conflict centering on property purchases led the French minister, Frédéric-Albert Bourée, to complain in early 1882 to the Zongli Yamen. On February 5 the Zongli Yamen replied that local officials must be informed of pending sales to the Catholic Church to ascertain that the transactions conform to Berthemy Convention stipulations: the deed must note the seller's name and list the new owners of the property as the collective members of the local church. According to the Zongli Yamen, and this was a new point, the deed must also be presented to local officials who would affix a seal or stamp on payment of the stamp fee. Without an officially stamped deed as proof of ownership, there could be future controversy and litigation. The Zongli Yamen believed that this procedure, which came at the end of the transaction and which amounted to a sort of title search and recording in modern terms, would help eliminate fraudulent sales and later regrets (i.e., law suits) by the purchaser. The Zongli Yamen stated that this fully conformed with the spirit of the Berthemy Convention and certainly was not a contravention of it or any treaty article.[20]

Minister Bourée wanted to clarify that the buyer's payment of the stamp fee and local official's stamping of the deed came at the end of the transaction. In other words, local officials did not actually approve the sale. The Zongli Yamen, provincial authorities, and local officials all thought otherwise. In November 1891, Liu Kunyi, the superintendent of trade for the southern ports, ordered that pending property sales to missionaries must continue to be first reported to local officials for approval.[21] Although the French consul at Shanghai later protested that this procedure was not part of any Sino-French agreement, the Chinese apparently ignored him.[22]

There matters rested until yet another property dipute, this one in Lezhi County, Sichuan, caused the French minister, A. Gérard, to send a communication in July 1894 to the Zongli Yamen.[23] The Lezhi case precipitated a general discussion of the Berthemy Convention and led to its revision.

The Gérard Convention, 1895

Over the next year, the Zongli Yamen and the French minister exchanged communications on the issue of property transactions. Each side dug deep into its respective files for information to support its position. The Zongli Yamen brought up the Shengjing case of 1868, stating that property purchase regulations stipulated a seller must, prior to the sale of property to missionaries, report the pending sale to local officials for approval.[24] Minister Gérard replied by quoting the text of the Berthemy Convention and by pointing out that no such statement existed. Gérard also brought up the efforts of the former French minister, Bourée, to settle this same question. According to Gérard's understanding of Bourée's communications and the Zongli Yamen's replies, only after the consummation of the sale would the buyer submit the deed to local officials in order to pay the deed stamp fee and have the deed stamped. Gérard conceded that this complied with Chinese law and did not contravene any treaty article. By handling it this way, local officials need not get involved prior to a sale or provide their approval of it. To eliminate further misunderstandings at the local level, Gérard requested that the original text of the Berthemy Convention be copied off to the provinces so that high authorities there could in turn order local officials to cease requiring prior notification and approval of property transactions.[25]

On October 15, 1894, the Zongli Yamen again attempted to explain to the French the Chinese view of the property purchase procedure. The requirement that real estate transactions be reported to local officials for approval arose because common people often traded property that had several deeds or because a village or a lineage held property in common. By having local officials first investigate and approve the proposed sale, these details as well as possible fraud and other abuses could be discovered. Thus, Chinese officials made this requirement to protect missionaries from deception and financial loss, not to create difficulties for them.[26] Gérard replied that, in his opinion, if missionaries had to first obtain official approval to purchase a piece of property, local officials would block the sale. Given his expectation of outright discrimination, Gérard naturally saw no other solution except strict compliance with the treaty agreements.[27]

Compliance with the treaty agreements, to Gérard, included the Berthemy Convention. In 1894 Gérard complained to the Zongli Yamen about altered versions of the convention possessed by officials in different parts of China. These versions included added sentences that required sellers to obtain, prior to a sale, the approval of local officials.[28] On February 7, 1895, Gérard wrote to the Zongli Yamen to complain that the magistrate of Poyang County, Jiangxi, used a version of the Berthemy Convention that included the added language, and would not agree to or announce locally the deletion of it.[29]

The slowness of the Chinese response to such complaints and the difficulty encountered by the French in their attempts to change a thirty-year-old bureaucratic procedure apparently led Gérard to conclude that a new, clearly worded agreement on the property purchase procedure should be made. On March 28, 1895, the French minister sent the following text to the Zongli Yamen:

> Hereafter, if French missionaries enter the interior to purchase land and buildings, the seller (insert the name) shall specify in the deed of sale that he sold the property to become part of the collective property of the Catholic church of that place. It will be unnecessary to record the names of the missionary and the [Chinese] Christians. The Catholic mission after the execution of the deed, will pay the registration fee assessed by the law of China on the deeds of sale and at the same rate. The seller shall not be bound to give notice to the local authorities of his intention to sell or to apply for a previous permit.[30]

This new text became known as the Gérard Convention and the Zongli Yamen accepted it as a solution to the ongoing controversy regarding the payment of stamp (registration) fees and the timing of local officials' involvement in property purchases. The Catholic Church would pay the fees at the regular rate and local officials would not be involved in a transaction until the sale had been closed.

On April 8, 1895, the Zongli Yamen sent the Gérard Convention to all high provincial officials for their notification and further distribution within their respective jurisdictions.[31] Per Gérard's request, the Zongli Yamen on May 26, 1895, sent out a second copy of the convention, this one affixed with official seals, to the various provinces.[32] The Chinese agreed that these regulations would govern all subsequent property transactions between Chinese and Catholic missionaries. On the French side, the minister had the communications between the legation and the Zongli Yamen printed in two booklets that he distributed to his consuls.

The minister apparently also sent it to various bishops for their information and reference.[33] The last page of the second booklet had in bold type "Definitive Text" with the full text in Chinese below; it is not hard to guess its intended use.[34]

Local Concerns Over Property Ownership, Church Location, and Purchase Procedures in Jiangxi

To representatives of the French government in China the Gérard Convention and earlier agreements regarding missionaries' rights asserted their national interest in the promotion and protection of Catholicism. In the *jiao'an* documents, the missionaries' position often appears legalistic and oblivious to Chinese sensitivities and the practical aspects of property cases. Chinese officials, for their part, acted formalistically, imposing their own interpretation of treaty articles and agreements in adjudication of disputes involving missionaries and Christians. The following cases reveal the bureaucratic mind-set of both sides, as well as issues that immediately concerned rural people, such as land rights and access to resources. In all these cases we not only find Catholics in typical dealings with non-Catholics, but we also see both sides working together to solve problems.

Who Owns This Land? Disputes Over Property Rights at Pinglushang, Gan County, 1886–1896

In late June 1886 Bishop Géraud Bray of the Vicariate of Northern Jiangxi informed the daotai at Jiujiang that a church in Ganzhou Prefecture had been destroyed and a priest had disappeared. At about this time Bishop Bray's confreres in the Vicariate of Southern Jiangxi wrote letters to Europe stating that a violent, horrible "persecution" had occurred in the Ganzhou area when the magistrate and some gentry had set a large crowd upon the Catholics. The crowd pillaged and dispersed four large congregations, destroyed Church property including the bishop's boat, as well as capturing and beating a priest. The priest escaped and fled along with numerous Catholics. Losses had been heavy.[35]

Provincial authorities in Nanchang quickly met to discuss the situation.[36] The governor realized that local officials might not have properly protected the Christians.[37] Because of this concern, and the fact that it looked like a difficult case, the governor wanted to assign a capable deputy with prior experience in handling *jiao'an*. The only man available with such qualifications was Cai Shichun, the Nanchang first class subprefect (*tongzhi*). Cai left immediately, traveling nonstop more than three hundred miles to arrive at Ganzhou as soon as possible.[38]

Background to the case. High-level officials in Nanchang already knew something about the situation, for they had received a report from Magistrate Li Tingchun of Gan County. Li stated that at Pinglushang, the general name for a rural marketplace situated about seven miles south of the city of Ganzhou, there had previously been trouble between a large Catholic family named Xie and local gentry.[39]

The Xies had moved to Gan County from neighboring Xinfeng County about one hundred years earlier and had lived for at least two decades on a hillside farmstead at Longwang, one-third of a mile from Pinglushang. Beginning in 1860 the Xies tangled with Yang Chusan, a local man who held official rank, over various problems arising from the land the Xies worked.[40] In February 1873 the Gan County magistrate, Cui Guobang, ordered runners to summon both parties for trial regarding those disputes. Yang and the Xies each submitted several deeds and contracts. Based on the evidence, the magistrate ruled against the Xies, ordering them to halt construction of a building located on Yang's property and to pay Yang back taxes on other land. The magistrate also ordered Xie Lanren, a catechist, to repudiate any intention of constructing a chapel building. The catechist refused and the magistrate had him imprisoned.[41] According to the magistrate, the Xies had not stated in any previous litigation that they intended the unfinished building to serve as a chapel; only after Yang Chusan died in March 1873 did they abruptly make this claim. Later Bishop Bray would accept this claim as fact, wrongly believing that government interference prevented the building's use as a chapel. However, this was just one of several thorny issues that prevented the resolution of this case.[42]

The bishop's interest in this case also had to do with the long history of Catholic activity that, in this part of Gan County, dated back at least to the 1790s. Missionaries had had some success over the years, since many people with the surname Xie came to practice Catholicism.[43] By the late 1870s, the "mission of Pinglushang" consisted of four congregations with a total of 280 Catholics.[44] Exactly where the early priests held religious services is unknown. We do know, however, that a Franciscan priest purchased property from the Xies and established a church around 1825.[45] In 1871 the Vincentians established a replacement or new church despite the opposition of Yang Baoguang, a local *shengyuan* degree holder and member of a family feuding with the Xies.[46]

Over the next four years locals slandered and libeled the Catholics. In 1876 Bishop Bray obtained a copy of a placard, signed by the elders of six local villages, circulating in the Ganzhou area. The placard referred to the Xies as outsiders and blamed them for attracting "the propagators of a perverse religion." Moreover, the placard said the Xies had stolen land from the Yangs. Only because Xie Yingping, a Catholic *shengyuan* degree holder, had written to the "chief of the sect," that is, to the bishop, had officials intervened to thwart local sentiment and permitted a church there.[47] A Vincentian priest working at Pinglushang reported that about the time of his departure for a retreat, held during September 1876, local gentry hired three hundred men to scare him off and to expel Catholics from the area. When the gentry discovered that the "foreign devil" had already departed, one goal seemed fulfilled. However, the resistance of the numerous Catholics to bullying at the urging of a Chinese priest and the Catholic *shengyuan* may have also given pause to the local gentry and actually contributed to the disbanding of the hired thugs.[48] There were no further problems until the 1886 incident.

The Xies versus the Yangming Academy. In 1886 at the behest of Bishop François-Adrien Rouger who had visited the previous fall, the Xies began to construct at Longwang a European-style building they intended to use as a Catholic charity school (*yixue*).[49] The director of the local Yangming Academy (*shuyuan*), Shi Zhaohua, a *gongsheng* degree holder, apparently jealous of the new structures, not only claimed ownership of the Long-wang property for the academy, but also objected to the style of this unauthorized building. In addition, the academy contended the Xies were several years in arrears on rent payments.[50]

The first real hint of trouble came at the time of the prefectural *sui* examinations when a large number of students from the area and neighboring counties gathered in Ganzhou.[51] Most likely candidates from the Yangming Academy brought the local building problem to the attention of their peers, but the personal intercession of Magistrate Li

Tingchun prevented them from going to the building site and starting trouble with the Catholics.[52] To help smooth ruffled feelings the magistrate ordered the Xies to halt construction and sent runners to guard the building materials and watch for mischief-makers. The magistrate also sent *baojia* gentry (*shenshi*) to the various rural districts to restrain the people as well as to announce that there must be no further incidents.[53]

On June 21, 1886, Magistrate Li Tingchun began proceedings to settle the property dispute between the Xies and the Yangming Academy even though three Catholics from the Xie family defied summons to appear. This already complicated case became muddled further on June 25 when local people discovered a dead man lying outside a wall that enclosed the Xies' home at Longwang. Blood oozed from the corpse's mouth and people who saw the body presumed that the death had been violent.[54] Before the magistrate and a coroner arrived on the scene to make inquiries, the European-style school building caught on fire and suffered damage. A small church at nearby Cangliaoqian was also damaged that same day. Two Catholic priests and some of the Xies fled the area.[55]

Louis Boscat, a French priest stationed at Ji'an, wrote in a letter to Chinese officials that these events could be linked to Bishop Rouger's earlier visit. Bishop Rouger wanted the small church at Cangliaoqian replaced by a larger one and ordered a new school built on land already purchased at Longwang. But in an effort to tarnish the local Catholics' reputation, someone dumped a corpse outside the Xies' residence. Soon afterward, Father Boscat noted, a crowd of more than one thousand commoners assaulted the local priest, robbed Catholics, and set fire to the church and the school building. The Catholics had reported everything to local authorities, yet they did nothing. Father Boscat wanted the local Catholics protected.[56]

When Magistrate Li Tingchun visited the scene of the trouble at Pinglushang on June 28, he noted minor fire damage to the Xies' house and questioned neighbors about it. They told him that people saw the Xies start it. A Catholic woman named Xie and a local government functionary, probably a *dibao*, both confirmed this.[57] However, the magistrate still had many questions about the fire, the apparent homicide, and the land dispute. If he were to find the answers, hold a new trial, and reach a judgment, he needed time. He requested that there be no administrative deadline set for closing the case.[58]

The deputy sent from the provincial capital, Subprefect Cai Shichun, arrived in Ganzhou in early August 1886. Together with Ganzhou prefect Cui Guobang, who had been involved in the property case in 1873 as magistrate, and two locally assigned deputies, Cai went to Pinglushang on August 9.[59] The entourage was one mile from its destination when Li Tonghong, a local elder, and eighteen men approached with a petition. They claimed that local Catholics had insulted them and requested official action to stop it. The officials said they would investigate the matter but, in the meantime, the men should restrain their juniors and neighbors from taking independent action; everyone should mind his own business.[60]

At Pinglushang, the prefect and subprefect found the titles to properties held by Catholics at nearby Longwang and Cangliaoqian at the center of the turmoil. The Xies' deed to the Cangliaoqian land was dated and recorded in 1797.[61] However, the Yangming Academy had a document for the same property dated 1844 and another deed for the Longwang land dated 1876.[62] The academy had purchased the latter property from a family named Guo, and a tax-seal showed that the academy had properly registered the deed. This and other evidence convinced the officials that the Xies had actually been leasing the land at Longwang.[63] Although they had not signed a new lease with the academy in 1876, they had continued to pay the same amount of rent as before.[64]

The prefect and subprefect ruled that both the Longwang and Cangliaoqian properties belonged to the academy. The European-style building under construction at the Longwang location was to be removed and the fields returned to the management of the academy.[65] Upon learning of this decision, the Xies counterclaimed that "it was a Jiangxi custom that in renting land, the skin was acquired, not the bones." They owned the "skin" or surface rights; the academy owned the "bones" or subsoil rights. If they surrendered their surface rights without compensation, argued the Xies, there would be no money with which to acquire new "skin." Moreover, there was no place locally to resettle.[66] The officials replied that the Xies had insufficient proof to substantiate their claim, but the Xie lineage could discuss it further and petition again within five days. In the end, the officials just told the Xies not to depend on foreigners for help, not to insult the local people, and not to resist appearance in court if officially summoned.[67] They did not order the properties immediately returned to the academy, and the Xies retained possession.[68]

The Ganzhou prefect and the Nanchang subprefect no doubt realized that the entire problem at Pinglushang could have been avoided if the priests had only followed properly land-purchase procedures. Local and provincial-level officials pointed out that in 1865 with the Berthemy Convention the French agreed to report Church property transactions to local officials for approval. It was their understanding that officials would determine if the seller had clear title and if any obstacles to the sale existed. Then, and only then, could the transaction be consummated, with the collective members of the local Church listed on the deed as the new owner rather than individual priests or Catholics.[69] No one on the Catholic side at Pinglushang had complied with these regulations, probably, in part, because of the long history of Catholic churches in the area. Jiangxi officials requested that the Zongli Yamen pursue this with the French minister in order to secure his agreement and missionary compliance with the Berthemy Convention. The officials also hoped that the minister would order the bishop in Jiangxi to instruct the Xies to return the property voluntarily to the control of the academy.[70]

Instead of a direct reply from the French minister, the Chinese received an indirect response from Bishop Jules-Auguste Coqset—newly promoted to that position for the Vicariate of Southern Jiangxi—who went to Ganzhou during the spring of 1888. The bishop intended to see the damaged church at Cangliaoqian repaired,[71] and thus ignored not only property purchase procedures, but also the official ruling that the property belonged to the academy. Clearly, the bishop considered the cause above Chinese law. Probably because of his position, the Xies decided to ignore the February 1887 deadline for payment of overdue rents to the academy and removal of the European-style building.[72]

Such defiance directly challenged government authority. The Catholics' decision to restart work on the European-style building on lunar New Year's Day, February 9, 1891, compounded the problem.[73] The local people roared in protest. Ganzhou officials reported that control had become difficult.[74] Governor Dexing stated that

> If the earlier decision [of the prefect and subprefect] was overturned and [Catholics] planned construction, then inevitably there would be friction

between the [local] people and Catholics. The Ganzhou people are truculent, determined, and unified. If a crowd starts a disturbance, local officials will not be able to protect [the Catholics].[75]

With local feelings nearing the boiling point, Bishop Coqset added fuel to the fire. He demanded, with support from the French minister, that Ganzhou officials arrange a meeting for him with the academy so that each side could examine and compare the other's property deeds. Ganzhou officials thought this unnecessary unless the bishop had a deed not submitted earlier. Furthermore, reopening the case would alienate the already agitated academy students.[76] In broader terms, the governor feared that the French were trying out a new way to coerce the Chinese side and that a precedent once established would be hard to live with.[77]

The dilemma was one confronted elsewhere. One official move disturbed those influential locally; the countermove exacerbated Sino-Western relations.[78] The Ganzhou prefect and the Gan County magistrate did not let this paralyze them. They worked with *baojia* deputies to impress upon the local people just what was at stake.[79] To be sure, the conduct of the academy's students at examination time would remain a concern, but officials placated them for the time being by arresting three Xies for disobeying the earlier trial settlement and ignoring the February 1887 deadline for compliance.[80] By the time Chinese authorities reluctantly agreed to the French demand for the face-to-face comparison of deeds in 1891, tempers at Pinglushang presumably had cooled off.[81]

A surprising conclusion. What transpired between Catholics and non-Catholics in this part of Gan County over the next five years is unknown. A sort of stalemate must have existed because French and Chinese officials did nothing more about the case and reported no new problems. Then, in 1896, Daotai Huang Zunxian of the Nanjing foreign affairs bureau received a commission as deputy to handle *jiao'an* for five provinces. The governor of Jiangxi ordered Expectant Magistrate Xu Baolian to take the various open case files for Jiangxi to Shanghai and assist the daotai in his investigations. The Gan County property disputes for Pinglushang were among those files.

At Shanghai, Xu reexamined the evidence and, supported by Daotai Huang, ruled that the Cangliaoqian property in fact belonged to the

Church.[82] Although the Xies could not prove undisputed ownership, missionaries did have tax receipts dating back to 1825, indicating clearly that Franciscans had purchased the property at that time.[83] From this finding the daotai agreed in an exchange with the French consul-general to have Gan County officials issue a replacement deed (with stamps) that indicated the property's boundaries. The new deed would clarify the size of the property and its ownership. Officials also agreed to permit the Catholics to proceed with their building plans without further obstruction and with official protection. The French in turn assured the daotai that the architectural style of the school and hospital the Catholics intended to construct would not be European; instead, they would follow Chinese building styles in accord with local customs.[84]

This case tells us several things about a rural situation over an extended period of time. First, it illustrates how people in the Pinglushang area of Gan County struggled over land resources. It has been noted that litigation between the Xies and the Yangming Academy over back rent payments predated the 1886 conflict. The official ruling that the Xies had no rights to the land caused them real concern. As much as the immediate monetary loss, the Xies feared the unavailability of other farmland. With this in their minds and with the trial settlement hanging over their heads, the Xie family could only cling tenaciously to the land. The academy accused the Xies of forcibly occupying the property, but just how they held off the academy is unclear.[85] The academy, which enjoyed the support of local degree holders, was unable to collect back rents from their tenants, nor could it intimidate them. Ultimately, it looked to government officials for resolution of the conflict and enforcement of the judgment.[86]

Although in 1876 Catholicism itself was raised as an issue in this case, this concern quickly gave way to first the land resource issue then to criticism about the style of school building under construction. While members of the Yangming Academy and local people successfully stopped the school's construction, the conflict around it did not escalate to include claims that a Catholic school would be potentially disruptive or that Catholic doctrine was a problem. Opposition to the Church was active enough in the 1880s, but I believe its proponents proved ineffective because the social context was one in which the local Catholics were a known part of the community. After all, they had already coexisted with people in the area for some one hundred years by the time the trouble began. And like everyone, whether Catholic or non-Catholic, gentry or commoner, their concerns were ultimately practical ones—property control, rents, and land resources.

The Improper Sale of Lineage Property to a Missionary, Lüqi County, 1894

This case, too, centers on the control of property. In 1864 Lin Wenyu, a military *juren* degree holder, contracted with Lin née Chen for the purchase of a building and land. Lin Wenyu did not make full payment so the seller retained the property deed and received annual payments, part of which went to pay taxes. After the government revoked Lin Wenyu's degree he fell upon hard times. Needing money but without clear title, he sold this property to a Catholic missionary; the precise date of the sale was not disclosed, but it was probably in the early 1890s. Father Antoine Tamet later repaired the building and began to use it as a church.[87]

In the spring of 1894 the Lüqi County magistrate received a complaint about the legality of the transaction from the property's original owner, one Lin Chunfa, a relative of Lin née Chen and possibly her heir. In addition, members of the Lin lineage complained that Lin Wenyu owed them grain and that he acted in a hostile manner towards them. Father Tamet further complicated the situation by writing in 1894 directly to the Jianchang prefect regarding the Catholic Church's claim to the property. The prefect ordered a thorough investigation and assigned a deputy to assist the magistrate adjudicate the dispute.[88]

Although various local gentry and common people petitioned the magistrate and deputy that the property had special geomantic character-istics, the two officials evidently dismissed those claims. Rather, they con-centrated their investigation on the ownership question. According to the deposition of Lin Chunfa, the property actually belonged to the Lin lineage. In fact, the Lins had already held public discussions about turning the building into a lineage hall.[89] Lin Wenyu also testified on the purchase details and admitted that his sale of the property to the missionary had been a mistake.[90]

After weighing the evidence, the magistrate reached a decision. He ordered Lin Wenyu to return the purchase money to the missionary, which would, in effect, void the sale. Lin, however, did not have the money to return. Father Tamet, for his part, refused to cooperate, probably because he had already invested money in repairing the building. The priest held onto the deed he had received from Lin Wenyu. Faced with these problems, the magistrate decided to validate the sale to the missionary and provided an official seal for the deed.[91] This action closed the case.

The governor of Jiangxi informed the Zongli Yamen of these details in October of 1899. By that time officials noted that the case had been concluded several years earlier, that the local people and Catholics coexisted peacefully, and that there had been no further problems in the area.[92] Although we may ask what legal justification the magistrate had for allowing the missionary to keep property with an unclear title, the significant fact remains that the Lin lineage accepted this settlement and the local community returned to life as usual.

Firewood as a Resource Issue: Local People Worry About Access to Mountain Land Leased by British Missionaries, Dehua County, 1895–1896

In early 1895 a commoner named Wan Dongfu and other land-owners agreed to give long-term leases of land, concentrated mostly at a mountain spring area called Changzhong, to a British missionary named Edward Little.[93] According to Reverend Little, they concluded the transaction only after the property owners agreed and prominent gentry approved as well as guaranteed it.[94] Reverend Little and other missionaries planned to develop this cool highland location in northern Jiangxi, then generally known as Guniuling—today part of an area known as Lushan—into a health retreat from the summer heat and a vacation resort for Westerners' use. But when the missionaries began to construct houses, local common people opposed it and destroyed their building materials.[95]

The daotai at Jiujiang ordered the acting magistrate of Dehua County to conduct an official inquiry. The acting magistrate, after consulting with local gentry and elders, verified the validity of the lease agreements between Wan Dongfu et al and Reverend Little. Furthermore, neither the gentry nor the common people could find any reason, including geomancy, to prevent the construction. However, the locals of the area did have one concern—they feared that British control of the mountain land would mean an end to their firewood gathering activities there.[96]

In the negotiated settlement of the case Chinese officials agreed that Reverend Little and other missionaries could lease and develop the property at Changzhong. The Chinese side also permitted the British to open a mountain road to the property and construct buildings, including bathhouses. As tenants, they would have full control of the property. The missionaries, however, would permit local people to continue to gather firewood from the area.[97]

When the British consul attempted to use the Changzhong case to wrangle leases for neighboring property, he did not succeed nor did he intimidate local officials. The consul received an indemnity of 3,455 silver dollars for the destroyed building materials, and the magistrate obtained British agreement that in the future missionaries would first notify local officials of construction projects so they could take precautionary measures to prevent further incidents.[98]

This case illustrates clearly a situation that involved commoners directly and gentry only indirectly. Neither group voiced any objections to Christianity as a religion nor did they complicate the case with claims of geomantic problems.[99] For people of the Changzhong area their primary concern was about local resources that had financial and convenience implications for their everyday lives. British missionaries understood this and exhibited flexibility about granting access to the area. Reverend Little also volunteered that the Chinese could freely use the newly built road. This eased tensions with the community, and there was no further trouble. The Protestant missionaries went on to develop Changzhong and nearby areas, which Reverend Little cleverly named "Kuling" (cooling), into a popular vacation spot. Within a few years, a priest purchased property there and Catholics also began to use it during the hot summer months.[100]

Resolution of a Catholic Complaint about Property Purchase Procedures in Rural Yongxin County, 1896–1897

In May 1897 Bishop Jules-Auguste Coqset telegraphed the French minister that during the previous year officials in Yongxin County had attempted to collect from Catholics three times the usual fee for stamping a deed on property purchased for Church use.[101] The minister protested to the Zongli Yamen that this contradicted the terms of the Berthemy (actually, the Gérard) Convention, which stipulated that fees would be paid in accordance with Chinese statutes and without discrimination against Westerners.[102] In July of that same year the French acting minister wrote to the Zongli Yamen stating that he believed the convention, as it applied to the purchase and ownership of property by the Catholic Church, had never been publicly announced in Yongxin County. The acting minister specifically requested that local officials properly stamp a deed to Church property recently acquired at Zhanghuwei in Yongxin.[103] He made no statement regarding fees, but implicitly connected the bishop's complaint of May regarding overcharges to the situation in Zhanghuwei.

Yongxin's location in far southwestern Jiangxi near the border with Hunan put it on the administrative periphery and made it possible that successive magistrates there were not familiar with the purchase procedures specified in the Berthemy and Gérard Conventions. More likely, the subcounty officials who administered Zhanghuwei, a remote rural area far from the county seat, did not know the rules about property purchased by Catholics. Consequently, the Zongli Yamen urged the Jiangxi governor to distribute copies of the Berthemy and Gérard Conventions to the various magistrates for public posting in the counties.[104] The governor complied and ordered provincial-level officials to take measures that would ensure compliance with the deed–stamp regulations.[105]

On September 19, 1897, the acting minister again complained to the Zongli Yamen about the Yongxin magistrate's delay in stamping the deed for the property in Zhanghuwei.[106] What the acting minister perhaps never knew, or at least failed to mention, was that the Yongxin magistrate and a deputy were investigating the Zhanghuwei property transaction because of an allegation that it had been sold fraudulently.[107] The two officials found irregularities in the sale, but they decided to allow the Church to keep the property rather than requiring the selection of another site.[108] If they felt any pressure to settle this case promptly, they never hinted at it. To avoid further complications, the magistrate ordered the deed to the property stamped, apparently with assessment of the customary fee. At this time the magistrate took official notice of the property purchase regulations for Catholics and announced them locally.[109] Local people and gentry raised no other issues and agreed to the Zhanghuwei settlement.

The Fraudulent Sale of a County Jail Warden's Office
To Catholics, De'an County, 1899

In 1899 Father Louis Fatiguet set out to purchase a building located in De'an County from one Liu Qianji. Before they completed the transaction, however, county officials challenged the validity of the sale. Father Fatiguet appealed to the French consul in Hankou for assistance. The consul's intervention in turn led to the involvement of the daotai at Jiujiang, who ordered an official investigation.[110]

The daotai learned from the De'an magistrate's investigatory report that the building Liu had sold to the missionary belonged to the county jail warden (*dianshi*); for over forty years, successive jail wardens had used the building as a government office. Bandits had destroyed a building that actually belonged to Liu in 1855, according to evidence the magistrate found in old files.[111]

The daotai endorsed the magistrate's findings and conveyed the information to the French consul and, through him, to the missionary. Father Fatiguet contested the magistrate's report, raising specific questions such as where was the jail warden's deed, and, if this building had been a government office, why was its architectural style the same as that of an ordinary house? Father Fatiguet argued that Liu Qianji was the rightful owner and his sale of the property to the Church did not break any law. He added indignantly that the Catholic Church would not condone the illegal purchase of any property. Since he had not broken any laws, why not let them close the deal? Why did Chinese officials want him to select other property to purchase?[112]

Neither the daotai nor the magistrate chose to answer the questions. Instead, the daotai wrote to the French consul that he found the evidence in the case, as reported by the De'an magistrate, to be accurate and so could not ignore it. The Chinese officials would not back down. The magistrate returned the money paid for the property to the local church manager and voided the sale. The church manager accepted the money and returned the deed to the magistrate. The daotai also informed the consul that the missionary, if he so desired, could send someone to meet with the magistrate and discuss the purchase of other property.[113]

This case is noteworthy as much for what was not said as for what was. Both sides stuck to factual arguments and neither side expressed any concern that somehow the dispute involved anti-Catholic sentiment. In addition, no one representing the local community complained about the building becoming Church property or about possible fengshui considerations. This dispute was of a purely secular nature and Chinese officials adjudicated it based on the facts. The Catholic Church simply could not buy the county jail warden's office because it did not belong to Liu Qianji.

Geomancy as an Issue in Property Transactions

Missionaries frequently claimed that Chinese used their belief in geomancy as an excuse to obstruct the sale of property to them, whereas the real reason was simply opposition to the Catholic presence. It is thus important to clarify how the parties involved in property transactions—missionaries, Catholics, Chinese officials, and non-Catholics—viewed and dealt with the geomancy issue. The cases below provide a unique opportunity to observe how local communities, while still retaining their beliefs in geomancy, accommodated the location of new church structures and outsiders who did not share those beliefs.

For many Chinese geomancy was an important way to interpret the physical world. They adjusted their presence and use of space according to its principles to harmonize with the forces of nature manifested in an area's topography.[114] People chose a propitious site with proper orientation for new buildings because of the direct effect fengshui was believed to have on the fortunes of the owner, or resident, his neighbors, and their respective progeny. Buildings not suitably located, moreover, could conceivably impair local geomantic currents and thereby influence an entire community's well-being.

People in Jiangxi's urban and rural locales believed in the power of geomantic forces, and it was an important element of dispute in some property transactions. Father Antoine Anot, for example, bought vacant land in 1882 from a Chinese family for use as a church site at Dongqi, a rural community in Anren County. Neither the priest nor the owner reported the transaction to local officials for review and approval. Subsequently, the local gentry and people formally complained to the magistrate that "the excavation to build the church harmed the fengshui and injured the people's fates."[115] Officials quickly recognized that apprehension about geomancy could destroy community harmony. The daotai who adjudicated the Dongqi case made the argument,

> [If] that priest will accept return of the original price, [he] can still locate another site for [church] construction. This way the fengshui of that locality can also be preserved and there will be no worries about harm to peoples' lives. The people and Catholics can then be eternally peaceful and [live] without incident.[116]

A cynic might believe, as did some Westerners, that the Chinese adroitly used geomantic beliefs to mask opposition to the establishment of churches. Regarding the trouble at Dongqi, a French consul stated, "The claim of fengshui [obstacles] is frivolous and obviously an excuse. It is a scheme to obstruct [church construction]. If property is bought or sold, it should depend on those involved. Bystanders should not interfere [by raising geomancy as an issue]."[117] An absence of outside interference certainly would have simplified life for missionaries who faced the difficult decision of whether to doggedly pursue a purchase or choose another site. On the one hand, if they accepted the explanation that their church would be incompatible with local geomancy and selected another site, their acquiescence might be interpreted as the acceptance, in their estimation, of superstitious beliefs. This was clearly an inappropriate position for the Church. On the other hand, if they insisted on obtaining and building on a property and the public perceived this to be geomantically injurious to the community, mission work might be hampered by prolonged feelings of animosity.

Life for Catholic missionaries sometimes entailed compromise and flexibility. Using houses as chapels or expanding existing structures into churches provided one way to deal with geomantic issues. Although they may not have liked to admit to such an approach, still, using an existing building evidently saved them trouble by guaranteeing that any fengshui problems would have already been resolved. Wherever Catholics used houses as chapels or converted existing buildings into churches, geomantic obstacles in fact did not surface.[118]

Wrangling over Property and the Establishment of a Church at Yingtan, Guiqi County, 1877–1898

Located about fifteen miles to the east of the Guiqi county seat and nestled against the banks of the Xin River, Yingtan served as an important market town for the area. Its place on a main trade artery linking eastern Jiangxi and Poyang Lake made it easily accessible by traders and missionaries alike. Not surprisingly, Catholic priests concentrated their attention there and hoped to construct several churches in the area.

According to a report made by the daotai at Jiujiang, the first attempt at establishing a church at Yingtan was made by a French missionary in the 1870s.[119] The priest wanted a church built because many Catholics, especially from the local Gui lineage, lived there.[120] Through the assistance of some of these Catholics, the missionary succeeded in purchasing various properties, including an old cemetery that belonged or had belonged to the Gui lineage. When local residents learned of these transactions, they protested that if Catholics constructed a church at any of the property sites, it would disturb the geomancy of the entire town.[121]

Among the leaders of the opposition to the church was Gui Caohua, a *shengyuan* degree holder. He filed a formal complaint with the Guiqi magistrate, stating that Gui Liangcai had fraudulently sold property that did not belong to him and that two other Gui kinsmen had improperly sold fields owned by the lineage to the Catholic Church. The *shengyuan* contended that the transfer of this property and subsequent construction would disrupt the geomancy of the Gui lineage's ancestral graves.[122]

Official investigations of the situation in Yingtan revealed that the first property transaction occurred in 1877 when Gui Dongxi sold his property at Shatanshi, a location within Yingtan, to the local Catholic Church. Later, in 1882 and 1883, other people bearing the Gui surname sold to the Church more property at Shatanshi and another location in Yingtan called Hujiajing.[123] Sometime during 1883 a missionary purchased lumber, tiles, and other building materials for a new church. At that time the *shengyuan* Gui Caohua ordered the materials, valued at 102 taels, destroyed.[124] Officials could blame this man for part of the case, but they still had to determine whether or not the property sales involved jointly-held lineage land and therefore constituted fraudulent sales or whether they were simply unfinished or poorly handled transactions. Officials also wanted to determine whether Sino-French agreements on property purchase procedures had been complied with.[125]

On April 22, 1884, Father Antoine Anot met and discussed the Yingtan case with Zhang Pengchang, the Guiqi County magistrate. Magistrate Zhang urged Father Anot to return to him all property deeds in exchange for the original purchase price. The magistrate would then permit him to select other sites, thereby settling the controversy and minimizing the possibility of open conflict with Yingtan residents. Father Anot seemed receptive to this solution, according to the magistrate, and agreed to consult with his superiors for approval. Magistrate Zhang expected that they would approve, so he proceeded to collect the money from the sellers for return to the Church. The sellers would thus regain possession of their various properties. Father Anot's superiors disagreed, however, and the priest retained the deeds.[126]

The case remained unresolved and dragged on over the next two decades with Catholic missionaries and French consuls periodically demanding settlement. From 1877 to 1898, numerous Chinese officials attempted to conclude what had become a most difficult case. Some officials found the details of the repeated investigations too numerous and confusing to sort out. One official commented that by the 1890s the written materials and documents for the case stood over two feet high.[127]

Father Alexandre Dillieux, who had been in Guiqi County for many years, took the initiative in 1896 to go to Yingtan and seek out the properties purchased in 1877, 1883, and 1884 to determine exact property lines and establish boundary markers in preparation for the construction of a church and other buildings.[128] Magistrate Yang Hun of Guiqi, fearing that the priest's actions would precipitate trouble in the community, decided to reverse the unsatisfactory position taken by his predecessors. Magistrate Yang would find a way to overcome the objections of Yingtan residents and allow the priest to formally take possession of the properties.[129]

The magistrate must have been surprised to learn that Yingtan's residents had already reached an agreement regarding ownership and possession of the properties. Dan Xibin, a local *jiansheng* degree holder and a Catholic, submitted a document to the magistrate indicating that the local people and their Catholic neighbors had decided to settle the problem out of court.[130] The local Church had made payment to the owners for the properties and residents of the area had agreed that the missionary could proceed with his construction plans.[131] The magistrate ordered the Guiqi assistant county magistrate (*xiancheng*) and the Yingtan subcounty magistrate (*xunjian*) to meet with Yingtan gentry and elders.[132] These officials confirmed that an agreement had indeed been reached. They also observed that the earlier complaints about fengshui problems now seemed uncertain and in any case were much less an issue.[133]

Most cases did not go unresolved for such a long time. The repeated official investigations and attempted settlements from 1877 into the late 1890s must have placed Yingtan's residents under a certain amount of strain. Perhaps this explains why the gentry and elders of the community finally agreed to the missionaries' persistent attempts to buy property. However, it does not explain why the initial geomantic objections disappeared. Perhaps, since the issue had clearly been resolved through private negotiations, the Catholics had given assurances regarding the exact location, size, and style of the buildings to be constructed. In the county seat of nearby Guiqi, Catholics responded to community sensitivities by erecting a Chinese-style church.[134] People in Yingtan most likely knew this, which would have helped allay the concerns of those involved.

That the community succeeded in settling this case where local officials had failed is certainly a significant point. As time passed the property-transaction side of the case became exceedingly complex because of the numerous investigations and the voluminous documentation. In the end, local officials could only validate the agreement formulated within the Yingtan community. They also formalized the Gui lineage's transfer of a piece of land adjacent to property purchased by the missionary as compensation for Gui Caohua's destruction of building materials in 1883.[135] This satisfied Father Dillieux, who signed a statement that he considered all cases dating from 1877 onward closed.[136] He later began the construction of a church, employing workers mostly from the Gui lineage.[137] As far as Chinese sources reveal, there was no further trouble.

A Fengshui Dispute Leads to a Property Exchange, Fengcheng County Seat, 1898

In 1898 a Catholic missionary paid one thousand *yuan* for a vacant lot in the Fengcheng county seat. The priest intended to use the property, located behind the county government yamen, as the site for a new church. It is unknown whether the priest abided by property purchase regulations in acquiring the title or whether local officials had any prior notification of the transaction. Difficulties arose almost immediately when local gentry and people voiced opposition to the construction of a church there based on fengshui considerations. According to the Nanchang prefect, Fengcheng residents believed that the land sat on the county yamen's geomantic "pulse" and feared that a building there would obstruct the entire county seat's fengshui.[138]

Magistrate Wen Jukui of Fengcheng and Father Aimé Braets, however, easily settled the dispute. On December 12, 1898, the magistrate offered in exchange for the lot a house located near the front of the county yamen. He further agreed that the priest would possess full ownership authority and could turn the house into a church by making needed repairs, or he could rebuild.[139] Local Catholics clearly benefited from this deal. They acquired not only a more prominent location with a usable building but also one without fengshui problems. Moreover, as the magistrate pointed out, the value of this property exceed that of the lot. The magistrate stated that to demonstrate his friendly intentions, the Catholics would not have to pay him the difference in market value between the two properties.[140] High-level officials in Nanchang approved, repeating the old Confucian aphorism about treating kindly men from afar (*huairou yuanren*).[141]

This property case was concurrent with but otherwise unrelated to a conflict that occurred at Qijiaxu, a rural community in Fengcheng County (see chapter 6). In the agreement that ended that case, Father Ambroise Portes proposed that the compensation paid by the Chinese for the Catholics' injuries and damaged property be reduced by one thousand *yuan*, the amount Catholics had originally paid for the lot in the Fengcheng county seat. Father Portes intended the reduction to offset, presumably, the magistrate's claim that the Catholics had received at no extra cost a higher value property for their church. The priest qualified his apparent magnanimity, however, when he stipulated that he wanted to purchase additional property for construction of a Catholic school at the county seat. The magistrate agreed.[142]

In Fengcheng Catholic missionaries showed flexibility and willingness to negotiate even though the main point of contention involved geomancy. This approach avoided extended negotiations and demonstrated Catholic sensitivity to community concerns.

Catholics Destroy a Rural Shrine, Linchuan County, 1898–1899

Bishop Casimir Vic of the Vicariate of Eastern Jiangxi wrote to the French minister that Father Claudius-Louis Gonon had been assaulted while in Chongren County. The bishop specifically blamed the county magistrate for inciting the local people to such action.[143] After receiving this information, the French minister contacted the Zongli Yamen, which in turn instructed the Jiangxi governor to order an official inquiry. The subsequent joint investigation by the magistrates of Chongren and Linchuan counties, together with a deputy assigned to the case, confirmed that Father Gonon had suffered injuries. The circumstances leading to the injuries, it turned out, revolved around a dispute between a local Catholic named Dong Youfa and members of the Li lineage.[144]

Dong Youfa resided, not in Chongren County, but in Linchuan County's 109th *du*. He owned some rural property on which there were two very old trees and a small stone shrine.[145] Animistic shrines devoted to imposing natural objects and their spirits were commonplace in China.[146] Adjacent to Dong's property was a lineage cemetery belonging to the Lis of neighboring Chongren County.

After Dong converted to Catholicism, he destroyed and removed the shrine. Many years later, in June or July 1898, the Lis hired workers to build a replica of the shrine at its original site. The Li lineage did this without Dong's permission.[147]

Dong Youfa waited, however, until Father Gonon visited the church at nearby Hangbu before protesting the Lis' actions. The day after hearing Dong's complaint, December 3, 1898, the priest accompanied Dong and other Catholics to the shrine; they destroyed it and chopped down the two old trees as well. According to Dong Youfa, "Thereupon, the Lis, using fengshui as an excuse, schemed to take over the [shrine] site." They also beat and injured Dong, the missionary, and the others.[148]

Based on a joint statement four members of the lineage made in court, the Lis felt that the removal of the trees and destruction of the shrine on property adjacent to their lineage cemetery would "disrupt the fengshui."[149]

A group of kinsmen went to discuss the matter with Dong Youfa at his home. When they arrived, they found the priest and other Catholics with Dong. The two groups argued. The Lis took the position that because Father Gonon "was at the scene helping" they would not give in to the Catholics.[150] Soon the argument turned physical and someone struck Dong Youfa on the head with a bamboo stick while other unidentified persons threw stones that hit the priest on the head and the Hangbu church manager on the forehead. In addition, someone else either set loose or stole livestock belonging to Dong Youfa. The incident ended with the intervention of the local *dibao* and others. Everyone then dispersed.[151]

The three officials who investigated concluded that no property ownership dispute existed because both sides already knew the legal land boundaries. Instead, they sustained Dong Youfa's claim that the Li lineage used geomancy as a convenient excuse to try and take over his property at the site of the shrine. The officials ruled:

> The Lis are from now on to manage the cemetery in accordance with the old boundaries. [They] are not permitted to use [the excuse that] the cemetery is influenced [by the situation involving the shrine] to forcibly occupy Dong's property."[152]

As punishment and warning against further action, the officials sentenced the four Li kinsmen, who had summoned earlier to testify, to wear the cangue. Upon their release from the cangue, the lineage was to shoulder responsibility for supervising their behavior. Last, the officials awarded Father Gonon and the Catholics 2,400 taels as compensation for their injuries and medical expenses.[153] Father Gonon consented in writing to this settlement and the officials closed the case.[154]

The two magistrates and the deputy handled this potentially difficult case with great tact and skill. How they resolved the entwined issues of property ownership, a local animistic shrine, and a lineage's attempt to use fengshui concerns to justify their actions is especially noteworthy. Since the rural property clearly belonged to Dong Youfa, officials did not challenge his right to remove the shrine and the trees. Neither the officials nor anyone else chose to focus on the shrine itself or the beliefs associated with it. The Li lineage only stated that the changes to the property had an effect on the local geomancy. Yet, one must wonder, given Dong Youfa's removal of the shrine many years earlier, why the Lis waited so long to rebuild it. To Dong Youfa, it was clear that the Lis used fengshui as a convenient excuse for an attempted land grab.

Although the officials sided with Dong Youfa regarding the fengshui issue, they couched their report carefully. They evidently did not want to say specifically that they considered fengshui irrelevant. Rather, they implied that in this instance the Li lineage needed a stronger defense for its actions. Officials had difficulty discounting fengshui arguments entirely, as we have seen elsewhere, when the gentry and other residents of a locality claimed that a church building's location, for example, affected the entire area's fengshui. In the case at hand, only one lineage was concerned. Moreover, the focus of the dispute was an isolated rural area, and this made a difference. Officials thus could rule in favor of Dong Youfa without really having to deal with the validity or influence communitywide of the fengshui issue. This decision and the officials' actions directly contradict the bishop's complaint that the magistrate had incited local people against the Catholics. The case was therefore easily resolved and ended quietly.

★   ★   ★   ★   ★

According to the French, various local officials in Jiangxi deliberately created obstacles for Catholics pursuing property transactions, either from ignorance of or disregard for the Berthemy and Gérard Conventions. Whatever the hurdle encountered, missionaries ultimately saw it as an official or local tactic to impede their proselytizing work. But this view discounts the fact that as newcomers to a community, missionaries must have seemed easy prey to local hustlers. In their hurry to purchase property and establish churches, missionaries sometimes ignored a basic principle of the marketplace—*caveat emptor*, let the buyer beware. Consequently, fraud and improper transactions led to property disputes such as those in Lüqi and De'an counties. The significant fact in these cases seems to have been the buyers' business acumen rather than their nationality or religious beliefs.

The French presumption of official interference or local hostility also ignored the complexity of Chinese society and the fact that in counties like Gan and Dehua a common element of concern was the control of surface rights to land and access to local resources like firewood. These cases suggest that in the countryside the issues at hand were often practical, rather than religious.

I want to emphasize that all these cases involved numerous people, arose from a complex social context sometimes complicated by the belief in geomancy, and touched on many interrelated issues. Although many people believed that a building's location, orientation, and use affected the well-being of everyone in the community, this did not mean that solutions could not be reached when problems arose. In Yingtan worries that the location of a proposed church would harm the geomancy of the Gui lineage cemetery as well as the entire town, evolved over two decades into a matter community leaders chose to handle out of court. The Catholics were permitted to construct their church at the originally selected location, proving that both lineages and communities were open to compromise, even on the issue of fengshui.

Missionaries and Chinese officials could be flexible, too. In the Fengcheng county seat a missionary agreed to another site for a new church after residents opposed the first location, which interfered with local geomancy. In rural Linchuan County when members of the Li lineage complained that Catholics had harmed the fengshui of their nearby cemetery, local officials deftly sidestepped the issue of geomancy and ruled that the Catholics had acted within their property rights. The point that emerges from these cases is that geomancy, like other issues between Catholics and non-Catholics, could be successfully negotiated. In the tight fabric of rural society both sides often saw accommodation as a preferable alternative to conflict. After all, whether a church was built or not, everyone remained part of the community and life went on.

Chapter 6

Local Security Issues and Christians: Their Involvement and Impact

Throughout China during the 1850s and 1860s Qing officials, the gentry, and common people associated Catholics with sectarian groups or illegal activities. For example, confusion about the Taipings' version of Christianity put Catholics under a pall of suspicion; many people could not or chose not to distinguish between Catholic religious beliefs and those held by the rebels. The association of Catholics with dangerous sectarians continued for the remainder of the century—even after the Taipings had been defeated—and was compounded by a general deterioration of social order. The perception that Catholics were a threat to order and security of course affected them directly, bringing them an additional level of official and community scrutiny.

Government authorities in Jiangxi were sensitive to Catholics' activities and their movements. In centrally located Ji'an, officials reported in late 1861 that a strangely dressed man claiming to be a Catholic priest appeared outside the city. According to the officials who investigated, the man "is sympathetic to the rebels; [he] is indeed suspicious. It is difficult to guarantee that [he] is not a Taiping in disguise going to various places to spy."[1] Farther north in the urban Nanchang area, local people worried about their safety because of the long yet unsuccessful Taiping siege of the capital. Some feared that wily rebels pretending to be Catholics might try to sneak into the city unless authorities took special measures to block them.[2] Others thought that if rebel forces entered the city or if Catholic priests attracted more rebels to the area then all would be lost.[3]

Such feelings made it easy for authors of anti-Christian literature to link Catholics with any group rebelling against the dynasty. Jiangxi's gentry reprinted inflammatory tracts written by counterparts in Changsha, Hunan, and circulated them widely in the Nanchang area during the early 1860s.

One, the "Public summons [issued] by the entire province of Hunan" (*Hunan hesheng gongxi*), contained a variety of wild accusations against Christianity. Another promoted the view that Taiping and Christian beliefs were similar; therefore, rebel and missionary activities were linked.[4] In 1866 at Ganzhou similar publications appeared, calling for the death of "Catholic sectarian bandits" (*Tianzhu jiaofei*). The authors of such pieces stated that their aim was "to protect the villages and prohibit heterodoxy."[5]

In some rural areas we find similar sentiments. For example, in late 1866 in the village of Xujia, near Nanchang, one villager, Wei Zhengren, observed about ten people lighting candles and reciting scriptures with a stranger at the home of Xu Taifang, a local Catholic. Wei suspected that the visiting stranger, a Chinese Catholic priest, was actually a Vegetarian bandit. According to a joint statement made by several villagers, "[If a sect member] was permitted to stay in one home, the neighbors would be implicated." Xu reassured his neighbors that everything was proper, but they remained suspicious and said they intended to keep an eye on the situation.[6]

Jiangxi governor Liu Kunyi summed up the populace's distrust in a report written in 1870 and addressed to the Zongli Yamen: "Most [Catholics] are vagrants [whose] social standing is disreputable. . . . [Their] movements are secretive and many are bandits."[7]

To be sure, during the second half of the nineteenth century Catholics were at times implicated in illegal activities and did commit crimes. However, the *jiao'an* materials for Jiangxi do not support the claims of active engagement between Catholics and Taipings or any other sectarian group. These suspicions nonetheless influenced many and impacted virtually all localities, forcing officials—and Catholics—to deal with the tension they generated. For officials this complicated the already challenging task of local control and made security a prominent issue in their case reports about Catholics.

The deterioration of the *baojia*, of course, did not make maintaining local control any easier for Qing authorities. According to one scholar, by this time the local security system had become "utterly ineffective."[8] Out of necessity officials improvised with all types of measures and personnel while dealing with various local exigencies. They also had to manage affairs carefully to reduce Sino-Western tensions exacerbated by disturbances that involved Christians. The dynasty's very survival ultimately depended on the actions and success of local officials.

I find it notable that in the settlement of cases involving Christians, government authorities used the same techniques and personnel applied generally to stabilize local society. Despite their general prejudices against Christians, officials treated them as part of the communities in which they lived rather than as segregated or special entities. We may observe this below in cases that revolve around law and order and mutual security— issues of utmost importance to everyone and everyday life.

Christians in Urban Areas: Local Security Measures and Government Efforts to Prevent Conflict

Earlier studies show how gentry instigated conflict with Christians in Nanchang during the 1860s; but other, later urban cases have not been addressed and no one has determined whether those cases reveal a pattern of behavior across Jiangxi. Furthermore, once we consider the overall situation from the perspective of local security and control, other questions present themselves. First, did the gentry of Nanchang export their anti-Christian sentiments to other cities? Second, how did government officials respond to incidents involving Christians, and what measures did they take to contain them? We begin by turning to cases that occurred in and around the provincial capital of Nanchang, the prefectural cities of Ji'an and Ganzhou, and the county seats of Yihuang and Yongxin.

The Control Crisis Created by Anti-Catholic Agitation In the Nanchang Area and in Wucheng, 1862–1872

Nanchang was the administrative home of the governor and several other provincial-level officials. One prefecture and two counties also located their government offices there. No other city in Jiangxi had such a concentration of political power and personnel, not to mention large numbers of gentry. In addition, Nanchang played an important role as the province's chief financial and commercial center. Situated near the Gan River, which connects the southern reaches of the province with Poyang Lake and the Yangzi River, Nanchang's location allowed it to dominate Jiangxi's water-bound trade and economy.[9]

Given Nanchang's political and economic importance to the Qing and its access to the agricultural riches of northern Jiangxi, there is little wonder that the Taipings targeted the city in 1853. Their attack and continued fighting in Jiangxi drew the attention and presence of Zeng Guofan, a high-level official and the Qing's most important regional leader.[10] However, it was Nanchang County native Liu Yuxun (a *juren*) who played the crucial role in saving the capital from rebel occupation. Liu molded northern Jiangxi local militias into a large and credible fighting force that kept rebel forces at bay at Nanchang.[11]

Throughout the 1850s Taiping and Qing armies fought for control of various parts of Jiangxi. At Wucheng, an important trading center strategically located on the shores of Poyang Lake some sixty miles north of Nanchang, rival forces crisscrossed the area. Everyone suffered, including local Catholics who had established a church there as early as 1834. In 1857 when Qing forces moved into Wucheng, an officer ordered his men to kill the church caretaker and raze the church along with Catholic-owned shops because he suspected Catholics sided with the Taipings.[12]

During the next decade problems revolving around the presence of Catholics and missionaries in the greater Nanchang area multiplied for Qing officials. Catholics' supposed connections with Taipings and suspicions about the mistreatment of children under Church care became volatile issues and led to recurring violence. This presented government authorities with serious challenges to law and order. Within the extensive documentary material for events that occurred in the Nanchang and Wucheng areas from 1862 to 1872 we find an unusually close view of the problems officials had in maintaining order and dealing with Catholics.

Trouble in Nanchang began with the arrival of Father Fang Anzhi, a French-speaking Chinese priest who often interpreted for his European confreres. In late 1861 he purchased a building within the city walls at Kuaizi Lane that would serve as a residence, chapel, and orphanage. With the help of several local Catholics, Father Fang began providing care for young orphans brought there from other localities.[13] Father Antoine Anot soon joined him. Probably for security reasons, they kept the main entrance tightly shut, coming and going via a small rear door.[14] This permitted only limited observation by neighbors and the curious.

Since the priests had essentially closed the orphanage to public scrutiny, local residents' suspicions about the care of the children began to merge with existing popular concerns over Catholic sympathies towards the Taipings. With Qing forces engaging the Taipings a mere one hundred miles away, and with Catholics operating behind closed doors, some people in Nanchang felt threatened from within and without. The governor knew this and assigned two deputies, Xia Xie and Zhang Guojing, to investigate.[15] Xia Xie noted that Father Fang and other Catholics could enter or leave the city without restriction. Xia proposed that the Catholics be required to register at public offices (*gongsuo*) located within and outside the city. There they would be issued waist badges (*yaopai*), a sort of identity card that would be checked by functionaries stationed at the city gates.[16]

These public offices appear to have been involved in registration work before the arrival of Father Fang; they had been set up as part of a general effort to keep track of people's movements and secure the city against troublemakers. Ordinarily, the registration and control of all residents fell within *baojia* purview, but there is no mention in the official documents of a *baojia* network fulfilling such duties in Nanchang. Moreover, singling out Catholics this way was a new twist.

Before long the closed-off orphanage spawned rumors that the priest and other orphanage workers mistreated the children in their care. Anonymously written placards that imaginatively embellished upon this story began to circulate. One public summons (*gongxi*) from Hunan in particular graphically described the horrible mutilations that Catholics supposedly inflicted on orphans.[17] Matters came to a head over a few days in mid-March 1862 when indignant residents destroyed the building at Kuaizi Lane, a church-orphanage at Yuanjiajing, and a church-orphanage about two miles from the city at Miao Lane. These same crowds also pillaged the stock of storekeepers who did business with the Catholics. The prefect ordered runners to make arrests, but darkness allowed members of the destructive crowd to scatter with impunity. Local Catholic orphanage workers then took the orphans southeast to a church at the city of Fuzhou and the two priests fled north from Nanchang.[18]

A *dibao* from the Miao Lane area promptly reported to officials that there had been no way to prevent the sudden destruction of the church there.[19] Local officials ordered secret inquiries. Another *dibao*—this time from within the city—reported that babies at the orphanage did not have wet nurses. He stated that the public summons from Hunan had aggravated existing suspicions regarding Catholic activities. Civil-service examination candidates in Nanchang became curious and went to the Kuaizi Lane orphanage to inspect it. When the Catholics refused to allow them inside, they raised a commotion that attracted a crowd of onlookers and eventually led to the destruction of the building.[20] The *dibao*'s report, which the governor cited at the beginning of his communication to the Zongli Yamen, also mentioned that people had found suspicious looking items inside the orphanage.[21] In addition, a prominent family in Nanchang claimed to have found evidence of murdered infants in the form of bone fragments at Father Anot's residence.[22] In the heat of the moment, people gave credence to these rumors of missionary misdeeds and took action.

These events and the flight of Fathers Anot and Fang from Nanchang began a long and acrimonious struggle between Chinese and French authorities over missionaries' right of access to the provincial capital. Through the remainder of 1862 and into 1863 various Nanchang officials fretted about tensions in the community and about their exceedingly tenuous control of the populace. Prevalent sentiments of government partiality towards foreigners, according to Governor Shen Baozhen, eroded the people's confidence in government. At that time, the people and officials could only be described as opponents.[23] One anonymous placard called for the death of the rebels, Anot and Fang, and for village lineage leaders to execute local Catholics without bothering to inform officials.[24] To Shen, it was critical that the government win back the hearts and minds of the people if it hoped to maintain local order.

Governor Shen's sensitivity to Nanchang public opinion led him to order a secret inquiry. Several of his non-Jiangxi confidants dressed in the garb of visiting merchants and went to various wine and tea shops in the city. Their report is significant because it records, with unabashed candor in their own colloquial Chinese, the actual feelings of some local residents.[25]

> Question: You have all discussed it intensely and you all say that you want to fight off, at the risk of death, the French missionary [Antoine Anot]. Why?
> Answer: He [Anot] wants to take away our publicly established orphanage and [he] also wants us to compensate him with a great deal of money. Moreover, he is telling the [local] Catholics to take over our stores and land. [He] also says that [French] gunboats are coming to oppress us. If

we give a step, they always advance a step. Afterwards we cannot live in peace. How can we not risk our lives [to oppose Anot and the French]?

Question: We have come from Shanghai where there are many Catholic churches. [Catholics] all claim to exhort men to do good. For instance, are the [Catholic] orphanages here not a good thing?

Answer: Our own orphanages all take children in and [have women] nurse them. In their church [orphanages], all are boys and girls ten years old or so and all are purchased [for the orphanage]. You consider it: Is [their purpose] to care for children or is it to mutilate them? And what's more, the Taipings are all Catholics. They [the missionaries] must propagate their religion inside the city and near it. If [missionaries] entice the Taipings to enter [the city], our homes and lives will be in jeopardy.[26]

These vocal informants felt they had few options. To them, it appeared that no one cared about their fate so they vowed to resist on their own, even if it meant sacrificing many men to eliminate just one Taiping or Catholic.[27] An anonymous placard posted in the Nanchang area echoed these same sentiments. It stated that the people of Jiangxi were united in opposition to Catholicism and the return of missionaries to Nanchang.[28]

To prevent further conflict with Catholics, however, the Zongli Yamen called for decisive action by Jiangxi officials. At this time, France was rendering assistance to imperial forces fighting rebels near Shanghai and Ningbo. Therefore, the Zongli Yamen told the governor to swallow his pride and treat the missionaries politely should they return to Nanchang.[29] It also suggested that Jiangxi officials make any reparation payment for the destroyed church secretly and that they have the missionaries relocate their church to a safe distance from the city.[30] In an effort to give Jiangxi officials more time to reassert government authority in the Nanchang area, the Zongli Yamen instructed Hubei provincial authorities in Wuchang to delay Father Anot when he passed through that city on his return passage from Beijing to Nanchang.[31]

Despite such tactics, Father Anot soon returned to the Nanchang area where he found that a few Catholics had reopened their shops amidst continued tension.[32] At the time of Father Anot's arrival in May of 1863, someone posted a large banner near the city gate boldly declaring that French "barbarians" could not enter the city.[33] The seriousness of the situation became apparent when townspeople, sensitive to any official contact with Catholic missionaries, stoned a yamen runner sent by the prefect to help Father Anot find lodging. Realizing the danger, Father Anot departed at once for Jiujiang. Nanchang residents blamed the local Catholics for the missionary's return and proceeded to destroy the Catholic-owned shops in the area.[34]

When Liu Kunyi assumed the governorship of Jiangxi in mid-1865 he quickly realized how difficult governing the local populace would be.[35] The atmosphere at Nanchang was so charged with hatred that the return of a single missionary would be enough to spark numerous incidents. Fortunately, missionaries appear to have made no further attempts to enter the capital through 1870. In that year, however, Governor Liu still considered Nanchang unsafe for missionaries. Liu also noted that the large numbers of people drawn to the city during the various upcoming civil service examinations would be difficult to regulate.[36] The governor clearly knew that examination candidates had been involved in the 1862 destruction of Catholic property. Last, but not least, the governor considered the route from Jiujiang to Nanchang to be hazardous. A recent drought had filled the area with multitudes of displaced, hungry people, and both civil and military officials would be hard-pressed to protect any Westerners in the area.[37] In fact, rampant banditry in northern Jiangxi had caused the government to revive militia activities.[38]

The French chargé d'affaires, Julian de Rochechouart, did not believe these warnings. Aboard a gunboat, he sailed from the Yangzi River into Poyang Lake in early 1870. Although his boat ran aground, he reached Nanchang by other means. An unfriendly throng numbering in the tens of thousands awaited him.[39] Governor Liu immediately dispatched Green Standard soldiers and averted trouble. Unimpressed by the numbers of Chinese opposing them, the French still demanded access to the city. The Chinese continued to be adamant, even when the French threatened to station gunboats on Poyang Lake.[40] The governor finally conceded that missionaries and Westerners would eventually be permitted to enter Nanchang. First, officials had to quiet the agitated gentry and local people and establish a better relationship with them. Qing officials knew that if they lost the people's hearts, the dynasty would suffer.[41]

The difficulty of calming the populace soon became apparent in Wucheng. Strong anti-Catholic sentiments were fueled in large measure by placards that appeared after the Tianjin Massacre of June 1870.[42]

Catholic concerns about personal safety proved warranted as Wucheng townsmen destroyed the church there in September. According to a missionary on the scene, tremendous property damage and severe personal harassment forced many Catholics to flee the area.[43]

During the investigation ordered by Governor Liu Kunyi, the first class subprefect at Wucheng determined that the incident had actually been precipitated by the presence of kidnapping bandits (*guaifei*) who used medicines to drug and abduct young children. Prior to the destruction of the church a *dibao* and local gentry had requested that the subprefect order the arrest of the kidnappers.[44] Although the subprefect dispatched runners to find the lawbreakers and instructed the community to ignore all rumors, Wucheng residents remained tense.

On September 10 a beancurd vendor spotted a child who appeared to be drugged. The vendor threw water in the face of the youngster, who then awoke and cried out. The would-be kidnappers, according to several eyewitnesses, ran to the vicinity of a church still under construction and vanished from sight. Because the building site appeared to be their hiding place, the frustrated pursuers destroyed it in a vain search. As these events unfolded, the subprefect, the registrar (*zhubu*), and the battalion commander (*yingdu*) of the Green Standard garrison happened to be elsewhere distributing rations to hungry people. By the time the news reached them, they could not prevent the destruction.[45] Nevertheless, they ordered armed runners and Green Standard soldiers to make arrests, which they did with some success.[46]

Not mentioned in the provincial-level reports on this incident was a significant fact provided by the British consul at Jiujiang: anti-Christian materials printed elsewhere in Jiangxi had been distributed daily in Wucheng prior to the incident.[47] Among these was the slanderous *Bixie shilu* (A true record to ward off heterodoxy), which was similar in scatological content to a circular seen in Nanchang.[48] The Zongli Yamen remarked in a communication to the Jiangxi governor that if local officials did not prohibit the distribution of such materials, trouble would surely result.[49] The daotai at Jiujiang investigated and found the Wucheng subprefect negligent for not halting their circulation. Upon the daotai's recommendation, authorities dismissed the subprefect from office.[50]

These actions aside, through 1872 the Jiangxi governor still felt that the government retained only tenuous control in the Wucheng area.

Governor Liu ordered additional measures and specifically instructed the new subprefect to be certain he restrained clerks and runners as well as members of mercantile circles.[51] The subprefect assured the governor that he would take precautions and smother false stories regarding Christians wherever they appeared.

Given the shaky nature of local control in and around Nanchang, it is not surprising that Governor Liu sought to change the opinions of the local elite and the common people, whom he blamed for the earlier troubles.[52] Mary Wright has noted that "the most serious problem the Restoration government faced was the increased xenophobia of the local gentry."[53] This certainly appears to have been true in Nanchang. Officials found the exclusion of all Westerners from the city the obvious and easy solution. Yet the need to instruct, soothe, and calm the common people remained. Usually, the local elite assisted in this, but now certain influential local degree holders like Xia Tingju (a *jinshi*) and Liu Yuxun did the opposite by sponsoring the 1862 reprinting of the public summons in Nanchang.[54] Given the proximity of Wucheng and Nanchang it is reasonable to assume some sort of sociopolitical connection between the elites of those two areas, but their exact role in the Wucheng incident in 1870, where we find anti-Christian materials similar to those seen earlier in Nanchang, cannot be determined. Provincial-level officials, made nervous by the local elite's position and presumed role in these events, did not enlist them or their militia to help deal with the new threat—assertive Catholic missionaries supported by the bellicose French.

Officials had to deal no less carefully with the local gentry than they did with the missionaries. The joint settlement of the Wucheng and Nanchang incidents reveals this clearly. In the 1863 agreement worked out by Father Anot and Acting-daotai Cai Jinqing, the Chinese paid compensation for the two churches destroyed in Wucheng. Officials returned one site to the Catholics and permitted them to select a replacement site for the other location. The Chinese paid 17,000 taels to the Catholic Church and local Catholics for their property losses and other expenses in Wucheng and Nanchang. This included payment for the building destroyed at Kuaizi Lane, the church at Yuanjiajing, and the church at Miao Lane. The Chinese took possession of these three Nanchang sites but agreed that Father Anot could purchase replacement property at quiet, out-of-the-way places for a new orphanage and church.

Governor Shen Baozhen thought the case was closed and communicated the details to the Zongli Yamen who informed the French minister.[55]

Chinese officials, however, considered Nanchang unsafe for the return of Catholic missionaries through 1870. That year Bishop François-Ferdinand Tagliabue tried unsuccessfully to initiate discussions with officials about reestablishing a church in the city.[56] The Chinese solution continued to be one of preventing conflict by keeping missionaries out of the city, and no missionaries meant no churches. This approach apparently succeeded because officials reported no other incidents involving missionaries or Catholics in Nanchang through the rest of the nineteenth century. The two previously Catholic properties in the city were adapted to other uses: one site became residential while the other was used as an ancestral hall. Chinese also took over the old church site at Miao Lane on Nanchang's outskirts.[57]

There matters stood until April of 1897 when the French minister, A. Gérard, reopened the case. Minister Gérard, through the French consul in Shanghai, informed the governor of Jiangxi that officials still had not returned the three old church-owned properties in Nanchang where incidents had occurred in 1862.[58] Officials in Jiangxi were incredulous. They claimed, and quickly located old files as proof, that Father Anot and Acting-daotai Cai had agreed upon a settlement and closed the case in 1863.[59]

In October 1897 the acting French minister stated that the money the Chinese had paid earlier compensated Catholics for damages not property. The Chinese had not returned the three property sites, but had usurped control of them.[60] In March 1898 the French revealed the kernel of the issue: British and American Protestant churches had been established within Nanchang yet no Catholic church existed there. The French could find no reason for this and the exclusion of Catholic missionaries from within the city walls.[61] Finally, Bishop Paul Ferrant worked out an agreement with the Nanchang prefect whereby the Church received property inside and near the city's Yonghe Gate while the Chinese retained control of the properties located at Kuaizi Lane and at Yuanjiajing.[62] The prefect ascertained from a local *dibao* that the Catholics had previously established a cemetery at the Miao Lane property. Because of this fact, the prefect ordered the property returned to Catholic control.[63] Bishop Ferrant and the prefect put their agreement into writing on October 24, 1898. The bishop stated that he considered the Nanchang case now fully resolved and that he would inform the French minister.[64] On May 6, 1899, the Zongli Yamen communicated to the French minister that they considered the case officially closed.[65]

Unruly Examination Candidates at Ji'an, 1868–1869

In 1865 Father Antoine Anot sent another priest, Fu Ruhan, to the prefectures of Ji'an, Ruizhou, and Linjiang to propagate Catholicism. Although a group of villagers in the countryside of Lüling County assaulted the priest for reasons now unknown, this did not deter him.[66] By 1868 Father Fu Ruhan had moved into a commoner's house located in that same county near the west gate of Ji'an. With donations from local Catholics, some of whom traced their faith back five generations, he remodeled the house and enlarged it into a church mission complex.[67]

As we saw earlier (chapter 3), local officials in Ji'an did not have a high opinion of the local Catholics.[68] Civil service examination candidates shared this opinion and vowed to destroy the church after they had completed the 1868 prefectural-level test. The prefect learned of the plan, however, and with the help of local gentry prevented trouble.[69] In August a local Catholic discovered a Ji'an printing shop preparing plates for publication of defamatory claims aimed at Catholics.[70] Although the man personally confiscated and destroyed the plates, the acting magistrate still sent out runners with a warrant for the arrest of the printer. The printer readily confessed to his own role and furnished the customer's surname, but authorities made no other arrests.[71] Even so, the daotai at Jiujiang stated confidently in April 1869 that anti-Christian literature had not reappeared in Lüling County.[72]

The scheduling of another examination again generated anxiety about possible friction between the examinees and Catholics.[73] Officials decided to take all possible precautions despite the acknowledged likelihood of incurring the ill will of a large number of degree holders. The prefect told county educational officers to instruct their subordinates (*baoyue*) to prevent the candidates from causing trouble. Concurrently, runners would monitor local sentiments and discourage agitation when necessary.[74]

Nonetheless, following the completion of the examination on May 12, 1869, candidates started an altercation with Catholics, but dispersed without serious trouble. The next day, according to the prefect, he was just ordering *baoyue* to investigate that incident when news arrived that candidates had started a disturbance at the church.[75] Catholics had tried to prohibit the examinees from entering the church grounds and during the ruckus that followed someone set fire to the church. By the time civil and military authorities arrived to supervise the fire fighting, the examinees had scattered.[76]

The Ji'an prefect and the Lüling acting magistrate jointly ordered runners and Green Standard soldiers to make discrete inquiries, gather relevant information, and arrest the examinees involved. Considering their dim view of Catholics, it is surprising to find them confidentially instructing Wu Aiyao and other local Catholics to observe the candidates carefully when they appeared for the next examination. If they could identify any who had participated in the church's destruction, they could submit a petition at any time. Officials would then incarcerate the accused.[77]

Provincial-level officials were supportive of these efforts. They instructed local officials to have the various educational officers advise *baoyue* on the need for greater control of future examination candidates.[78] In addition, a deputy, Expectant Magistrate Zhang Guoying, was dispatched from Nanchang to investigate. Zhang summoned Catholics to court for questioning, but the scanty information they provided disclosed nothing substantial about the incident. Dissatisfied with his understanding of what had happened, Zhang made a personal inspection of the church site. He then consulted a local *dibao*, but the *dibao* could add nothing new.[79] The examination candidates remained the prime suspects, although Zhang and his colleagues never located any of the responsible parties. Little else could be done but to continue to use *baoyue* to inquire discretely and, if necessary, make arrests.

The Zongli Yamen wondered why local officials had repeatedly ordered the conflict suppressed, with no apparent result.[80] In defense of the prefectural and county officials it must be remembered that at examination time, not only candidates from across the prefecture, but also numerous merchants, entertainers, service dealers, and other outsiders poured into Ji'an. This situation stretched public security resources to their limit. In 1868 government contact with local gentry had succeeded in forestalling violence and officials had stopped the publication of anti-Christian literature.[81] But because government control of the examination candidates could not be sustained by educational officers and *baoyue*, the 1869 disturbance had erupted despite official efforts to prevent it.

Assault of a Missionary: A City Gate Incident at Ganzhou, 1873–1874

Citing information provided by Bishop Géraud Bray for conveyance to Zongli Yamen, the French legation reported in September 1873 that Father Alexis Sassi had been in China for thirteen years. At one time he had tried to build a church inside the city of Ganzhou, but the magistrate prevented its construction by confiscating the deed to the building site.[82] In June 1873 the priest returned to the Ganzhou area to resolve this problem, as well as another involving disputed property owned by Catholics, and a third one that concerned the construction of a chapel at nearby Pinglushang (see chapter 5). Seated in a palanquin and accompanied by eight Catholics, Father Sassi headed for Ganzhou. He carried a copy of a letter from the daotai at Jiujiang, which he hoped would help resolve matters.[83] At the city gate a local official empowered to inspect and question those entering the city blocked Father Sassi's way and seized his passport and various papers. According to Father Sassi, the official shoved him, thus initiating a violent attack.[84] Assailants grabbed the priest's hair, threw him to the ground and beat him. A crowd soon gathered and threw rocks at him, shouting that they wanted to drown him in the river. Although the crowd prevented him from going to Pinglushang, they did not stop him from traveling down river on a small boat. He later stopped at a village where Catholics loaned him clothing and money. Father Sassi was physically able to continue, and after resting a bit, proceeded to Ji'an.[85]

Chinese officials thought Bishop Bray exaggerated the account of the incident and Father Sassi's injuries because he wanted to gain better leverage for his missionaries in their dealings with Ganzhou authorities.[86] The Chinese also believed that the bishop had focused on the area because of Gan County Magistrate Cui Guobang's earlier ruling against the Catholics of Pinglushang and termination of the chapel's construction there. By directing Father Sassi to go to Pinglushang, Bishop Bray planned to resume active proselytizing in the Ganzhou area.

The incident at the city gate reveals how fragile control was and how quickly local insecurities could embroil visitors to the area. According to Magistrate Cui's description of Father Sassi's arrival, a Catholic priest, wearing unusual apparel and riding in a small palanquin, arrived un-announced at Ganzhou on June 7, 1873. The priest's journey through the countryside had attracted about one hundred curious people, who tagged along behind him. As the priest approached the city gate a large number of people surged forward and blocked the path. The priest decided to walk into the city with his porters and a local man leading the way. Suddenly, the crowd grew larger and noisier. The commotion brought the gate inspectors, Deng Yaozeng (an expectant official the prefect had assigned to this task as a deputy), Liu Fengren (a local *shengyuan* who was at the gate in an official capacity), as well as Yao Guocai (a *dibao* whose jurisdiction included the area outside the gate) to the scene. This trio saw the size and unruliness of the crowd as a security problem generated by the missionary's presence. They persuaded him to leave the area immedi-ately, and after Deng and Liu personally escorted him safely away, the crowd dispersed.[87] Chinese officials did not mention any violence or injuries to the priest.

The bishop's complaint, registered at the Zongli Yamen, led Governor Liu Kunyi to order local officials to apprehend the instigators of the city-gate incident. The Gan County magistrate selected capable runners to investigate and make the necessary arrests. The *dibao* cooperated with these runners and helped identify the main culprit, who succeeded in fleeing the area. When he returned to Ganzhou in November 1874 an alert *dibao* and runners quickly arrested him.[88]

As in Nanchang during the early 1860s, authorities considered traffic in and out of Ganzhou a major security problem. When trouble started at a city gate, three types of personnel went into action: the expectant official from the regular bureaucracy; a degree holder working as a low-level official, but also representing the local elite; and the *dibao* from the county subbureaucracy.[89] The gate incident of June 1874 points to the con-siderable collective local authority needed to maintain order. In the face of an unruly crowd numbering well over one hundred people, and without the assistance of soldiers, these three men probably saved the missionary's life and avoided the serious consequences that would have followed.

Catholics, a Crime Wave, and Revitalization of Militia
in the Yihuang County Seat and Surrounding Area, 1874–1875

Through the entire month of April 1874 a crime wave swept over a rural area near the county seat of Yihuang. Then, within the county seat itself, two major daytime robberies, one of a wealthy lower degree holder, nurtured the seeds of panic. Men identified as Catholics were determined to have committed these crimes. However, French missionaries quickly claimed that the problems in Yihuang were really a result of yamen runners' harassment of local Catholics. When the Catholics stood up to them, the conflict escalated, with reprisals coming from a yamen clerk who attempted to discredit local Catholic litigants and from gentry-led militia that sought to persecute all Catholics.[90] Missionary claims thus complicated the official investigation that followed. Nevertheless, the energetic efforts of an able and experienced official, Magistrate Xia Xie, led not only to the completion of a competent investigation, but also to the restoration of law and order.[91]

The following description of the various incidents in Yihuang comes from the depositions of the main characters involved. In a hamlet of the rural Tanfang area, about seven miles from the county seat, trouble began during February 1874 when a Catholic, Zou Jiaqi, contracted to purchase land from an older cousin and non-Catholic, Zou Jiaxiang. Zou Jiaqi's failure to make proper payment sparked repeated requests for fulfillment of the agreement. Exasperated and sick, Zou Jiaxiang had his mother-in-law file a complaint with the magistrate for the prosecution of his cousin.[92] A week later Magistrate Xia Xie issued a warrant to runners Zhou Xin, Chen He, and Wu En to summon Zou Jiaqi for trial. On April 13 the three runners confronted Zou and ordered him to surrender. Zou refused. The runners decided to try again the next day and, along with two other runners on a separate assignment, spent the night at a local inn. Early the next morning Zou led six Catholic friends in a surprise seizure of the five runners.[93]

Zou and his cohorts tied up the runners and took them to Longqi, a market town about six miles north of the Yihuang county seat, where Catholics regularly met. With one Catholic sitting as judge, the men stripped Chen He and Wu En naked and flogged them. Another Catholic wrote a formal apology and a monetary IOU for each runner; each approved the documents before his release.[94] The runners hastily returned to the county seat to inform the magistrate of their humiliating and painful mistreatment. Xia personally observed the marks left from the beating.[95]

On April 18, four days after the altercation with the runners in Tanfang, Zou Jiaqi visited at the home of Zou Yaya, a Catholic catechist. They chatted idly until Zou Huaichu proposed the idea of raiding a rice-transport boat. That same day eight Catholics, each carrying poles and baskets, went to a riverbank location where rice-transport boats could be easily boarded. A boat appeared and the Catholics raided it without resistance from the crew. Each man carried away one picul of rice, which they sold at a nearby village for a total of thirteen strings of cash.[96]

Three days later, You Pingli, another catechist, initiated the scheme of extorting money from a local pawnshop owner. This time the Catholic band of eight gained a prize of over ten strings of cash.[97] On April 25 the same group extorted forty strings of cash from a family at the village of Chankang.[98] The following day, twelve Catholics, some carrying knives, entered the Yihuang county seat. They robbed a well-to-do family of clothing and cloth and extorted an IOU note from them for one hundred strings of cash.[99]

Zou Jiaqi had masterminded the first Yihuang county seat intrusion and he led the Catholics back a second time because Zhang Bashi, a Catholic tenant farmer, had been evicted by his landlord and cousin, You Longbao, a *jiansheng* degree holder. Zou and his Catholic cohorts offered Zhang a share of the loot in exchange for guiding them to You's house. Zhang at first refused but the explicit threat of death quickly changed his mind.[100] After leading the band to You's home, Zhang, who did not participate in the robbery, spied his cousin sneaking out the back way. Zhang joined You and together they went directly to the county yamen for help. The magistrate immediately dispatched runners and Green Standard soldiers to apprehend the robbers.[101] Several of the Catholics resisted arrest using knives and sticks, but the runners and soldiers easily subdued them. Only Zou Huaichu and one or two others escaped arrest.

The attack on the pawnshop and on a wealthy family, which included a degree holder, spread panic among the county seat's gentry and elders. Local gentry, ninety-four of them holding official rank, publicly petitioned Magistrate Xia. They stated their concern about the victimization of villagers by the Catholic "gang," Catholics' disregard for authority, and especially the fearless way the robbers had entered the county seat itself.

Government authorities needed to arrest and punish the offenders if they intended to keep this type of activity from growing out of control.[102] Moreover, rumor had it that the Catholics who had escaped were already planning to form an even larger group to liberate the prisoners. Residents of the county seat were thoroughly frightened, and some had left Yihuang for safer quarters.[103]

Steps to restore order were taken promptly. The magistrate "summoned and instructed gentry managers (*shendong*) to organize militia with real power."[104] The gentry received orders to manage the *baojia*, assemble militiamen to patrol the area, take necessary precautions, and suppress any suspicious activity so as to calm the fears of local residents.[105] Gentry action on these fronts, apparently funded by the government, brought the Yihuang troubles to an end.[106]

During the 1870s, some new converts acted aggressively and violently as we saw in Yihuang County, but not in response to religious conflict.[107] Their success as a group perhaps gave them collective confidence and was a contributing factor to their predation on local people. Another factor was unemployment and poverty: eight of the ten Catholics arrested did not have jobs, while the other two were laborers. I believe the economic hopelessness of their lives rather than their Catholicism is the key to their actions. It is surely relevant that all but one of the men had only recently "converted,"[108] that no one mentioned their affiliation with any rural congregation, and that missionaries did not know who they were. It is also worth noting that older Catholic families of the area did not participate in the illegal activities.[109]

Motivation of the bandits aside, the crime wave did reveal the weakness of local control organs and the lack of security felt by the area's residents. The pawnshop owner, for example, stated that he dared not file a complaint against the men who extorted money from him.[110] He either feared official inaction or believed the Catholics would avoid arrest and return to extort more money. According to testimony from nine of the ten men arrested, *baojia* system personnel simply did not know about their actions.[111] Xia Xie's successor at Yihuang concluded that local personnel were guilty of negligence, but not concealment.[112] Negligence was in some sense the worse offense because it meant that such personnel ignored or did not know about criminal activity in their jurisdictions. As a result, crucial information regarding important local trends failed to make its way to the magistrate. The magistrate had no choice and dismissed from service the negligent parties.[113]

As to informal control mechanisms, rural gentry of the Zou lineage stated that these Catholic members of their kinship group simply came from a "bad class," and they expressed thanks to the magistrate for his arrest of the criminals.[114] If these lineages lacked sufficient means to control unruly members, then they probably also lacked the inspiration to turn the various incidents into an opportunity to target other Catholics. The rural gentry, like the gentry and elders of the Yihuang county seat, do not seem to have been in a position to organize or direct any anti-Catholic movement on their own; instead they looked to the county government for restoration of order.

Controversy Over How to Control Catholics at Yongxin's County Seat, 1897–1898

On May 1, 1897, Bishop Jules-Auguste Coqset sent a telegram from Ji'an to the French minister in Beijing. He complained that Yongxin gentry had incited local people to start quarrels with the Catholics and to rob them or destroy their property.[115] The bishop repeated this complaint in a second telegram on July 19, in which he blamed Long Xuezhen, a *juren* degree holder, and other gentry for instigating the conflict. The bishop also castigated local officials for not dealing with these serious matters.[116] That same month Bishop Coqset obtained two written documents that, he believed, revealed the true nature of local official bias and the reason behind the Yongxin County gentry's opposition to the Catholics.[117]

The first document represented itself as the last testament or report (*yigao*) of Yan Xian, a former magistrate of Yongxin. According to this document, Yan had committed suicide in desperate protest at the way missionaries forced him to adjudicate court cases involving Catholics. Although written in the first person and emotionally loaded, Bishop Coqset asserted that the document had actually been fabricated by Li Fangxin, a director of Yongxin's Xiushui Academy, to publicly libel Christianity and precipitate disputes with Catholics such as the one over property ownership at Yangjiang in 1897.[118]

The second document contained a general statement against Catholics and a list of four regulations drafted by a member or members of the Yongxin *baojia* bureau. Bureau gentry ordered these regulations circulated and posted to discourage or terminate certain objectionable activities of the local Catholics. The bishop contended that these regulations contravened Sino-Western treaty agreements and contradicted the imperial edict of toleration for Christianity.[119]

These documents are significant not only for their emergence in connection with recent and notorious property disputes, but also for their emphasis on the issue of local control. In other words, the so-called last testament of Magistrate Yan Xian and the *baojia* bureau's regulations voiced, for at least some of the gentry, pressing concerns about the behavior of missionaries and Christians in Yongxin County.

The last testament began by pointing out that treaty articles prohibited missionaries from interfering in public affairs. The first issue centered on missionary and bishop-level protection of Chinese Catholics involved in litigation. The author(s) contended that too many "shameless and vile" officials capitulated to the missionaries and, as a consequence, the local people suffered. When officials stood their ground, the missionaries simply appealed to the French consul in Shanghai or to the minister in Beijing for assistance. This invariably led to greater difficulties for the magistrate and the inevitable coercion of large indemnities from the Chinese. This document stated that if missionaries succeeded it would certainly disrupt local law and order and lead to unsettled feelings, even renewed conflict. "To toady to the foreigners is to arouse the masses' anger," summed up the author(s).[120]

The second major issue raised in the testament grew out of the first. When missionaries interfered in legal disputes too often and bishops had too much power, the magistrate faced a serious administrative problem. If people saw that Catholics usually won in court, more people would convert to Christianity to obtain this advantage. The document stressed that to enforce laws, officials must be able to conduct trials and to cross-examine plaintiffs and defendants no matter what their religious affiliation. Without unencumbered judicial power, officials would not be able to distinguish the facts of a case, maintain community stability, and protect the public welfare.

To remedy these problems the last testament proposed that the Chinese set a precedent by prohibiting the construction of churches in Yongxin County. The author(s) clearly presumed that if no churches existed, there would be no missionaries and no new converts. Without missionaries and Catholics, there would be no riots and all related misfortunes would vanish. The problem of what to do with the existing churches in the county and its various Catholic residents, however, was passed over without comment.

A solution to this problem was articulated in the Yongxin County *baojia* bureau regulations. A general statement that echoed the last testament prefaced the regulations: that is, treaty articles prohibited missionaries from interfering in Chinese court cases. But because missionaries interfered, Catholics were encouraged to act improperly, too. The bureau identified several Catholic "ruffians" by name and pointed out how these men had used their religious affiliation to start trouble, and because of it how they had acted recklessly and enticed others to do likewise. These ruffians behaved like virtual gangs in their efforts to control (*baolan*, literally, monopolize) all new litigation. When they succeeded, they turned justice upside down, cheated the people, implicated the gentry, pressured government officials, and, in essence, managed public affairs. People from all over the county had complained about these improper activities. The Yongxin *baojia* bureau regulations also asserted that since the Catholics were not subject to limitations, the good and the weak alike had no place to hide.[121]

Feeling they needed to do something, the bureau gentry decided to first investigate the overall situation then expel these Catholics from the public arenas where they exercised undue influence. The bureau gentry also announced that a fee they would collect directly from the public would subsidize expenses connected with this effort.[122]

The bureau leaders reinforced this general strategy with four regulations devised to control local Catholics. First, Catholics were not permitted to interfere in court cases or bring up their religious status in order to gain an advantage in litigation or cause trouble. If Catholics formed gangs and acted perversely or violently, the bureau would punish them. Second, when government officials reached a decision on quarrels that involved property, marriages, or other matters, all parties must obey the decision. The Catholic Church must not interfere. If Catholics did not obey government orders and official decisions or attempted to monopolize litigation, the bureau would expel them from the county. Third, since Catholics disavowed their ancestors and lineages, they should not be permitted in lineage halls or to have formal contact with their lineage. Common people should have no contact with Catholics in matters of marriage, funerals, and other affairs. In addition, since Catholics did not pay miscellaneous fees (*zafei*) to the county they should receive no assistance for civil service examination expenses. If Catholics choose to correct these various deficiencies and fulfill their proper duties, then everyone would treat them with courtesy. Fourth, Catholics and non-Catholics should attend to their respective affairs and duties. If there are problems, either side may come to the *baojia* bureau to file suit; the bureau would judge impartially.[123]

Both the *baojia* regulations and the magistrate's last testament revealed the concerns of the local elite regarding Catholic missionaries' behavior and local Catholic activities. Both documents contained similar introductory statements about Sino-Western treaty stipulations barring Catholic interference in court cases and both referred to some of the same examples chosen to demonstrate such interference. These similarities are more than mere coincidence and either point to real problems with the Catholics in Yongxin County or suggest that some local gentry had decided to take the lead in finding answers to perceived problems.

The official investigation into the Yongxin County situation revealed that Li Fangxin and other gentry had visited the magistrate in 1897 to complain about the breakdown in law and order. According to Li Fangxin, night prowlers and roving gangs of men had infested one area adjacent to the county seat itself. Also, hustlers pretending to be Catholics had sought to control or monopolize litigation materials that were sent into court. Previous magistrates had instructed the gentry to determine the effectiveness of the *baojia* in curbing such illegal activities.[124] This initial official encouragement perhaps led the *baojia* bureau gentry to create a list of regulations.

Given Li Fangxin's identifiable role in Yongxin's *baojia* activities, the contextual connections between the *baojia* regulations and the magistrate's last testament, and the bishop's accusation that Li Fangxin had composed the latter document, investigatory officials took a closer look at the facts. First, the Ji'an prefect determined that Magistrate Yan Xian had died of an illness, not suicide.[125] Since Li Fangxin seemed to be the leading suspect as author of the testament, officials summoned him for questioning. Although the details of his deposition were not preserved, officials ruled that Li Fangxin had acted improperly, presumably for his role in the publication of the two documents, and ordered him punished.[126] Last, local officials nullified the *baojia* bureau regulations and reminded Yongxin gentry and elders that an imperial edict prohibited anonymous postings that libeled Christianity. The gentry agreed to obey the edict.[127] Any gentry interest in pursuing their complaints seems to have disappeared as Yongxin officials took full charge of local security matters.

Christians and Security Issues in Rural Areas

In the cases presented above the relationship between Qing officials and local elites in Jiangxi's larger cities was strained and sometimes difficult when it came to the question of dealing with missionaries and Chinese Catholics. Still, the gentry of those urban locales do not appear to have mounted a cohesive campaign to oppose Christianity. But what happened in the small county seats, towns, marketplaces, villages, and rural districts where control or security problems involving Christians were equally challenging and collectively no less important than the cases that occurred in the cities?

Cases from rural locales also show officials, and sometimes gentry, attempting to contain specific security problems and stabilize the local situation. The roles played by Catholics in these cases are difficult to generalize. In one county, for example, Catholics refused to join a militia to fight sectarians, while in another a Catholic led his local militia in doing just that. Qing officials were understandably uncertain and uneasy about the political reliability of Catholics. Catholic refusal to participate in *baojia* security registration led to suspicions and embroilment in other disputes. The cases presented below take us deep into the countryside and give us another view of how security issues affected the lives of local Catholics.

Suspicions Regarding a Catholic Militia Director, Nankang County, 1869

In April 1869 Bishop Jean-Henri Baldus complained to the daotai at Jiujiang that the magistrate of Nankang County in southern Jiangxi accused Catholics of being Vegetarian sect bandits. The bishop asserted that Nankang officials had arrested Chen Yuanyou and Wang Xiuke, two prominent local Catholics, and were mistreating other Catholics. Further, local non–Catholics had stolen church construction materials and posted a placard on the city gate libeling Catholicism and offering a fifty-tael reward for the capture of a missionary. Runners had "arrested [Catholics] and extorted money [from them]."[128] When the governor learned about these accusations he ordered local officials to investigate.

According to Magistrate Shen Enhua's inquiry, militia bureau gentry (*jushen*) accused Chen Yuanyou and his nephew Chen Jinxin, both *shengyuan* degree holders, of being Vegetarian sect members and engaging in secret activities. The magistrate summoned them on several occasions for questioning, but the two men refused to admit to any wrongdoings. Magistrate Shen thought they were using the privileges of their lower degree status to be evasive. He therefore sought annulment of that status so he could interrogate them effectively.[129] After the Liangjiang governor-general approved his request, the magistrate ordered runners to summon the Chens. The same treatment was given to another senior Catholic, Wang Xiuke, who held a *jiansheng* degree.

In the meantime, provincial-level officials commissioned Wang Mingfan (an expectant magistrate) as deputy to work with Magistrate Shen. They convened court and obtained depositions from the principals. Chen Yuanyou testified that he and his family had been Catholics ever since the conversion of his grandfather many years earlier. When Vegetarian sect bandits appeared in 1856 in Tankou, a town thirteen miles northeast of the county seat, community leaders responded by establishing militia in the various rural districts, and requested that those within Chen's *jia* (a *baojia* division of one hundred families) become part of a militia bureau.[130] Chen felt that his refusal to join had sparked hatred against his family. Moreover, because his brother taught family members how to wield cudgels, a sort of martial art, local people became suspicious and complained to the magistrate. The testimony from Chen Jinxin supported this statement.[131]

Wang Xiuke, a third generation Catholic, corroborated Chen's recollection of Vegetarian sect trouble in Tankou. In contrast to Chen's unwillingness to cooperate with local defense, Wang served as the principal director (*shoushi*) of a militia bureau, and in that capacity he stored military weapons and the militia's banners at his home. Sometime in 1868 officials ordered Wang to turn over the weapons, but a year later he had still not complied.[132]

The official investigation discovered that the Chen family had for years been engaged freely in martial training and this in combination with Wang's possession of military equipment made non-Catholic residents nervous. When people filed a complaint with the magistrate, Chen Yuanyou counterclaimed that the magistrate had been arresting Catholics for no reason and that yamen runners had stolen and destroyed their property. Although these very claims led to missionary involvement, the two Chens and Wang later admitted they were all false. Magistrate Shen and Deputy Wang ordered the Chens to stop their training and had Wang's equipment confiscated. They concluded, however, that Chen Yuanyou, Chen Jinxin, and Wang Xiuke were not Vegetarian sect members. Still, they were to be kept under surveillance, and if they exhibited proper behavior, their degree status would be restored.[133]

Several facts regarding local society and government may be deduced from this case. First, when the well-known Taipings and other smaller rebellious groups threatened rural society in the 1850s it was the local elites who led local defense efforts in Nankang County, just as in many other counties. Philip Kuhn has pointed out how existing *baojia* divisions in northern Jiangxi served as organizational units for local militarization. The same appears true for southern Jiangxi, where Nankang militia bureau leaders sought unsuccessfully to enlist Chen Yuanyou's *baojia* group. Wang Xiuke, on the other hand, as militia bureau director had played a role in maintaining the status quo. Although clearly a local leader and a man of means and influence since he held a purchased degree, Wang was accused of arousing the mistrust of the "entire county" by virtue of his control of weapons stored at his home.[134]

On balance this situation seems unlikely. Here it was actually other bureau leaders who had urged the investigation of Wang. Although the exact status of other militias in the area is unknown, I believe this case stemmed from a local power play complicated by the fact that Wang's rivals did not have sufficient militia clout to handle him themselves. Consequently, bureau leaders appealed to the magistrate for assistance. When the magistrate asserted his authority by summoning the Chens and Wang to court, they first sought to protect themselves using their privileged degree status and by falsely claiming that they and other Catholics were being harassed because of their religion. The bishop believed these claims, although I find no evidence that official and gentry actions led to a general persecution of Catholics in the area. The bishop's introduction of a religious issue to a case in which none apparently existed, however, does obscures the point that Wang had earlier played a leadership role in maintaining law and order.

Revival of the *Baojia* and the Catholic Response, Chongren County, 1872–1874

On March 13, 1873, a French legation interpreter in Beijing personally delivered to the Zongli Yamen information received from missionaries in Jiangxi. The missionaries drew attention to Qiuqi, a marketplace twenty miles northeast of the county seat of Chongren where repeated and large-scale persecutions of Catholics had allegedly occurred. According to Fathers Antoine Anot and Fu Ruhan, after Catholics erected a church at Qiuqi in February 1872, local gentry, led by a man named Wang Po, sought to extirpate Catholicism and set a date on which the church would be destroyed. The prefect of nearby Fuzhou, however, had stepped in and prevented the destruction. Subsequently, contended the priests, Wang Po had organized a militia, cast cannons, and procured weapons to be used against local Catholics. In addition, the county magistrate had dispatched Wang by official palanquin to four rural militia bureaus, and villagers had then launched an anti-Catholic campaign. Incidents of robbery and arguments over unpaid rents and loans ensued, but local officials ignored Catholic complaints. Father Anot claimed that it was open season on Catholics. The conflict climaxed on December 14, 1872, with the collapse of the Qiuqi church in a fiery heap.[135]

In a letter written to a confrere in Paris, Father Anot described the conflict in detail. Over the previous three years, priests had attracted nearly one thousand people to Catholicism in Chongren County. Wang Po had been startled by their rapid progress and declared himself the sworn enemy of Catholicism.[136] Wang held a *gongsheng* degree and was clearly a powerful local leader. During the Taiping Rebellion he had commanded a local militia that had been instrumental in expelling rebels from a two-county area.[137] In other words, he had successful experience in organizing, financing, and leading effective militia forces. He thus began again to levy taxes in the area, using the revenue to make weapons and pay new militiamen. According to Father Anot, Wang's militia scoured the countryside for Catholics. Those caught were dragged to local temples and beaten until they disavowed God or died. Wang Po wanted to eradicate all traces of Catholicism in his area.[138]

The Zongli Yamen enjoined the Jiangxi governor to ascertain the relevant facts quickly.[139] The governor learned that in April of 1872 the Chongren magistrate had been officially instructed to determine the condition of the local *baojia* and take appropriate measures to revive it. The magistrate ordered the gentry of various rural districts to register residents for the *baojia* and search out any outlaws (*feilei*).[140] The magistrate designated Wang Po and unnamed others as *baojia* directors for Qiuqi. Their duties, all typical for this role, included inspecting local households, distributing gate cards (*menpai*) that listed the names and occupations of each resident, and determining the population.[141] The directors learned that local Catholics, among them Zhang Jianming (a catechist), Yu Wuxing, and others had blocked the registration inspection and rejected the standard gate cards.[142] They claimed they took this position because of their religion. The matter of their cooperation with local security efforts stood at a stalemate.

During the autumn of 1872, following local custom, organizers prepared for a year-end festival that included theatrical performances. In October Wang Po, Xu Puchu, a commoner, but local lineage head, and others began assessing and collecting fees from residents to pay for the festival. Once again Zhang, Yu, Xu Houxing, and other Catholics claimed exemption on religious grounds. They resisted successfully, in part, by enlisting the services of Father Fu Ruhan who protested by letter to the Fuzhou prefect. The Chongren magistrate then summoned Wang Po, and sixty to seventy Catholics followed him to the county yamen. Although the magistrate persuaded the Catholics to leave the yamen compound, they remained in the vicinity with the intention of beating up Wang. Only with the arrival of "able-bodied" *baojia* men from Qiuqi to serve as an escort did Wang safely return home.[143]

No one reported any other trouble until the theatrical performances began in early December. Wang Po went to see one at the Wanshou Temple and, much to his surprise, he spotted Yu Wuxing, a Catholic, in the audience. Wang could not resist calling Yu a freeloader, and then each spat curses at the other while bystanders urged them to calm down and leave.[144] Wang Po withdrew to a teahouse to cool off. Suddenly Yu, together with Zhang Jianming and Zhang's son, entered the teahouse, hopping mad. Insults again filled the air. Now armed with a butcher knife, Yu attacked Wang. Zhang Jianming brought out his own knife and joined the melee.[145] Wang fell to the floor bleeding before the Catholics ended their attack.[146]

The local *dibao* reported this assault to the magistrate and Wang Po also lodged a formal complaint. Due to Wang's condition he could not travel to the county yamen for verification of his injuries, so the magistrate went to Qiuqi.[147] In addition to two local degree holders' description of what transpired,[148] we also have Zhang Jianming's own testimony. Zhang's age (sixty-one *sui*) and status as a Catholic catechist made him an important man in Qiuqi. Although not gentry, he appeared to be, in a sense, a rival of Wang Po. After the verbal altercation at the temple, Yu Wuxing immediately sought Zhang out to complain about Wang's public humiliation of him. Zhang then conceived the idea of revenge.[149] Their assault on Wang, of course, made Zhang and Yu vulnerable to prosecution. To protect themselves, they declared that Wang Po was trying to eradicate Catholicism from the area. Clearly problems already existed, but proof of their accusation came dramatically two days after the assault when, according to local Catholics, *baojia* directors ordered their men to raze the Qiuqi church.[150]

The destruction of the church, which appears to have been the work of Wang Po's men, did not erase the crime of assault committed by Zhang Jianming and Yu Wuxing. Runners arrested and detained them for trial at the county yamen. The arrival of a large group of Catholics at the yamen, shouting and demanding the release of Zhang and Yu, changed matters, however. The Catholics apparently intimidated the magistrate or at least gave him second thoughts about the potential scope of the trouble. He released Zhang and Yu technically on bail to Wang Jiarui, a *jiansheng* degree holder and catechist from neighboring Linchuan County.[151]

The governor deemed the initial report from the Chongren magistrate and the Fuzhou prefect insufficient and assigned a deputy to reinvestigate. Before the deputy could schedule an inquest, *baojia* directors voiced fears that Catholics would intercept, and perhaps harm, witnesses presenting evidence to the investigating official. However, after provincial-level officials dispatched irregular troops (*yong*) from another county to Chongren to serve as escorts for witnesses, eight or nine people came forward to make a statement.[152] The arrival of additional military forces also made possible the second apprehension of Zhang and Yu, whom runners again took to the Chongren County yamen. Several hundred menacing Catholics watched their departure from Qiuqi, but the military guard discouraged trouble.[153]

High provincial officials summoned witnesses to Nanchang for a third inquest. County authorities feared that Catholics might try to rescue Zhang and Yu and asked superiors to dispatch trustworthy troops (*liangyong*) to accompany the party to the provincial capital.[154] Provincial authorities ordered other soldiers stationed in the Chongren county seat for security purposes.[155] This transfer of military personnel led the Catholic missionaries to complain that "the provincial capital dispatched five hundred soldiers (*bingyong*) to assist Wang Po in apprehending Catholics."[156] Privately, Father Anot complained that the various military forces acted like brigands, pillaging everything owned by Catholics and forcing many from a large area to flee their homes.[157]

At Nanchang the Jiangxi judicial commissioner decided punishments for this case: Zhang Jianming was sentenced to one hundred blows with the heavy bamboo and three years' penal servitude; Yu Wuxing got ninety blows with the heavy bamboo and two and one-half years' penal servitude. Given the origins of the Chongren conflict, the judicial commissioner ruled that the Catholics should not be required to register for the *baojia* nor should they be required to contribute money for performances connected with local temple festivals.[158] This flexibility on the part of Qing officials did not satisfy Father Anot who demanded the release of Zhang and Yu. The governor refused this on the grounds that the investigation of the case had been thorough and the adjudication fair. Governor Liu Kunyi believed that overturning the sentences would only lead to further complications,[159] and the Jiangxi authorities did not release the Catholics.

Father Anot continued to labor on behalf of local Catholics. In December 1873 the French minister forwarded to the Zongli Yamen a copy of a report by Father Anot that described how from January of 1873 to year's end Catholics in Chongren had suffered assault, robbery, and extortion on more than thirty occasions.[160] In May of 1874 the acting magistrate of Chongren responded to these allegations. In the county yamen files for 1873 he found thirty-four cases involving Catholics, eight of which he summarized briefly for the governor.[161] Information from one of these eight cases is especially important to our story here.

Wang Po's nephew, Wang Ximing, also served as a *baojia* bureau director. When Zhang and Yu assaulted Wang Po, a number of local Catholics observed the incident. Thinking that Wang Po might die of knife wounds and that a murder charge might implicate them, Catholics went repeatedly to the local *baojia* bureau to inquire about Wang's recovery and deliver medicines or money for the purchase of medicines for his use. Wang Ximing interpreted the Catholics' evident concern as an opportunity to squeeze them for money. Subsequently, using his uncle's name cards to verify his relation to Wang Po, he extorted cash or IOUs from many Catholics.

Although Wang Ximing claimed to have done this on his own,[162] another possibility is that he did it because his bureau was financially strapped. A letter written by Wang Po to another *baojia* bureau director leaves the clear impression that such extortionary tactics were necessary to raise revenue for the bureau.[163] Other schemes involving Wang Po or his name probably generated additional money.[164] Access to such revenue had allowed Wang Ximing to organize a militia band whose purpose, claimed a priest in Fuzhou, was to terrorize local Catholics.[165] After one Catholic, Hua Menglan, filed a complaint against Wang Ximing, the acting magistrate ordered Wang to return all money he had taken. Eventually, the air cleared and the various tensions disappeared.[166]

Indeed, by the spring of 1874 peace had returned to Qiuqi. Thanks to the money provided by the new county magistrate, according to Father Anot, the rebuilt church in Qiuqi was three times more beautiful than the previous one. In early 1876 Father Anot gloated that conversions in the area were increasing rapidly. In one village he opened a catechumenate. Wang Po, who lived in a nearby village, could now hear people chanting Catholic prayers. Wang's neighbors and, reportedly, even his parents converted. It appears that these new circumstances constrained him from further anti-Catholic activity.[167]

The trouble in Chongren County during 1872 and 1873 centered on local security and reveals how difficult the task had become for officials. Remember that the Catholics' refusal to register with the *baojia*, complicated by their refusal to contribute to the theatrical performances, preceded their aggressive action toward Wang Po. Other subsequent problems led the judicial commissioner to observe that "the animus between commoners and Catholics runs deep." The various cases involving Catholics and non-Catholics needed to be closed and public feeling soothed.[168] To accomplish this Jiangxi authorities had to intervene militarily, bringing in troops from outside the county to rearrest Zhang and Yu. Although an expensive solution and not practical everywhere, the transfer of military personnel to Chongren County allowed officials there to reestablish order. Catholics, who had clearly been part of the Qiuqi community before the trouble, settled once again into their old patterns of contact and peaceful relations with non-Catholic relatives and neighbors.[169]

A Brotherhood Band's Interest in Catholics, Wuning County, 1874–1875

In a rural area of Wuning County during October and November 1874, five men met with Yu Yichang, a martial arts expert who made his living by teaching the use of cudgels. The men soon became close friends with Yu acting as the group's leader. Yu eventually proposed that they form a sworn brotherhood (*jiebai dixiong*) and look out for one another.[170] All concurred and each man contributed one hundred copper cash to purchase incense, candles, wine, and meat for formal rites. On December 2 the men gathered to formalize the brotherhood: each knelt and paid obeisance to the others. Members addressed Chen Lunhe, the oldest of the group, as eldest brother.[171] The other men used the labels second brother, third brother, etc., according to their age relationship to Chen.[172] One day after dining the men chatted. According to Chen Lunhe,

> We each talked about [our] extreme poverty. Yu Yichang said that he had once studied fortune-telling and could interpret the heavenly constellations. [He also said that] he had witnessed the appearance of a new star, the brightness of which portended a military catastrophe. [Yu] knew that there were numerous rich merchants at Wuning's county seat, [so he] conceived the idea of gathering people together to attack and pillage the city with [all of us] sharing the loot.[173]

Thus inspired, the brotherhood planned to recruit as many followers as possible before setting a date for the attack on the Wuning county seat.

But by January of 1875 few people, if any, had been attracted to this plan. Yu and Wang Hongyong then discussed an alternative tack.

Yu and Wang, like others who had lived through the Taiping Rebellion, believed Catholics to be members of "sectarian bands" and assumed that those living in the nearby prefectural city of Jiujiang would want to participate in their uprising.[174] Since they did not know any Catholics in Jiujiang, Yu and Wang felt that a formal letter of introduction and invitation was needed to sound out their interest. If a favorable reply came, Yu would go to Jiujiang and make detailed arrangements for the attack on Wuning. Wang Hongyong then composed a letter in which he falsely stated that several thousand people would gather at a certain place in the county. The uprising would occur in the spring of 1875 and, as soon as it began, they wanted the "various [Catholic] teachers" to join in. To give the letter a proper, formal appearance, Wang stamped the letter with a chop used by his grand uncle, a Taoist priest.[175]

On January 10, 1875, Wang Hongyong personally delivered the letter to the church in Jiujiang.[176] While Wang waited for a reply, Bishop Géraud Bray obtained the letter, which he forwarded to the nearby daotai. The daotai promptly dispatched runners and Green Standard soldiers to arrest Wang. Wang, however, had hidden in the British settlement area. Once the daotai's deputy received approval from the British vice consul, Chinese authorities entered and took Wang into custody for questioning.[177]

Acting on the information obtained from Wang by Jiujiang officials, the Wuning magistrate ordered runners and Green Standard soldiers to make arrests.[178] Altogether, authorities apprehended four brotherhood members and the Taoist priest whose chop had been used on the letter and took them first to Jiujiang then to Nanchang for trial. Provincial-level officials commissioned the acting prefect of Nanchang, Rong Shou, to try the five men. Rong worried that another gang might still be at large. He repeatedly questioned the men on this point, but no new information came to light.[179] Finally he ruled the men, excluding the Taoist priest, guilty as accomplices in a conspiracy to revolt. Rong sentenced each man to one hundred blows with the heavy bamboo and a four-character tattoo on the face (*baimeng feifan*, brotherhood outlaws). After officials had administered these punishments, they banished the men to a distance of one thousand miles. Because of the crime's seriousness, Rong specifically requested that neither of the two general imperial pardons be applied to these criminals; the risk of further trouble from them seemed too great.[180]

Provincial-level officials retried the case and endorsed the acting prefect's judgment.[181] They additionally ruled that Wuning County *baojia* personnel had been negligent in discovering and reporting on the brotherhood's activities; they should be punished according to the statutes. Although an imperial pardon exempted the *baojia* personnel from a beating, officials still enforced their dismissal from service.[182] Of the five men arrested, only Chen Longhe was not a native of Wuning. The *baojia* personnel of Ruichang County, his original home, had no way to monitor his actions in Wuning, so officials absolved them of responsibility.[183]

Jiangxi officials had been lucky that the brotherhood band had not attracted supporters and that the bishop had quickly tipped off the daotai regarding Wang Hongyong's presence in Jiujiang. High-level authorities found the entire matter related not to suspicions about Catholics, but rather to the deficiency of the *baojia* system, whose personnel had not reported the brotherhood in the first place. Clearly, the local security system had not functioned as intended. Unless responsible and informed subcounty personnel reported rural crimes and rumblings of discontent to the magistrate, he faced great difficulty in taking timely measures to check disturbances.

This case is most remarkable because it shows the actual birth of a brotherhood cell. Such occurrences, I suspect, were common in rural China. In this instance, respect for Yu Yichang's martial abilities initially brought him followers.[184] With the formation of a teacher-student bond, feelings of mutual concern naturally developed between Yu and the other men. With poverty weighing heavily on their shoulders, the men gained hope and inspiration from Yu's claimed ability to read the stars and prognosticate the future. He gave the brotherhood a common purpose and target—the county seat's rich merchants. The brotherhood did not inspire an uprising or engage Catholics at the church in Jiujiang to its cause. Local Catholics were clearly not interested in fomenting rebellion.

Investigating Catholic Problems in Anren County, 1874–1876

In August of 1874 the French minister in Beijing informed the Zongli Yamen that at Dengjia, a market town in the southern part of

Anren County, a church caretaker had been murdered, a church had been burned, and sixty Catholic families had been robbed.[185] The conflict there, as I described it in chapter 3, involved various minor and specific secular disputes rather than broad religious issues. Below I will provide additional information that foregrounds the rural Catholics and how authorities investigated their claims of persecution.

Governor Liu Kunyi first furnished the Zongli Yamen with a short summation of the Dengjia situation based on the report of the Anren County jail warden in September of 1874. The governor then obtained more information from an experienced deputy assigned to the case and the new, acting-magistrate of Anren.[186] Last, to double check, the governor ordered the case reinvestigated and those involved retried in Nanchang. The judicial commissioner assigned the case to Dexing, the acting prefect for Nanchang.[187] The information available regarding the events in Anren County thus appears quite complete and reliable.

Acting-prefect Dexing began his report by citing a statement from a *dibao*. According to Song Chang'an, on May 4, 1874, Kong Lienfa and other Catholics seized Wang Changsheng, head of the local Wang lineage, and dragged him off to their church. The Catholics kept Wang securely tied up there until they decided to parade him through the market town's streets and lanes. After subjecting Wang to public humiliation, the Catholics forced him to remain at the church.[188]

Three days passed before Wang's brother and a group of men went to the church to demand the prisoner's release. The Catholics barred the gate while several men climbed atop the church; from this vantage point they hurled roof tiles and insults down at the Wang group. Suddenly, the church was ablaze and the men were forced to scramble down. One of them, Wu Liansheng, the church caretaker, in the course of his descent slipped and fell on a sharp object. He later died from a deep stomach wound.[189] The assistant magistrate and a Green Standard lieutenant directed soldiers and runners in fighting the fire, but their efforts proved futile as the flames devoured the church.[190]

Because the Anren magistrate was away in Nanchang on official business, the county jail warden apprised the Fuzhou prefect of the incident. The prefect named a deputy to investigate but the magistrate returned to Anren before the deputy had arrived. The magistrate immediately launched his own investigation. A coroner performed an autopsy on

Wu Liansheng, determining that a penetrating wound to the stomach had caused his death. The coroner also examined Wang Changsheng and found a large bruise, three stripe-like wounds on his back, and rope burns on his wrists.[191] The magistrate, however, did not understand the trouble's origins until he took testimony from the central characters. The following account has been compiled from their depositions.

Around year's end in 1873 Wang Kaixiu, a Catholic, saw his wife die of kick injuries inflicted by a kinsman, Wang Jiaoda. Wang Kaixiu was a poor man and considered this both a personal and economic loss. After reporting the murder to a *dibao*, he tried to blackmail Wang Jiaoda. The head of the Wang lineage, a commoner named Wang Changsheng, heard about the blackmail and intervened on Wang Jiaoda's behalf.[192] No one, however, reported or filed charges regarding either the murder or the attempted blackmail.

A detail not mentioned by either the lineage leader or by Wang Kaixiu was the sexual aspect of the relationship between the murderer and his victim. According to officials, the two had been romantically involved and when Wang Jiaoda refused to loan money to his lover, a fight ensued in which he brutally beat the woman.[193]

Wang Kaixiu's wife was dead and the murderer had gone unpunished, in part because of lineage intervention. Wang Kaixiu now became sensitive to lineage actions. During Qingming of 1874, the Wangs followed local custom and went to their lineage hall to pay respects to their ancestors and to receive free lineage pastries.[194] When Wang Kaixiu asked for his allotted share of pastries Wang Changsheng firmly refused to give him anything. The Wang lineage denied Wang Kaixiu these group benefits because they felt his belief in Catholicism had led him to disregard their ancestors.[195]

In early April, according to Wang Kaixiu and others, after worship at the Dengjia church several Catholics gathered to chat. The topic turned to the troubles between Wang Kaixiu and Wang Changsheng. Kong Lianfa, a Catholic with a reputedly violent temper, became upset at the humiliating treatment Wang Kaixiu had received. Kong swore to exact revenge for Wang, even though Wang attempted to dissuade him.[196] Several other Catholic men agreed to help Kong out of personal fear for his temper.[197]

Not long afterwards, Kong Lienfa and the other men caught sight of Wang Changsheng walking alone. They seized and detained him at the church. The next day, Kong and his friends beat Wang about the shoulders as they paraded him through Dengjia. The men wanted this treatment to serve as a warning of what would happen to other people who mistreated Catholics or tried to eradicate Catholicism from the area.[198]

Motivation for Kong's actions arose in part from a desire for revenge and in part from greed. He demanded a ransom of fifty strings of cash for Wang's release. Wang's wife could not raise the money and instead unsuccessfully offered the deed to two *mou* of farmland.[199] After the mediation of a local Catholic with bureaucratic rank failed to gain the lineage leader's release, his wife sought assistance from the lineage organization.[200] When Wang's younger brother, older cousin, and other kinsmen proceeded to the church, the Catholics greeted them with a closed gate and a shower of roofing tiles. In the excitement of the ruckus, a rubbish fire burning in the church courtyard went unattended and spread to the church, bringing the Catholics down from the roof in a hurry. It was then that the church caretaker slipped and fell. When the Catholics opened the gates to get help putting out the fire, the Wangs rushed in to rescue their lineage head.

Runners arrested everyone involved except Kong Lienfa, who had escaped. Provincial-level officials found Wang Kaixiu guilty and sentenced him to eighty blows with the heavy bamboo, which a general imperial clemency later voided. They found Wang Changsheng innocent and freed him; they decided to try Wang Jiaoda separately, but the outcome of that trial was not preserved in the *Jiaowu jiao'an dang*.[201] Provincial-level officials ordered *baojia* personnel dismissed from service for being remiss in enforcing prohibitory regulations, a reference to the illicit sexual relationship between members of the Wang lineage and the kidnapping of Wang Changsheng.[202]

The Dengjia affair did not die, however. Father Anot wrote a long report in January of 1875, which the French minister forwarded to the Zongli Yamen. Father Anot's information came from his own personal inquiry and from the investigation made by two Catholics he sent to Dengjia. They said that Wang Kaixiu's wife did household work at the home of Wang Jiaoda and one day he attempted to rape her. When she resisted Wang kicked her, and these blows to the stomach proved fatal.[203]

Due to poverty, the widower agreed to accept money from Wang Jiaoda, with a portion earmarked for the magistrate, presumably, as a bribe to forestall any investigation. The money arrived with the stipulation that Wang Kaixiu needed to renounce his Christian faith. When he refused to do this the money went back to Wang Jiaoda.[204]

Father Anot also contended that from 1873 to 1875 there had been numerous instances of persecution targeting Catholics (see chapter 3). Furthermore, although the church fire had occurred in the very neighborhood of the assistant magistrate's office, local officials sat idly by and did nothing. When they finally did make arrests, it was Wang Kaixiu and other Catholics who were imprisoned. Officials had tortured them and forced them to state that the church fire started accidentally and that the caretaker died of a mishap. Father Anot thought this was a travesty of justice,[205] and Bishop Bray also believed there was an organized movement against them.[206]

In November of 1876 acting governor Liu Bingzhang reported the Anren magistrate's findings to the Zongli Yamen.[207] Although the magistrate found that almost all of the complaints were false, it is possible to sift out from his records bits and pieces of information about local security operations relevant to both Catholics and non-Catholics.[208]

Subcounty functionaries investigated the complaints, most of which came from residents living in one rural area, the thirteenth *du* of Dengjia, where the trouble among the Wangs had occurred. In two instances, *linbao* recovered items that had been lost but were reported as stolen.[209] On one occasion, a *baolin* went to court to provide information and twice *dibao* investigated complaints.[210] Song Chang'an, the *dibao* mentioned earlier, apparently had jurisdiction over the second *jia* while another *dibao* had responsibility for a village.[211] Besides these men, the various gentry and *baojia* heads (*geshen baojiazhang*) of a village located three miles from Dengjia also provided information and assistance in the investigation.[212]

Along with *dibao*, yamen runners carefully but unsuccessfully combed an area within a radius of seven to ten miles around Dengjia for the alleged plaintiffs and defendants, or even anyone with a similar name.[213] Qing statutes pointed to the obvious: there could be no trial without plaintiffs and defendants.[214] *Dibao* and runners thus constituted the magistrate's principal means of searching the countryside for people and information. This thorough and broad search convinced Father Anot to drop his allegations.[215] The priest's new position relieved pressure on Jiangxi authorities and in turn on officials at the Zongli Yamen. The careful work of local-level security personnel could thus have an impact on high-level relations with the French.

A Case of Extortion and a *Dibao's* False Report, Jinqi County, 1874

On July 17, 1874, eight men who identified themselves as "[militia] bureau troops" (*juyong*) from Anren County went to the home of a Catholic in Jinqi County. They accused Fu Jialao of using his religion in unspecified ways to extort money from other commoners. They intended to arrest him and take him to a militia bureau for punishment. Fu appealed to a *dibao* named Fu Zuoran—no relationship indicated—for help, and he advised a settlement. The Catholic man agreed to give the militiamen three strings of cash but since he had no money, he substituted one long cloth gown and some small pieces of jewelry. The eight men spent the night at the Catholic's home, departed the next morning, and were not seen again in the village.[216] Although there are no other reports about this band of men among the *jiao'an* documents, they probably struck elsewhere, too.

Fu Jialao later pressed charges against the extortionists directly with the county magistrate. The magistrate ordered the *dibao* to ascertain the names of the men so he could issue warrants for their arrest, threatening severe punishment if he failed.[217] Fu Zuoran, according to the official report sent to the Zongli Yamen, feared that the magistrate would summon him to court because he could not determine the men's names. Somehow, Fu knew the names of five men involved in the Dengjia case and turned in those names, plus three others, for the crime committed against Fu Jialao.[218]

The Jinqi magistrate checked with his counterpart in Anren County and learned that one of the men named by Fu Zuoran had been sent to Nanchang for trial. In other words, it was impossible for that man to have been involved in the Jinqi incident. Similarly, the other seven men were cleared of blame. The Anren magistrate also stated that militia bureaus no longer operated there, meaning that the extortionists were frauds.[219]

On determining that the *dibao* had submitted false information, the magistrate summoned him to court. According to the statutes on major wrongful acts, the magistrate sentenced the *dibao* to eighty blows with the heavy bamboo and the cangue for one month. The judicial commissioner reviewed the case and concurred. Although an imperial rescript of late December 1874 provided clemency for many criminals throughout the empire, the *dibao* was not reinstated to his position.[220]

In other circumstances and elsewhere in China, *dibao* have been described as untrustworthy characters.[221] Operating on the fringe between law abiders and lawbreakers, *dibao* could be easily compromised by criminals. Confronted with eight intruders, the *dibao* chose to help arrange a peaceful settlement rather than attempt an arrest, which probably would have been physically impossible to carry out without backup. It is likely that the *dibao* received some sort of payment for this service, though it went unnoted, and the Catholic made no complaint about the *dibao*'s role.

Complications arose for the *dibao* because the magistrate depended on an honest and reliable informational agent at the local level. Only then could investigations proceed properly, without undue waste of time and energy. That the magistrate considered this extremely important is clear from the *dibao*'s anxiety at his failure to determine the identity of the extortionists. Quickly and cleverly, Fu Zuoran falsely substituted the names of men involved in another case. Logically he used the names of Anren people, since the extortionists claimed to be from a militia organization based in that county. Yet, it is surprising that a supposedly ignorant and isolated *dibao* knew the names of defendants in distant Dengjia. He apparently had his own channels of information, channels that led to the county yamen and from there to other yamens.

Although the victim in this case was a Catholic, the real issue was not his religion but his security—and the Jinqi magistrate was clearly concerned about that. But for him, and many other magistrates, maintaining law and order in the countryside was problematic especially where the *baojia* system had collapsed. Where the local elite's militia power had waned, all that was left was the magistrate, his staff, and local functionaries. Consequently, local *dibao* were critically important if the magistrate were to get accurate information and devise appropriate security measures. If one *dibao* failed, the magistrate had to punish him as an example to others; the magistrate could not afford to keep on unreliable men.

Illegal Catholic Activities in Anyuan County, 1881–1883

At Lotang, a busy marketplace fifty-eight miles northeast of Anyuan's county seat, *baojia* personnel neglected their security responsibilities with dire results. In early 1881 with no one acting to stop them, Zeng Dalian and eleven other Catholics kidnapped local residents, held them for ransom, and planned to privately collect local custom (likin) taxes for their own use.[222] The Ganzhou prefect, passing through Lotang in mid-April, heard about these illegal activities. He notified Anyuan magistrate Xie Ruochao who, accompanied by Green Standard soldiers and yamen runners, personally went to investigate. Over the next few days, soldiers and runners hunted for those involved. Rather than be captured, Zeng Dalian committed suicide while five of his accomplices slipped out of town. Soldiers and runners arrested the six remaining men and confiscated a cache of two pennants, two signal flags, twenty spears and knives, two sets of metal manacles, and two metal chains intended for use in the tax collection scheme.[223]

Two separate but almost identical trial reports, one from Magistrate Xie Ruochao and the other from his replacement, acting Magistrate Lu Chengshu, include depositions taken from witnesses and those arrested.[224] This information allows us unravel the tangle of events that occurred at Lotang.

In early March of 1881 Zeng Dalian returned home to Lotang after taking part in banditry in neighboring Guangdong Province.[225] Zeng was Catholic and regularly met with Catholic friends at a shop involved in the transporting of goods operated by a kinsmen, Zeng Shangkui. On March 4 Zeng Dalian announced around town that the bishop wanted a church built at Lotang. Zeng then forged a letter in which the bishop stated this intent and had a Catholic friend deliver it to the local congregation. Zeng designed his hoax to convince the congregation at Lotang that they needed means to finance the church construction. Zeng Dalian proposed establishing a custom house, but he did not tell the congregation at large that the money he collected would be for his and his cohorts' personal use. Zeng began to assemble the pennants and weapons to make the operation look official. He also recruited eight Catholics, all surnamed Xue, to serve as patrolmen (*xunding*) for the custom house, which Zeng wanted to open on April 17.[226]

In mid–March, however, another matter developed. Zeng Shangkui hired Lan Gaolang to transport rice to market. Instead of leaving Lotang at dusk, Lan spent the night at a restaurant-hostel owned by Lin Jinshou, a man he knew. That night thieves broke into the establishment and stole Lan's rice shipment. Lin assumed responsibility for the theft and paid Lan seven hundred copper cash in compensation.[227] But the matter only seemed settled. Zeng Dalian used the robbery as a pretext to detain and blackmail Lin. According to Lin Jinshou, on March 22 Zeng Shangkui and Yang Erzi (also a Catholic) accused him of harboring robbers, then seized him and held him for ransom.[228] Three weeks passed without any money being paid. When the magistrate arrived to investigate, Zeng Shangkui quickly released Lin unharmed.

These events show Zeng Dalian organizing local Catholics for criminal activities. Although Zeng's wife and a gentry of the Zeng lineage (*zushen*) testified that they knew nothing about his affairs, their statements must be considered self-serving given the risk of implication.[229] In the end, the magistrate acquitted the Zengs for their failure to control a lineage member.

The magistrate was not so lenient with Lotang's *baojia* personnel, who should have prohibited or at least reported the crimes. He sentenced the *baojia* elders (*fuxiong*) to a beating with the light bamboo then ordered them dismissed from service. An empirewide imperial pardon saved them from the first punishment but not the second.[230] In this case officials applied the Chinese principle of collective responsibility to the local control apparatus personnel and not to the lineage. The magistrate, however, did not hold the *baojia* of Yang Erzi's native place in Guangdong accountable for acts Yang committed while away from home.[231] Apparently no one locally considered Lotang's *baojia* system responsible for registering the presence of outsiders, once a prime security function.

For kidnapping with the intent to receive ransom, the magistrate sentenced the Catholics Zeng Shangkui and Yang Erzi to tattooing and banishment to a malarial region for military service. Authorities permitted no reduction of the sentence through the imperial pardon. Officials sentenced the four other Catholics arrested to forty blows with the light bamboo for consenting to participate in an illegal act that had not yet been perpetrated. The imperial pardon allowed them to be released on bail without flogging.[232] Anyuan magistrate Xie Ruochao anticipated that the Catholic Church might intervene to save Zeng and Yang from their punishments, so he requested that his superiors forward all the facts to the bishop.[233] By taking the initiative and making full disclosure of why these Catholics were being punished, the magistrate avoided further complications. The bishop apparently had nothing to say about the case and stayed out of it.[234] This, too, aided officials in reestablishing order in Lotang.

Protecting Catholics at Qijiaxu, Fengcheng County, 1898

Led by lower degree holders, a crowd assaulted Catholics at Qijiaxu, a rural marketplace located in the southern part of Fengcheng County in early 1898. This serious disturbance led to the magistrate and prefect taking measures to reestablish order and quell further trouble. After the French minister complained on February 27, 1898, Zongli Yamen officials became involved. They ordered Jiangxi officials to investigate and, at the same time, telegraphed Bishop Louis Fatiquet requesting information.[235] On receiving the report from local Jiangxi officials, the Zongli Yamen informed the French minister that the incident involved Catholics and Protestants who had boasted of their respective beliefs, then quarreled and fought, resulting in minor injuries but no deaths.[236] The minister flatly rejected this version of the incident and threatened that if Jiangxi officials did not protect Catholics he would dispatch a gunboat to that province.[237]

Bishop Fatiquet's description of the Fengcheng incident was based on details he learned from a missionary in that county. According to Father Ambroise Portes, on February 7, 1898, Zhang Su (a *shengyuan*), Yang Renzhai, and Yang Zilin (both *jiansheng*) aimed to eliminate Catholicism from the area and had led a crowd of two to three thousand people armed with sharp weapons against local Catholics. The crowd beat several Catholic catechists, calling them agents (*zhaoya*) of the foreigners; they injured other Catholics and killed three. In addition, the crowd burned houses and stole property belonging to local Catholics. The bishop stated that forty to fifty Catholics had witnessed these events.[238]

To restore peace to the Qijiaxu area, the acting magistrate of Fengcheng County summoned local gentry to discuss the situation and enlist their cooperation in preventing further trouble. The magistrate also admonished *dibao* to do more, the only mention he made of local security personnel. The Nanchang prefect, however, took action that was more forceful by dispatching soldiers and runners to the area.[239] Although they were employed only after the incident had occurred, officials clearly had the techniques and the resources to handle serious local problems.

Father Portes visited Catholics at Qijiaxu and outlying areas during March-April 1898 and monitored the progress made. There he found the situation peaceful and reported passing through the nearby market town of Xiucai without event. At Qijiaxu, Catholics formally accused Zhang Su, Yang Renzhai, and Yang Zilin of being the incident's ringleaders. The Fengcheng magistrate, based on his own investigation, agreed and began the procedure to strip them of their degree status as punishment. The magistrate thus contained provocative local elites and warned others against anti-Catholic actions. As compensation for their physical abuse and property losses, the magistrate and the missionary agreed to a monetary settlement of 12,000 foreign dollars. The magistrate ordered Zhang Su and his cohorts to pay the money to Father Portes in three installments. The Catholic priest accepted this arrangement, thereby ending the matter.[240]

★   ★   ★   ★   ★

In the greater Nanchang area during the 1860s and early 1870s, many people felt uncertain about Catholics' political loyalties. Anti-Christian materials playing on these sensitivities appeared there, in other cities such as Ganzhou, Ji'an, and Yongxin, and occasionally in rural areas. *Jiao'an* documents, however, show no clear trail from one city to another and no factual clues that the gentry of Nanchang, or any other Jiangxi city, masterminded and instigated an interconnected movement against Christianity.

Instead, what we find in Jiangxi through the remainder of the century were localized tensions and conflict, including that between Catholics and non-Catholics, over local security *and a variety of other non-religious issues.* During the mid-1870s personal problems in rural Yihuang County spilled over into the county seat, causing many to worry about their safety. Likewise, in Anyuan County during the early 1880s, various illegal activities in the countryside caused concern about maintaining law and order. Elsewhere we may note how basic community squabbles over unpaid rents and debts could escalate into something larger, in good part because of a weak or absent *baojia* security system.

In addition to the cases and problems discussed here, so-called sectarian bandits (*jiaofei*) lurked in practically every prefecture, and drought conditions spawned banditry in northern Jiangxi.[241] Highly capable governors like Shen Baozhen and Liu Kunyi struggled with the challenge of reasserting government authority in the post-bellum era. They found provincial administration to be one headache and crisis after another. At the local level, prefects and magistrates handled myriad affairs, including troublesome and tricky cases involving Catholics. Through the efforts of these various officials, we see more closely the Qing dynasty's local security concerns, and how Catholics played into them.

Responsive government officials regularly found and filled gaps in the administrative structure.[242] For the Nanchang area this meant reliance on public offices to register Catholics and others, too, given the absence of a dependable, up-to-date *baojia* network there. In Chongren County, the magistrate ordered the local elite to reinstitute the *baojia*. All over the province, officials used *dibao*, who knew local residents and were familiar with community affairs, to help with a wide range of administrative chores. Not surprisingly, *dibao* delivered important information to county and higher-level officials. Confidence in the reliability of *dibao*'s reports led to their citation in important communications sent to the Zongli Yamen. Overall, *dibao* appear to be a crucial security link between the magistrate and local society. The proper performance of the *dibao*'s duties was of the utmost importance to smooth county government operations.[243]

Besides relying on *dibao*, we saw in the events at Nanchang and Ji'an that officials also commonly called on Green Standard forces to maintain order. Governors Shen and Liu noted their importance and the need to continue efforts to improve their reliability, efficiency, and power.[244] In fact, new training programs and the acquisition of modern weapons continued to increase the Green Standard's usefulness.[245] Scholarly criticisms of these forces need reevaluation because officials all over Jiangxi indeed used them to control crowds, fight fires, investigate problems, and make arrests.[246] In conflicts between Catholics and non-Catholics, these soldiers probably proved themselves more reliable than local militia forces.

In fact, when disorder involved Christians, officials worried that gentry might compromise their use of militias. In the Nanchang area the local elite, especially degree holders, were openly hostile toward Catholics. Although the 1870 drought worsened security problems in northern Jiangxi, government leaders did not once propose the use of militia to control Catholics or counter the aggressive French; the risk of gentry-led militias turning on the Catholics was too great a risk. On the other hand, when officials were more confident of their overall management of local affairs they acted differently. With community security at stake in Yihuang County, not because of anti-Christian agitation but because of a crime wave, the magistrate used militias—and the local elite—to the government's advantage.

The correlation between government control of local society and gentry power is complicated by another factor: the attitudes of the common people. In the early 1860s, a conversation with anonymous informants in Nanchang was recorded:

> Question: What are the concerns of your local officials and gentry?
> Answer: Local officials and gentry always favor them [the missionaries]. Officials always hope there will be a day without incident so they can swindle [the government] of a day's wages. When a crisis occurs they simply leave—when are they ever concerned about the homes and lives of the common people? Gentry and officials are much alike, too. They [the gentry] also have property, yet they can move [safely] away [in times of trouble]. Those who suffer the consequences are the common people: what has any of this to do with them? Right now we do not want them [the officials and gentry] to handle anything; we will just mind our own affairs.[247]

This gap between officials and gentry on one side and the common people on the other in Nanchang existed in other parts of the province as well. As we saw in the county seat of Yihuang, once a crime wave had started there, it was the degree holders and wealthy people who were able to flee. But residents everywhere wanted to feel safe and secure.

Qing authorities had to reestablish government authority, order, and security. In many parts of Jiangxi, the government had accomplished this by the early 1870s. County magistrates proved to be the crucial variable in local control. Much depended on their administrative expertise, decisiveness, and flexibility. According to the situation and the resources available to them, magistrates employed *dibao*, Green Standard soldiers, local militias, gentry, and even Catholic commoners, to stay on top of the community scene. Few would deny the effectiveness of such tactics in maintaining some semblance of order in both urban and rural areas. During very difficult times and circumstances, the Qing officials did their job. As a result, Catholics did not suffer widespread persecution by the gentry.

Chapter 7

Another View of Christianity: Accommodation in the Countryside

For the late Qing a wide assortment of cases survive regarding Christianity in China. This study has concentrated on a province where our previous knowledge of Christian affairs came primarily from accounts of a serious conflict in the provincial capital during the 1860s. The Nanchang case points to central issues in the development of anti-Christian conflict for that place and time, but those findings should not be generalized to create the impression that elsewhere and at other times in Jiangxi the same pattern of events repeated itself, with the gentry instigating one anti-Christian incident after another. By investigating a full spectrum of cases, especially those that occurred in country towns and villages, I propose a different picture. The gentry presence, as well as that of officials and missionaries, was still important, but the precise roles they played varied from case to case. In rural Jiangxi's variegated social landscape it was mostly ordinary people and their usual concerns that precipitated conflict between Catholics and non-Catholics.

The conflict involving Christians came at a tumultuous time for China. During the late nineteenth century, the Qing had to contend with aggressive imperialistic nations, large-scale rebellions, and numerous minor insurrections, disruptions of traditional trade patterns, economic uncertainties, heightened competition for resources, rising unemployment, rampant drug use, and the effects of all these on lineage and family structures. From this perspective, *jiao'an* were but one part of a larger story of the country's disintegration over several generations' time.

Like a devastating flood, these events and changes swept through Jiangxi. Navigating these whirling, muddy waters is difficult. From a historical record that tends to privilege the difficult and more dramatic aspects of change, it is hard to get at the ways people managed to cope and harder to spot those islands and periods of relative calm and normalcy, even though these may have been larger and of greater length than one might expect. However, missionaries' passing comments, brief observations, and, occasionally, long descriptions help us move away from a conflict-oriented perspective to one that centers on rural locales in peaceful times. The account below provides information that leads to a more balanced understanding of life in the Jiangxi countryside for ordinary Catholics and gives new insight into their everyday affairs in rural places like Jiudu.[1]

Compromise and Coexistence in Jiudu

The village of Jiudu and other nearby rural areas in Jianchang Prefecture were home to hundreds of Catholics. Missionaries over the years had built extensive facilities in the area, living and working there on a regular basis. The *Jiaowu jiao'an dang*, however, contains not a single case of conflict between Catholics and non-Catholics for Jiudu over the forty-year period under study; nor do missionaries mention any prolonged sectarian tension in their letters addressing community-related problems.[2] What are we to make of this? Should we conclude that no conflict occurred or that where conflict did occur the participants resolved it privately? Given what we know about life in the countryside, the latter seems more likely than the former. Since most problems and quarrels were not litigated, and since officials could not and did not record every local altercation, it is not surprising that no official paper trail survives for customary relations between Catholics and non-Catholics.

Father João da Rocha arrived at Jianchang, a joint prefectural and county administrative center in eastern Jiangxi in 1616.[3] He made some converts in the city but had greater success about ten miles away in the countryside of Nancheng County, especially in and around Jiudu. Although a local gazetteer states that Father da Rocha converted 579 people at Jiudu, this figure probably included those who lived in nearby villages as well. Many converts came from Jiudu's You lineage, but not all. The priest made Jiudu a local Catholic center by constructing a church and other buildings there.[4] After Father da Rocha's departure in the early 1620s, other Jesuit priests came and went. The fall of the Ming and the struggle for dynastic consolidation meant times were insecure for all, but especially for Catholics. During the early 1660s, for example, Father Prospero Intorcetta's initially good relations with the magistrate turned sour due to dual concerns about the new church's impact on local geomancy and the priest's political reliability.[5] After the imperial proscription of Christianity in 1724, only a few priests remained in Jiangxi, moving secretively from one rural congregation to another. Even under these circumstances, the Catholics at Jiudu somehow maintained their faith.

Western nations' trade expansion in Guangzhou and increased interest in China during the early nineteenth century attracted European missionaries, some of whom reentered the hinterland. Father Bernard-Vincent Laribe became the first Vincentian to work in Jiangxi. In 1832 he traveled by boat from Macao to Fujian, then overland to eastern Jiangxi. This route took him to Jiudu, which became one of his regular stops as he visited the scattered and half-hidden Catholics of various rural areas.[6] Priests who visited him at Jiudu noted that the rural people displayed a favorable attitude towards Christianity. Father Laribe baptized many people and by 1838 Jiudu had become his base of operations. Approximately 1,600 Catholics lived in Jianchang Prefecture, with the majority in Jiudu and neighboring villages.[7]

Additional information on Jiudu and its Catholics comes from Father Évariste-Régis Huc, a Vincentian who passed through Jiangxi on his way to north China in early 1841.[8] According to Father Huc, Jiudu served as a marketplace for the area and about one-third of its residents were Catholic. A church, rectory, and school were situated on a hillside overlooking the village and a small valley of farm fields (see figure 2). Father Huc called the village an "oasis" and felt he could rest safely there. About that time Father Huc heard rumors of an imminent "persecution" of Christians in Jiangxi. Local Catholics, however, did not seem fearful and openly celebrated Easter. Country people from other villages came, some a long distance, to Jiudu for religious services and activities that lasted several days. The Catholics prayed, sang, participated in night services, and after Mass on Easter Sunday set off firecrackers.[9] Neither Father Huc nor Father Laribe reported any trouble whatsoever regarding Church services that year or mentioned any instances of conflict.

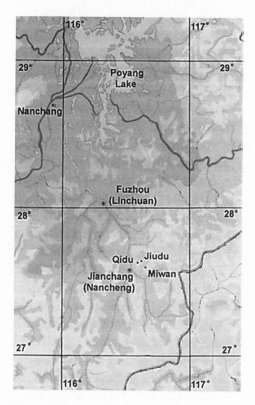

Map 2. Eastern Jiangxi and the Jianchang area

During the fall of 1842, however, a problem began to fester. Local non-Catholics started preparations for a festival. People in the Jiudu area, like people all across China, periodically organized festivals, usually to celebrate a temple deity's birthday or a temple's founding anniversary. Many people felt that such celebrations enhanced the deity's and temple's prestige, which in turn helped ensure the community's well-being. Because it was believed that everyone in the community benefited from these events, everyone supported them financially.[10] Festival organizers typically levied fees to pay for special feasts, theatrical troupes hired to perform on open-air stages, and other expenses such as the sweets and pastries distributed to the area's residents. All local people contributed something. The Church decided in 1769 that it did not want Catholics to support such "idolatrous" events.[11] Given the imperial proscription that had forced

Christians underground, many priests could not or did not enforce this prohibition. Father Laribe himself probably tolerated festival contributions by Catholics, if not their involvement in festival activities.[12] He had lived in the area since 1832, referred to the local festival neutrally as being an annual event, and mentioned no prior problems regarding it.

Fig. 2. Jiudu's Catholic church. The first church here dated to the 1610s; this church was constructed in 1903 and last restored in 1996. *Source:* Photo by the author

After the visit of Bishop François-Alexis Rameaux to Jiudu in 1842, however, Catholics, probably at the bishop's instruction, refused to pay to support the festival.[13] Father Laribe hoped that meetings between local Catholic leaders and non-Catholic village heads would generate a solution regarding whether Catholics could forego payments. But even after enlisting outside mediators, the two sides could not reach an agreement.[14]

The breakdown of negotiations led many Catholics to fear that those requiring support of the festival might turn violently against them. As a precautionary move and for safety's sake, they removed religious items from the church and from their homes. They met and decided not to defend the church; they would, however, protect their own homes. Since the dynasty still officially outlawed Christianity, the Jiudu Catholics thought that if it became necessary to appeal to the magistrate, their complaint could be better represented as an attack on private property than as an attack on an illegal religion. In late September, according to Father Laribe, a crowd of over one thousand people gathered in Jiudu. The crowd went first to the church, but they found it empty and undefended. Members of the crowd damaged the building, made various threats, and searched unsuccessfully for the priest whom they wanted to expel forcibly from the area. The attackers angrily proclaimed that they would "no longer permit [the priest and by implication Catholics] to draw water at the common wells," that is, be a part of the village community.[15]

Since the Catholics of Jiudu were outnumbered and could gain nothing by fighting, some headed for the nearby city of Jianchang. There they intended to hire "the guards, the lawyers, and even the higher men in office," presumably yamen secretaries and clerks, necessary to appeal to the magistrate for protection. More Catholics from Jiudu, including lower gentry, arrived and in a formal complaint stated outright that they as *"Pay-tchu-tee-gin"* (that is, *baizhuderen*, Catholics) had done nothing wrong yet others attacked them and their property. According to the missionary's account, the magistrate ordered yamen runners to go to Jiudu to stop the trouble, but they proved unable to control the situation. The conflict eventually ended with Father Laribe's voluntary departure from the area and the attackers filing a countercomplaint with the magistrate.[16]

The next year, 1843, Father Laribe returned. He learned that peace had been restored, but not by the magistrate. The Catholics and their opponents had evidently found the costs of dealing with the magistrate and going to trial too expensive. The gouging of defendants and plaintiffs alike at the yamen—typical conduct—did not surprise anyone, yet the amounts expended probably did. The magistrate chose not to prosecute the Catholics as members of a proscribed religion, an ancillary but relevant issue to be sure, and simply closed the case. The two sides then negotiated directly and reached an agreement. According to Father Laribe, the Catholics were "to be free both from all contribution towards the [festival] shows, and from taking any share in the superstition practiced in the village."[17] I interpret this to mean that the Catholics no longer had to contribute money to or participate in the festival, but would no longer enjoy any of the festival's benefits such as free entertainment and sweets.

Although in Jiudu financial support of the local festival was the central issue of conflict in the 1840s, missionaries in other rural areas of Jiangxi reported other types of problems, some of them quite serious. Officials and some Chinese confused Catholic religious practices with those of the illegal White Lotus sect, and rumors abounded about Catholics poisoning people. Missionaries unwittingly played into these rumors by having Chinese "medical practitioner-baptizers" (*médecin baptiseurs*) give out free medicines to the parents of sick children, while other Catholic workers tried to save the lives of dying children with medicine, or tried to save their souls with last minute baptism.[18] Opponents of Christianity at Jiudu could have easily thrown in any or all of these three accusations, yet they did not. Thanks to Christianity's long history in the area, non-Catholics apparently harbored no suspicions about missionary or Catholic activities. Both sides concentrated on the matter that concerned them, the local festival, and worked out an agreement.

After this episode, Jiudu continued to be a center for missionary work in eastern Jiangxi for several decades. In addition to the church, rectory, and school, Catholics at various times also built a seminary, an orphanage, and lodging for visiting priests. These facilities and the village went relatively untouched during the early years of the Taiping Rebellion in spite of nearby fighting. To express thanks for this good fortune, Father François-Adrien Rouger prepared a special celebration in 1859 to coincide with Corpus Christi (*Fête-Dieu*). He wanted to bolster the Catholics' spirits and at the same time show non-believers the greatness of a Christian feast. Father Rouger enlisted a Chinese priest, seminarians, and domestic help in cleaning the church and seminary, writing religious inscriptions in Chinese characters on colorful paper for mounting on walls, building temporary altars and religious displays, making ornaments, and sprucing up the grounds. He wanted everything clean, neat, and attractive.

The celebration began with Catholics filling the church to capacity. Father Rouger said Mass and then took those in attendance on a procession around the church, other buildings, and the gardens. With an old catechist holding candles of honor and standing at the priest's side, everyone walked from one special worship place to another, admiring the religious symbolism, the pious couplets, and the ornaments. Catholics chanted prayers and sang while in the background firecrackers and the church bell sounded. The congregation must have felt grateful and proud.

Non-Catholics in the village could not have missed the celebration, yet not one among them complained or made a disturbance about it.[19]

Father Rouger's expression of gratitude may have been premature, for the rebellion gradually engulfed Jiangxi and took its toll on rural areas like Jiudu. Priests did what little they could to help people and the orphanage took in many small children. In 1865 church facilities and the village lay in ruins. Later people rebuilt their homes and the priests returned to work. By 1872 the community had recovered and a wealthy Catholic merchant of Jiudu donated a large sum of money to construct a new church at the same site as the old one, on the hill overlooking the village.

Meanwhile, priests made new conversions to the faith in outlying villages. In nearby Miwan several families converted, and the priest later approved the marriages of women from the Jiudu orphanage to single men of these new Catholic families.[20] This created Catholic family units, which priests wanted, and linked the Miwan families to Jiudu, which made it easier for priests to monitor their religious faith and devotion. Identical motivations led priests to try to marry young women from the orphanage to Catholic men of the area. In eastern Jiangxi priests saw the marriage of a Catholic woman as a way to fortify the religious faith of her entire family.[21]

During the 1870s Catholics in Nancheng County lived in at least twelve rural congregations all directed by a priest who usually resided at Jiudu.[22] Jiudu, the largest congregation, had about four hundred Catholics, while the smallest had only seven or eight.[23] Catholicism's steady growth in Jiangxi led Rome in 1879 to split the province into two vicariates. The new bishop of the Vicariate of Northern Jiangxi made Fuzhou, a city about fifty miles west of Jiudu, his episcopal residence. From that time onward Jiudu lost personnel, funding, and facilities to Fuzhou but remained a well-known center for Catholics.[24]

In 1882 Father You Yong (André Yeou) went to Jiudu where his family lived and where he had been born in 1856. From his account we learn of changes that had occurred in the village. Father You wrote that in the past the Catholics and non-Catholics of his lineage had not gotten along. At one point, the non-Catholics had threatened to remove the Catholics' names from the genealogy. Catholic Yous did not take this threat lightly and some turned hesitant about going to Mass. No doubt, other threats and tensions with non-Catholic kin also made the Catholics' lives difficult. But times had changed and Father You observed that

Catholics in Jiudu now enjoyed "a peace and liberty that they had never known before." Village children attended the Catholic school without obstacle, and more importantly, the recently republished You genealogy not only included the full names of all the Catholics but also the names of four priests born there. I believe that this inclusion indicates a shift from tolerance to acceptance. Before Father You departed the village, the headman and older non-Catholic men came to pay their respects.[25] By prostrating (*ketou*) themselves before him, they demonstrated that they no longer disdained Catholicism. From this it appears that Catholics were integrated into the kinship and prestige systems of the village.

Father You's observations were corroborated by Father Antoine Anot, whose career in Jiangxi spanned from 1844 to 1893. Through the years, this most veteran of all French missionaries in China visited Jiudu periodically and resided there from 1887 until the year of his death. Father Anot remarked in 1890 that the inhabitants of Jiudu had been part Catholic and part "pagan" for twelve generations and over the last forty-seven years Catholics had lived in peace with their neighbors.[26] In other words, since the 1842-1843 incident over payments to support the local festival, the Jiudu congregation had seen no other disruptions.

I do not contend, however, that Jiudu was an idyllic Catholic congregation living in problem-free bliss. On the other hand, neither was it the site of continuous conflict brought on by an ever-hostile population agitated by local gentry. Without question, disagreements and problems arose between Catholics and non-Catholics, and probably between Catholics as well. If these led to litigation, the record of it no longer exists. What seems likely is that with time the non-Catholics gradually changed their expectations of Catholics and their sociocultural practices, and developed a more tolerant attitude. In other words, people adjusted to one another and their differences. In 1883 Bishop François-Adrien Rouger of the Vicariate of Southern Jiangxi commented that missionaries and those who had been Catholic for some time did not fear persecution. Recent converts, however, who had just ceased their practice of ancestor veneration and stopped making annual payments to support the "cult of idols," that is, local festivals, dealt with numerous and often cruel "vexations."[27] It took time for people to adjust their expectations of what Catholic membership in the broader community entailed, given that

Catholicism led converts to discontinue some long-standing and central cultural practices.

The Rural Catholic Experience

There are further possible explanations of how and why relations between rural Catholics and non-Catholics improved. Conflicts that occurred in major urban centers often arose due to people's concerns about what went on inside the churches and orphanages. We recall that in Nanchang anti-Christian publications during the 1860s condemned Catholic activities as barbaric.[28] Uncertain security and curious but unruly townspeople led priests to control access to churches and orphanages. Closed doors, however, just fueled suspicions. In the countryside circumstances were different.

First, anti-Christian literature and wild rumors were rare and seldom incited cases of conflict. Second, rural people had easy access to churches, chapels, and orphanages, which priests often located in preexisting buildings. Also, for lack of other facilities in the countryside, priests frequently said Mass in makeshift oratories, a room or part of a room located in a Chinese house. Sometimes Catholic and non-Catholic families shared these houses. One missionary described how Catholics created a temporary oratory in a rural home: they simply took the front door off its hinges and placed it on two stands to serve as an altar.[29] Priests felt lucky when swine and poultry did not wander through the open doorways in the course of a service. With doors and windows wide open, non-Catholics could easily peer inside or enter if they wanted to. Missionaries often did not appreciate these rural oratories, but they should have. The incidental observation and contact they allowed reduced the sort of rumor mongering and agitation successfully carried out in urban areas because of closed church buildings.

Third, special religious services or feast day celebrations such as the one described above for Jiudu involved public processions that exposed non-Catholics to rituals and actual worship practices. Moreover, villagers simply observing Catholics in worship probably already knew those participating. These factors all made a difference, as did the opportunity that non-Catholics had to casually watch the missionary's activities as he worked or visited families among them.

From the time missionaries first arrived in China, they showed special concern for the plight of children, especially those seriously ill. According to Church doctrine, baptism saved the souls of children near death. Priests, catechists, and the medical practitioner–baptizers treated and baptized as many sick children as possible. As more personnel, especially the Sisters of Charity, arrived in Jiangxi during the nineteenth century, and as funding permitted, the Church opened or expanded its orphanages. The larger orphanages were usually located close to the episcopal residence, which beginning in the 1870s tended to be in or near principal administrative cities. Priests ran smaller orphanages in rural areas where they had a good base of operations. By 1899 the Church operated eighteen orphanages in Jiangxi.[30]

The Church cared for and raised orphans and abandoned children in both urban and rural communities. Little girls greatly outnumbered boys. Unfortunately, the mortality rate among orphans was very high because the poor health and condition of the children when they arrived at the orphanage gave them low odds of survival. In the Vicariate of Northern Jiangxi from 1870 to 1886, the Church took in approximately six thousand children only to have four thousand die. Over the same period, Catholic workers baptized around 100,000 dying children.[31] Suspicions about the Church's connection to so much death led to the destruction of its orphanages at Nanchang in the 1860s, at Fuzhou in the 1870s, and threatened one at Jiujiang and one at Fuzhou in the early 1890s.[32]

The story in the countryside was somewhat different. Father Anot opened the first orphanage in rural Jiangxi at Jiudu in the 1850s. Often the orphanage had more children than it could handle. He and other priests hired local women, including non–Catholics, who suckled and cuddled the smallest children in their own homes. This hiring practice brought local non–Catholics into direct contact with the orphanage, gave them an opportunity to observe the treatment children received there, and, moreover, made them share some responsibility for the children's fate. Due to extreme poverty, some families in the area could not afford to raise their own babies. On occasion, priests found infants left anonymously at their gate. Sometimes people brought children to the priests and arranged for their admittance to the orphanage. The bishop of the Vicariate of Eastern Jiangxi, Casimir Vic, reported in 1886 that parents had left daughters at one orphanage with the stipulation that when the girls reached marriageable age the priests should find husbands in the area where the parents lived so they might have future contact with them.[33] Priests consented to this only if the natal family was willing to study Catholic doctrine. Priests also tried to arrange the marriages of young women from the orphanage to Catholic men. During the late 1880s, Bishop Vic counted more than two hundred orphans married mostly to new Catholics.[34] When circumstances left no choice, priests also permitted the marriage of orphans to non-Catholics, with the Church providing the bride's trousseaux and dowry. Marriage rites brought ordinary people into contact not only with the orphanage, but also with the priest and other Catholics. Generally speaking, rural people did not shun the orphanage or mistrust the work done there. Missionaries, naturally biased about their work, claimed that orphanages gained for them the sympathy and the respect of the people. In rural areas this claim appears to have had some validity.

Within the orphanages, missionaries emphasized the religious education and training of the young because they believed this would create solid and strong Catholics for the future. Priests lamented the fact that small children in the care of non-Catholic wet nurses missed basic Catholic education and instead received exposure to customs and practices not conducive to the formation of good Catholics. They worried that when the children returned to the orphanage there might not be enough time to fully inculcate Catholic values. On the other hand, priests sometimes took advantage of the strong bond that developed between non-Catholic wet nurses and infants. If the wet nurse approached the Church about adoption, the priest used this as an opportunity to draw a non-Catholic family into the Church and permitted adoption only after its conversion to Catholicism.[35]

Their emphasis on religious education led priests to establish schools. Father Laribe pioneered this work with his establishment of five village schools in eastern Jiangxi during the late 1830s. Priority for admittance went to Catholic children but if space permitted, non-Catholic children could attend. Students usually paid no fees. The school curricula, of course, emphasized Christian training while providing a basic education for many whom would not have otherwise had the opportunity to study. Where possible, as in Jiudu, priests established separate schools for boys and girls, which salaried Chinese schoolmasters and mistresses managed.

By 1899 priests had established 135 schools, most of them in the countryside.[36] The promotion of education clearly brought Catholics and non-Catholics into contact and probably led the latter to respect missionaries' efforts at increasing literacy. Significantly, Catholic education in Jiangxi was never a source of conflict and never came under direct attack by opponents of Christianity.[37]

Besides providing an education, the Church created a variety of employment opportunities for local Catholics and some non-Catholics, and patronized local trades and businesses. The remodeling of existing buildings or the construction of church buildings, usually supervised by priests, meant the use of local labor and the local purchase of materials. Once built, the mission centers, residences, and churches needed a domestic staff, watchmen, and others to operate and to maintain them. Also, priests hired sedan chairs, carriers, and porters for visits to their scattered congregations. In the countryside, priests paid small salaries to the numerous catechists, baptizers, and medical practitioner-baptizers so important to the Church's rural work.

Orphanages hired workers, too, and, as mentioned above, always needed wet nurses. Wet nurses in rural areas worked for less money than those in urban areas, an important consideration for priests on tight budgets.[38] When orphanages moved to new locations wet nurses sometimes made a commotion.[39] To be sure, they had strong affection for the infants under their care, but they also depended on the income. These women and most people working for the Church were extremely poor and had few employment options. Over all, it appears that income from the Church helped many rural people, and in the case of women, gave them additional opportunities that took them outside the home into positions such as baptizers.[40] Chinese women serving in this capacity or in orphanages and schools were never targeted for criticism in Jiangxi.

As mentioned above, Catholic women played a role in Catholicism's growth because in Jiangxi priests did not make conversions en masse but rather individual by individual and family by family.[41] Priests promoted the marriage of young Catholic women from the orphanages, calling them "little missionaries."[42] All Catholic women could play this role, winning over non-Catholic spouses, and bringing their children into the Church. During the 1850s in rural Nancheng County, a Catholic woman watched her daughter leave to marry a non-Catholic. The new bride found herself isolated from other Catholics, and it became difficult for her not only to attend Mass but also to make annual confession. She nonetheless managed to keep her faith alive and over a span of thirty years, with the help of her mother, made sure that eleven of her twelve children receive baptism. Eventually, her husband sat beside her in church.[43] Another Catholic woman helped to convert her husband, saw all her children received baptism, and found Catholic wives for her three sons. From the work of this one woman grew an extended family of seventeen Catholics.[44]

Catholic women who married Catholic men had the advantage of religious cohesion within the family. Catholic women who lived in villages with larger mission complexes like those at Jiudu, Sanqiao, and Daheli also had the advantage of access to religious training. In the Jiudu area this may account for the appearance as early as the 1840s of "consecrated virgins"—unmarried Catholic women who dedicated themselves to a Christian life.[45] Chinese women sometimes avoided marriage vows, but only an infinitesimal number made this choice because of the inherent difficulties that came with it.[46] Conversion to Catholicism presented this as a real option and, if circumstances permitted the women to live communally, the odds that they could win release from the constraints of male-oriented family life were even greater.[47]

The Church influenced other female Catholics in more subtle ways. Father François Dauverchain noted that female catechumens were often angry and vocal about their inferior position in Chinese society.[48] He implied that conversion helped eliminate those feelings. A Chinese priest, after traveling in three counties of eastern Jiangxi, commented that Catholic women greeted him without hesitation in public and spoke with confidence to him.[49] How some Catholic women developed self-confidence and self-esteem probably had to do with their attendance at Catholic schools and catechumenates. Prospective converts, many among them illiterate rural women with children in tow, stayed for a week or more at boarding-house style catechumenates. There they studied, prayed, and observed the example of Catholic women. Beginning in 1880, priests also conducted separate lay retreats for men and women at selected mission centers such as Jiudu.[50] Catholic women were able to spend several days refining their devotional practices, freed from regular household duties. Some women because of domestic responsibilities still returned home each night to cook, clean, and care for their families. To Chinese women, these were small but important steps toward education and self-improvement.

Not all Catholic women moved ahead and fared so well, however. In 1883 Bishop Rouger listed the practice of selling females and keeping concubines among his six main obstacles to Catholicism's growth.[51] Chinese men's treatment of women posed a stubborn problem both before conversion and afterward. Men typically considered women to be property and sex objects whose main purpose was to produce male heirs. Priests did not always succeed in eliminating these culturally dominant ideas from Catholic minds. One Chinese priest wrote from Fuzhou in 1880 that he knew of Catholics in rural areas who sold baptized women and girls from their families to non-Catholics. This priest, of course, did not condone the practice and tried to bring pressure from fellow believers to terminate it.[52] Since priests visited most rural congregations just once a year, it was up to local Catholics to detect such unacceptable practices early enough to prevent them. Interestingly, the priest's account makes no mention of formal Church intervention or excommunication as a punishment.

Although individual priests may have taken different approaches to supervising their congregations, all priests still knew the importance of Catholics, men and women, conducting themselves properly in everyday life. On the one hand, priests cared about believers as individuals and guided them to salvation through religious training and ritual practices. On the other hand, priests knew that the moral and behavioral standards of individual Catholics set an example for others and influenced what non-Catholics thought about Christianity; their actions had a ripple effect in the communities where they resided. For example, in 1836 a Chinese priest noted that bad or false Catholics who caused "scandals" gave non-Catholics a reason not to convert.[53] Catholics needed to lead virtuous lives because hypocrisy drove others away from Christianity—an age-old story, to be sure. As difficult as monitoring behavior proved, priests still did the best they could. In 1883 Father Nicolas Ciceri learned that a Catholic had married a non-Catholic woman whose husband was still alive. Church canon did not permit this and the priest wanted to show local Catholics how the Church dealt with "public sinners." The priest denied the sacraments to the Catholic man while seeking a solution. Father Ciceri contacted the woman's former husband and learned that he would neither convert to Catholicism nor, if his former wife returned to him, permit her to convert. Hearing this, the priest evidently decided that the woman would be lost to the Church unless he viewed her first marriage as over. The priest then sent the woman to the catechumenate to study doctrine. When she satisfied him of her sincerity, he baptized her and blessed her marriage to the Catholic man.[54] The impact of the priest's actions on the local congregation cannot be measured, yet his efforts stand as one example of how priests monitored and sought to correct the religious and behavioral practices of Catholics.

Priests' success in attracting "good" people and their diligence in supervising them leads easily to questions about the overall quality of Catholics and the type of people who became Catholic. We have seen in this study that Chinese officials generally viewed Catholics as people of questionable character. Nonetheless, one official with thirty years experience in Jiangxi said he had dealt fairly with all country people, whether Catholic or not. However, he asked missionaries to "be prudent, vigilant, and govern the Christians well because many are bad and under the pretext of religion trouble the people."[55] Undeniably, some Catholics did cause trouble and some had questionable motives for conversion. The bishop of the Vicariate of Eastern Jiangxi wrote in 1886 that if you asked new converts why and how they came to Christianity, you got answers such as, they did not know why they converted, they converted due to parents and friends' efforts, or they became Catholic because they wanted the priest's protection in the advancement of their secular affairs.[56]

The last answer suggests that priests attracted people with impure or ulterior motives. The reams of documentary materials at hand, however, provide no evidence that Catholic priests attracted new adherents based on their class standing, political attitude, occupation, residency, gender, age, or other attributes. Priests simply sought prospective converts everywhere, encouraged everyone who expressed interest, and accepted people from a cross-section of non-gentry society, since few gentry converted. Ordinary people, mostly farmers and workers, constituted the majority of people in China and also the preponderance of Catholics. In terms of personality or character, priests did not act selectively because they believed the study of Christianity and conversion would in any case reform and improve people.

Whatever the background or personality of a prospective convert, priests prescribed a course of religious training that led to baptism. Father Antoine Anot wrote in 1872 that in eastern Jiangxi some people had been catechumens for up to five years before being baptized. In the early 1890s the bishop of the Vicariate of Eastern Jiangxi held that two years of study at a catechumenate sufficient for a "solid conversion."[57] The degree of commitment needed to meet these standards must have discouraged many who expressed interest in Catholicism while harboring ulterior motives.

In spite of Catholic efforts to bring sincere converts into the fold, Protestant missionaries, like Chinese officials, criticized priests for working with people of dubious quality and especially for helping Chinese Catholics in legal disputes. To the Protestants, the inclination of Catholic priests to intervene in legal cases attracted the worst type of spurious Christian, and by intervening they obstructed justice. As a result, most Catholics tended to be dishonest or disreputable types dissatisfied with the sociopolitical status quo.[58] In fact, the materials consulted for this study do not bear this out. For the most part, Catholics were no better and no worse than their non-Catholic neighbors. Protestants, however, turned examples of "bad" Catholics and their behavior into a negative characterization of all Catholics, and that stereotype became part of their mission histories. With little or no qualification, later generations of scholars have accepted these generalizations as fact.[59]

From Protestant mission histories we also learn that priests created Church-protected enclaves of Catholics who lived apart from non-Catholics. But in fact, the scattering of small numbers of Catholics across Jiangxi did not lend itself to the formation of such enclaves. Early in the nineteenth century Catholics, who typically constituted a small minority of the residents of a village, continued to live with and labor alongside non-Catholics. In fact, when missionaries returned to Jiangxi during the early 1830s, they found that many Catholics had intermarried with non-Catholics. Although Bishop Bray reflected with satisfaction in 1884 that through time and patience the Church had "regularized" these marriages—that is, created Catholic families from previously "illegitimate unions"[60]—the percentage of Catholics in almost all villages remained low.

Like Jiudu, the village of Sanqiao was unique for its unusually large number of Catholics, and priests turned Sanqiao into a Catholic center. But Father Pierre Peschaud described a more typical situation when he wrote in 1839 that he visited small hamlets in which only four or five Catholics resided among all the other non-Catholics.[61] Decades later, in 1868, Bishop Rouger mentioned a similar situation in the countryside, where "in many areas, there is only a hamlet, a few families, or indeed just a single family, lost among the idolators."[62] Even in 1886 Bishop Casimir Vic commented that in eastern Jiangxi the Church had a Christian family here, two families there, and a few isolated ones elsewhere. He bemoaned the dispersion and isolation of Christians and the difficulties created by this situation.[63] These observations are congruent with data presented in chapter 2, which indicates that even at the end of the century most congregations were still small, averaging only eight Catholic families per village—and these so-called Christian villages were only a tiny minority among all villages.

It appears that in Jiangxi most Catholics could not have easily lived apart from non-Catholics because of their sparse numbers and because it was simply impractical. Even when a large number of Catholics lived in a rural area, as was the case late in the century at Daheli in Nankang County,[64] there is no indication that this community constituted an independent Catholic enclave. In fact, I find no evidence of any self-contained and independent Catholic communities in Jiangxi and no indication that, had they existed, they could have stood alone as social, economic, or religious entities.

The ultimate goal of the missionaries was, of course, to convert everyone; but until that day came, in recognition that real conversions came in small increments, priests knew that Catholics would be living in the same villages with non-Catholics. Priests often noted the close contact that came with Catholics renting housing from non-Catholics, or living with non-Catholic families in the same dwelling. In one instance, twelve families, two of them Catholic, shared a single building.[65] Chinese Catholics recognized the fact that in everyday matters they had little choice but to live and get along with their non-Catholic neighbors and kin. After all, they had to draw water from common wells and remained part of the village community, even after conversion.[66]

Catholics in the countryside saw a priest only once a year and otherwise depended upon the guidance of local lay leaders. Most congregations had only a small oratory in someone's house to use for worship, though most wanted a formal chapel or church. Cathechists sometimes lobbied priests for financial assistance and priests responded according to the need and the funds available. In Jiangxi the Catholic Church always operated on a tight budget so priests encouraged their congregations to donate the labor and materials to build and support their own establishments. In so doing, Catholics, by necessity, moved in the direction of self-support.[67] To be sure, Catholics gladly accepted whatever aid priests could provide, but their own contributions toward building churches, orphanages, and schools at home demonstrated to non-Catholics their commitment to the larger community in which they lived. These efforts kept the Catholics concretely linked to and part of the scene around them.

Disturbances in rural Jiangxi during the nineteenth century involving Catholics and other Christians usually ended after a short time. There were few lengthy *jiao'an* and few places where one finds trouble recurring. Based on the evidence, both Chinese and Western, the ordinary people of Jiangxi's towns and villages did not live embroiled in ongoing conflicts over Christianity. Rather, in time Catholics and non-Catholics were often able to find a middle ground that allowed them to live peacefully together and to adjust to the fact that they were equally part of one community.[68] A Chinese priest wrote in 1880 that the residents of a rural area of Lüqi County did not distinguish between who was Christian and who was not in their expressions of friendship.[69] In 1887 another Chinese priest commented that inhabitants of a small village in Fengcheng County were "polite and kind towards Christians."[70] Such observations about everyday life and normal relations between people during peaceful times may be easily overlooked because they do not seem noteworthy compared to an assault on a missionary or the destruction of a church. Nonetheless, common gestures of good will and the larger historical process of accommodation must also be recognized as elements of Christianity's presence in China during the late Qing.

Notes

Abbreviations

Notes to Chapter 1

[1] Kenneth Scott Latourette, *A History of Christian Missions in China* (London: Society for Promoting Christian Knowledge, 1929), chapters 17 and 19–20, especially, 279, 333–35, 348–50, 421–23, 467–68; and Paul A. Cohen, *China and Christianity: The Missionary Movement and the Growth of Chinese Antiforeignism, 1860–1870* (Cambridge, Mass.: Harvard University Press, 1963), chapter 3, especially, 86–87, 141. These books are representative of two different eras of scholarship. Also see Paul A. Cohen, "Christian Missions and Their Impact to 1900," in *The Cambridge History of China*, ed. Denis Twitchett and John K. Fairbank, vol. 10, *Late Ch'ing, 1800–1911*, pt. 1, ed. John K. Fairbank (Cambridge: Cambridge University Press, 1978), 556–60, 564–70.

The terms gentry and local elite are used interchangeably in this study. Broadly speaking, the gentry exercised power and influence in community affairs; they were the community leaders. For many, this status was a result of civil service degree status and the advantageous economic situation that led to and/or resulted from such achievement. Others possessed local power and influence because of wealth, education, experience, reputation, and position within a lineage or voluntary association.

[2] I do not deal with any cases or incidents that occurred in Jiangxi from 1900 to 1901. During these two years in north China the Boxer Uprising initiated new traumas for Christians there. For other areas, especially central and south China, this period and subject have not been researched. I do not believe this is the place to engage such a large and complicated topic, but hope my study may serve as necessary background for such work in the future.

[3] With the rise of Chinese nationalism, issues such as "local initiative," "self-support," and "control" of the church became prominent. For some early comments on these issues, see Frank Wilson Price, *The Rural Church in China: A Survey* (New York: Agricultural Missions, 1948), 165–69; and Latourette, *History of Christian Missions*, 801–22.

[4] Cohen, "Christian Missions," 544.

[5] Cohen, "Christian Missions," 564–66.

[6] Cohen, *China and Christianity*, 88–123, 263, 272.

[7] Frederic Wakeman, Jr., *The Fall of Imperial China* (New York: Free Press, 1975), 183–84.

[8] Cohen, *China and Christianity*, 3–60. In a long chapter entitled "The Anti-Christian Tradition in Chinese Thought," Cohen discusses examples of these materials. For a selection drawn from numerous Chinese sources see, Wang Minglun, comp., *Fan yangjiao shuwen jietie xuan* (Ji'nan: Jilu shushe, 1984). Materials that circulated in parts of Jiangxi appear on pages 21 and 114–21.

[9] Mary C. Wright, *The Last Stand of Chinese Conservatism: The T'ung-chih Restoration, 1862–1874* (Stanford: Stanford University Press, 1957; reprint, New York: Atheneum, 1969), 146–47 (page citations are to the reprint edition).

[10] Cohen, "Christian Missions," 572.

[11] *Jiaowu jiao'an dang*, series I, volume 1, document 21, pp. 7–9; and series I, volume 2, document no. 795, pp. 720–21. Hereafter cited as *JWJAD*. In future citations I will indicate, in abbreviated format, the series, volume, and document numbers, each separated by a slash mark; last come the page number(s). All dates from this source have been converted to the Western calendar. For more information regarding this collection, see n. 44 of this chapter.

[12] Cohen, "Christian Missions," 557, 567.

[13] Lü Shiqiang, *Zhongguo guanshen fanjiao de yuanyin, 1860–1874* (Taibei: Zhongyang yanjiuyuan jindaishi yanjiusuo, 1966), 130–94.

[14] Stephan D. R. Feuchtwang, *An Anthropological Analysis of Chinese Geomancy* (Vientiane, Laos: Vithagna, 1974), 172–75, 236–54. For one example, see *JWJAD*, IV/1/367, 454.

[15] John King Fairbank, "Patterns Behind the Tientsin Massacre," *Harvard Journal of Asiatic Studies* 20 (December 1957): 492–93; and Latourette, *History of Christian Missions*, 178–79.

[16] Cohen, "Christian Missions," 563, 566.

[17] Cohen, "Christian Missions," 566–72.

[18] Cohen, "Christian Missions," 556–57, 559–60, 567. Cohen's conclusion on this point seems influenced by the opinion of scholars such as Kenneth Scott Latourette (a former Protestant missionary). For example, Latourette characterized Catholic converts as coming from "the baser and more turbulent elements of society," "the lower economic and cultural strata," and "poverty-stricken groups." In short, they were "unpromising material." Latourette, *History of Christian Missions*, 333–34.

One wonders if Latourette, by implying that Protestant missionaries were concerned more with the quality than the quantity of converts, was attempting to explain the comparatively slow progress of Protestants in making converts in China. In fact, Protestant and Catholic missionaries alike worked among the same "kinds" of poor people.

[19] Cohen, "Christian Missions," 557.

[20] Paschal M. D'Elia, *The Catholic Missions in China: A Short Sketch of the History of the Catholic Church in China from the Earliest Records to Our Own Days* (Shanghai: The Commercial Press, 1934), 36.

[21] One of the few books on this subject includes a section on missionary work among the common people. Jacques Gernet, *China and the Christian Impact: A Conflict of Cultures*, trans. Janet Lloyd (Cambridge: Cambridge University Press, 1985), 82–104.

[22] Latourette, *History of Christian Missions*, 107.

[23] Latourette, *History of Christian Missions*, 129; and *Handbook of Oriental Studies*, ed. E. Zürcher, S. F. Teiser, and M. Kern, vol. 15/1, *Handbook of Christianity in China, 635–1800*, ed. Nicolas Standaert (Leiden: Brill, 2001), 382–86.

[24] French missionaries frequently referred to the Christians at a particular location as a *chrétienté*. One priest defined it as a *"station"* or *"loca missionum."* He also used the term "small parishes," which is technically incorrect because the Catholic Church did not yet have such ecclesiastical divisions in China. *Annales de la Congrégation de la Mission* 47 (1882) (Paris: Congrégation de la Mission), 269. Hereafter *ACM*, with volume number and year. I prefer congregation as the

translation for *chrétienté*. For further discussion of *chrétienté*, though of an earlier period, see *Handbook of Christianity*, 536–37.

[25] Latourette, *History of Christian Missions*, 182–83; and *Handbook of Christianity*, 383.

[26] Latourette, *History of Christian Missions*, 537.

[27] One source that provides a province-by-province total is Joseph de Moidrey, *Carte des Préfectures de Chine et de leur Population Chrétienne en 1911* (Chang-hai: Imprimerie de la Mission Catholique, Orphelinat de T'ou-se-we, 1913), 15.

[28] "Vincentian Missions in China," (Perryville, Mo.: St. Mary's Seminary, n.d.), 4–5. This manuscript is actually a history of Catholic missions in Jiangxi's Jianchang Prefecture through 1900. Context indicates the author was an Irish priest who served in eastern Jiangxi during the 1930s and early 1940s. He wrote it in 1942.

An untitled revision of this account may be found in the Archives of the Missionary Society of St. Columban, Dublin, Ireland (hereafter Archives, MSSC). This version continues the history into the 1930s. According to Father Luke O'Reilly, a Columban who also worked in eastern Jiangxi during the 1940s, the author is probably Father Joseph Mullen. I will refer to the untitled version as "Mullen's manuscript" (n.p., n.d.).

[29] In 1839 the vicar apostolic of Jiangxi and Zhejiang reported the number of Catholics for various parts of Jiangxi. Some of the numbers appear to be his estimates. *ACM* 9 (1843), 170–89. The numbers for this early period vary. For example, in 1849 another source counted approximately four thousand Catholics and twenty chapels. Latourette, *History of Christian Missions*, 238.

[30] In addition there were 15,333 catechumens. *Annals of the Congregation of the Mission* 7 (1900) (Baltimore and New York: Congregation of the Mission), 212–13; hereafter ACM-E, with volume number and year.

[31] Donald MacGillivray, ed., *A Century of Protestant Missions in China, 1807–1907* (Shanghai: The American Presbyterian Mission Press, 1907), 440.

[32] MacGillivray, *Century of Protestant Missions*, 144–45, 162.

[33] MacGillivray, *Century of Protestant Missions*, 453.

[34] Generally, I use the term Christian to refer to both Catholics and Protestants unless the context or source cited calls for a more specific usage.

[35] Since members of the Congregation of the Mission are known as Vincentians rather than Lazarists in the United States, I will use the former term here. The so-called secular priests, usually Chinese, were not members of the Congregation of the Mission but the vicar apostolic supervised and directed them. The Sisters of Charity are now known as the Daughters of Charity.

[36] Vincentians' reports and letters were published in *ACM* starting in 1834. In 1894 an English language edition appeared. Stored at the Mother House of the

Congregation in Paris are many unpublished letters, some predating 1834, and other materials related to China. In addition, *Annals of the Propagation of the Faith* (hereafter *APF*, Paris, [London: Society for the Propagation of the Faith, 1839–1901]) provides information sometimes not available in the Congregation of the Mission's sources mentioned in this note.

[37] J. Van den Brandt, *Les Lazaristes en Chine, 1697–1935: Notes Biographiques* (Pei-p'ing: Imprimerie des Lazaristes, 1936), 40, 48.

[38] I refer here to the *JWJAD* collection of documents and my own province-by-province survey of the documents' geographical distribution.

[39] Cohen, *China and Christianity*, 88–94.

[40] Ernest P. Young, "The Politics of Evangelism at the End of the Qing: Nanchang, 1906," in *Christianity in China: From the Eighteenth Century to the Present*, ed. Daniel H. Bays (Stanford: Stanford University Press, 1996), 91–113.

[41] Philip A. Kuhn, *Rebellion and Its Enemies in Late Imperial China: Militarization and Social Structure, 1796–1864* (Cambridge, Mass.: Harvard University Press, 1970), 152–64; and Cohen, *China and Christianity*, 88–94.

[42] In southwest and northwest Shandong, a weak gentry allowed the spread of sectarian practices that eventually led to violence against the orthodox order and conflict with local Christians. Joseph W. Esherick, *The Origins of the Boxer Uprising* (Berkeley: University of California Press, 1987), 7–37, 210–14.

[43] In Jiangxi, county magistrates did not automatically forward to superiors every legal case that involved a Christian. When magistrates settled disputes, especially civil ones, and when no one appealed, the files remained at the county yamen. Missionaries did not know of every case involving Christians and did not intervene in every dispute, legal or otherwise. Being a Catholic, and any implied status that came with it, was not necessarily relevant to all disputes and cases.

[44] *JWJAD*, Series I, 1860–1866, 3 vols.; Series II, 1867–1870, 3 vols.; Series III, 1871–1878, 3 vols.; Series IV, 1879–1886, 3 vols.; Series V, 1887–1895, 4 vols.; Series VI, 1896–1899, 3 vols.; and Series VII, 1900–1911, 2 vols. (Taibei: Zhongyang yanjiuyuan jindaishi yanjiusuo, 1974–1980). For a description of these materials, see Charles A. Litzinger, "Bibliographical and Research Note," *Ch'ing-shih wen-t'i* 3.1 (November 1974): 95–99.

Certain factors regarding use of the *Jiaowu jiao'an dang* require clarification. First, unfortunately for historians, *JWJAD* materials were not written for the purpose of preserving data on institutional and social change or on cultural history. The materials are mainly bureaucratic reports and the records of legal inquisitions and trials. The presence of relevant and significant historical information cannot be guaranteed, no matter how much documentation remains on a given case.

A second consideration is how this material relates to the bureaucratic structure. Even in densely populated counties averaging several hundred square miles, the magistrate was ultimately responsible for conducting trials, collecting all taxes, and maintaining the peace. Government statutes stipulated time limits for the completion of many duties, and the magistrate's administrative record was subject to annual review (*kaocheng*) by superiors. The likelihood of demerit or demotion was both real and frequent. See John R. Watt, *The District Magistrate in Late Imperial China* (New York: Columbia University Press, 1972), 174–76, 184.

One way the magistrate could avoid reprimand was to adjudicate legal cases as quickly as their investigation permitted. On one hand, this meant that the evidence gathered and the depositions given were often very fresh. On the other, with timeliness of such importance, the magistrate and his aides sought to minimize or eliminate contradictions of fact or opinion so as not to unduly prolong settlement and miss an administrative deadline.

Another reason for the magistrate's desire for speed and for congruence in the court records was that only a thoroughly investigated and clearly resolved dispute could win endorsement from higher-level authorities. In most cases that involved missionaries or Christians, the magistrate knew succeeding layers of the provincial government would scrutinize his records before sending them to the Zongli Yamen. Usually endorsement from superior officials did not come until they had commissioned a deputy (*weiyuan*) to reinvestigate the case with local officials. If the report produced jointly by the magistrate and the deputy was acceptable to superiors then the magistrate could rest easier. Other officials now shared administrative responsibility in the case, reducing the possibility of reprimand for any one official accordingly. As John King Fairbank noted, "self-confident officials sometimes took long chances in suppressing the report of grave events, but the usual practice seems to have been to err on the active side and announce even very slight matters. By so doing, an official could get his own version on record for the future and, by having his superiors accept and transmit his report, he could involve them in responsibility for whatever might thereafter occur." John King Fairbank, Edwin O. Reischauer, and Albert M. Craig, *East Asia: The Modern Transformation* (Boston: Houghton Mifflin Co., 1965), 104.

For the historian a crosscheck of the magistrate's report is possible via the missionary's account of the case submitted to Church superiors or to the respective Western legation. If the legation (for Jiangxi this usually meant the French legation) forwarded this account to the Zongli Yamen, officials there would in turn send it to provincial officials for verification. The missionary's version and the official Chinese records require careful comparison, but this in combination with the internal logic of the case itself usually makes it possible to determine the sequence of events, who was involved, and what happened. No small amount of historical detective work is required, particularly in examination of the testimony itself. On occasion, the recorded oral depositions of participants or witnesses are disquietingly similar in wording. The preservation of an accurate court transcript depended largely on the ability of the clerk-scribe to write quickly and precisely. No doubt clerks sometimes took shortcuts in recording the testimony of people with basically the same statement.

[45] For Chinese officials *jiao'an* referred to incidents that involved "heterodox" sects of all kinds. In this study I use *jiao'an* to refer to cases and disputes that involved missionaries and/or Chinese Christians.

[46] Britten Dean has examined provincial quarterly reports on Sino-Western conflict for 1868–1894 and determined that for cases involving Americans 37 percent centered on commercial issues and 23.4 percent on missionary (I would presume all Protestant) problems. See his "Sino-American Relations in the Late 19th Century: The View from the Tsungli Yamen Archive," *Ch'ing-shih wen-t'i* 4.5 (June 1981), 85–88.

Any attempt to compare statistically conflicts involving missionaries and Christians with other types of conflict is fraught with complications. One problem with this approach is that it makes all cases equal in significance. Some cases involved loss of life and/or property and led to many other problems that took much time and many resources to resolve, while other cases did not. Historians have tended to focus on the former and ignore the latter.

In *China and Christianity*, 272–73, 346 n. 13, Cohen writes that during the late nineteenth century there was more conflict involving missionaries than any other Western group. To support his contention he provides page- and volume-number comparisons. Later, Cohen seems to have revised his view, stating that "violence cannot be quantified. Nor is overt rioting necessarily its most significant expression. It is well to remember this when approaching the anti-Christian disturbances of the last decades of the nineteenth century." See "Christian Missions," 570.

[47] Cohen, "Christian Missions," 563.

[48] See for example, Philip C.C. Huang, *Civil Justice in China: Representation and Practice in the Qing* (Stanford: Stanford University Press, 1996), 21–50; and Matthew H. Sommer, *Sex, Law, and Society in Late Imperial China* (Stanford: Stanford University Press, 2000), 17–29

[49] In Jiangxi, circa 1900, there were about 27,000 Catholics (not including catechumens) and Protestants in a population of approximately 18 million. Christians constituted only 0.15 percent of the population and conflicts involving them were proportionately few in number.

[50] Jiudu is now known as Youjia.

Notes to Chapter 2

[1] Latourette, *History of Christian Missions*, 94–95; D'Elia, *Catholic Missions*, 36, 98; and S. Wells Williams, *The Middle Kingdom: A Survey of the Geography, Government, Literature, Social Life, Arts, and History of the Chinese Empire and Its Inhabitants*, vol. 2, rev. ed. (New York: C. Scribner's Sons, 1883), 290–91.

[2] Athanasius McInerney, "The Spanish Franciscans in the Province of Kiangsi, China, during the years 1685–1813" (Master's thesis, St. Bonaventure University, 1946), 11–18.

[3] McInerney, "Spanish Franciscans," 20–23, 39; and Bernward Willeke, "Fray Manuel del Santisimo Sacramento, the Last Franciscan in Kiangsi, China," *Franciscan Studies* 26.2 (n.s. 5.2; June 1945): 177. Willeke cites a mission report of 1765 that puts the number of Catholics at 9,713. Based on all other accounts, this number does not appear reliable.

[4] Latourette, *History of Christian Missions*, 118, 158.

[5] Willeke, "Fray Manuel," 178–79.

[6] Willeke, "Fray Manuel," 180–82.

[7] "Vincentian Missions," 2–3.

[8] Latourette, *History of Christian Missions*, 170.

[9] In "Christian Missions," 545–46, Cohen writes that "the more the Christian community was treated like a secret society, the more it was forced to act like one." However, I would venture that Christianity's existence during the period 1724–1844 was more analogous to that of a "religious sect" as described by Daniel L. Overmyer in his *Folk Buddhist Religion: Dissenting Sects in Late Traditional China* (Cambridge, Mass.: Harvard University Press, 1976), 7–11, 54–58, 102–8, 113–29.

[10] Archives, Congrégation de la Mission, Maison-Mère, Paris, France, "La mission des Lazaristes au Kiang-Si," 34–39. Hereafter cited as Archives, CM, with the archival reference number, if marked. "Vincentian Missions," 4–6. Another early estimate of Catholic numbers is ten thousand. See *ACM* 5 (1839), viii.

[11] *JWJAD*, I/2/969, 907. French First Secretary Kleczkowski reported that local officials ordered this church demolished in 1840.

[12] Latourette, *History of Christian Missions*, 230; and Cohen, "Christian Missions," 550.

[13] In 1696 the Pope demarcated for China seven vicariates apostolic; Jiangxi was one of the seven. Later, in Rome, Church authorities thought that better episcopal supervision was necessary and during the late 1830s and early 1840s made realignments. Jiangxi and Zhejiang were linked together in 1838 and then

split apart seven years later. Vincentian vicars apostolic (i.e., titular bishops) were placed in charge of both provinces. In 1879 Rome established another vicariate apostolic in Jiangxi and a third in 1885. The province was divided first into northern and southern jurisdictions and then the eastern half of the northern vicariate was split off. A variety of sources, which provided some slight discrepancies in dates, were consulted for this information. See Latourette, *History of Christian Missions*, 125, 232; *Album des Missions catholiques: Asie orientale* (Paris and Lille: Société de Saint-Augustin, 1888), 95; Joseph de Moidrey, *La Hiérarchie Catholique en Chine, en Corée et au Japon (1307–1914)*, (Zi-ka-wei: Imprimerie de L'Orphelinat de T'ou-se-we, 1914), 99, 102–3, 258–59; and *Mémoires de la Congrégation de la Mission (Lazaristes), La Congrégation de la Mission en Chine*, vol. 3, *Les Vicariats Apostoliques*, new ed. (Paris: La Procure de la Congrégation de la Mission, 1912), 190, 200.

[14] *JWJAD*, II/2/778, 994.

[15] Archives, CM, "Fruits Spirituels, 1841," C176-I-b-2-1.

[16] *ACM* 9 (1843), 169–91.

[17] *ACM* 11 (1846), 499; *ACM* 13 (1848), 296; *ACM* 15 (1850), 94–95; and *ACM* 16 (1851), 161.

[18] *ACM* 15 (1850), 94–95; and Latourette, *History of Christian Missions*, 238.

[19] *ACM* 18 (1853), 446–447. Latourette states that the number of Catholics was nine thousand in 1856; see *History of Christian Missions*, 323.

[20] *APF* 16 (1855), 45.

[21] *ACM* 22 (1857) 375–77.

[22] Latourette, *History of Christian Missions*, 295–302; and Jen Yu-wen (Jian Youwen), *Taiping tianguo quanshi*, 3 vols. (Hong Kong: Jianshi mengjin shu wu, 1962), 531–38.

[23] *ACM* 26 (1861) 281–99, 332, 335; and Latourette, who notes the decrease in Catholic numbers; *History of Christian Missions*, 323.

[24] Cohen, "Christian Missions," 563.

[25] For example, in Sichuan in 1769 officials arrested a European priest and imprisoned him for eight years because of supposed connections with the White Lotus. Latourette, *History of Christian Missions*, 165.

[26] These so-called Vegetarian bandits were members of a clandestine sect, which was probably an offshoot of the White Lotus Society. The sect was active in various parts of Jiangxi as well as in other provinces. See Mary Backus Rankin, "The Ku-t'ien Incident (1895): Christians versus the Ts'ai-hui," *Papers on China* 15 (December 1961): 34–35.

[27] *ACM* 12 (1847), 98. Perhaps the official confused Catholic abstinence from meat on certain days and during Lent with practices of Vegetarian sect members.
[28] ACM 58 (1893), 244.

[29] *JWJAD*, I/2/969, 907. The subprefect of Wucheng confirmed that the church was destroyed in 1857 because of suspicions that linked Catholics with Taipings. *JWJAD*, I/2/974, 910.

[30] *JWJAD*, II/2/778, 994.

[31] For example, in two north China villages in 1870 commoners, most likely members of a White Lotus sect, apparently had ulterior motives when they asked a Protestant missionary to visit them. John Fairbank saw in this "some support for the hypothesis that Christianity often aroused the most interest precisely among those elements of the Chinese populace that were least loyal to the established order." Fairbank, "Patterns," 492–93.

[32] *ACM* 21 (1856), 404.

[33] Keep in mind that the threat was potentially much larger than what we might assume because of the inconsequential numbers of Christians. After all, in 1885 there were only about thirteen thousand Catholics living in Jiangxi and by 1900 only about twenty-three thousand, plus around thirty-two hundred Protestants. Latourette, *History of Christian Missions*, 323; *ACM-E* 7 (1900), 212–13; MacGillivray, *Century of Protestant Missions*, 453; Bertram Wolferstan, *The Catholic Church in China from 1860–1907* (London: Sands and Co., 1909), 436–37, appendix, table A; and Samuel Yale Kupper, "Revolution in China: Kiangsi Province, 1905–1913" (Ph.D. diss., University of Michigan, 1973), 58.

When placed alongside the province's population figures, estimated at 24.5 million in 1851 and from six to eight million less after the rebellion years, Christian numbers are miniscule indeed. Dwight H. Perkins, *Agricultural Development in China, 1368–1968* (Chicago: Aldine Publishing Co., 1969), 202–14, appendix A; and Ping-ti Ho, *Studies on the Population of China, 1368–1953* (Cambridge, Mass.: Harvard University Press, 1959), 244–46.

[34] Brief biographical information about priests who served in China may be found in Van den Brandt, *Les Lazaristes en Chine*, passim; Robert P. Streit, *Bibliotheca missionum*, vol. 12, *Chinesische missionsliteratur, 1800–1884* (Freiburg: Verlag Herder, 1958). Very limited information is available for a few missionaries who served in Jiangxi in the personnel records of the Mother House's archives of the Congregation of the Mission in Paris.

[35] Latourette, *History of Christian Missions*, 343, 345.

[36] Latourette, *History of Christian Missions*, 337.

[37] *ACM-E* 3 (1896), 463.

[38] "Vincentian Missions," 5, 68; *ACM* 50 (1885), 210; and *ACM-E* 7 (1900), 212–13. Latourette mentions ten priests in Jiangxi during 1849. The Vincentians,

who worked in the provinces of Zhili (including Beijing), Zhejiang, Jiangxi, and Henan (until the 1860s), added fifty-two foreign and Chinese priests between the years 1843 and 1859. From 1860 to 1899, 235 more priests were added. Latourette, *History of Christian Missions*, 238, 321. According to Wolferstan in his *Catholic Church* (pages 436–37), Jiangxi's three vicariates apostolic in 1907 were home to forty-eight European missionaries and twelve Chinese priests.

[39] *JWJAD*, II/2/700, 879. We may observe in another instance during the mid-1880s that a bishop was responsible for three prefectures. *JWJAD*, IV/1/376, 510. This area was, in fact, the vicariate apostolic.

[40] *JWJAD*, II/2/765, 978.

[41] *JWJAD*, V/2/1054, 968.

[42] Latourette, *History of Christian Missions*, 335.

[43] Latourette, *History of Christian Missions*, 335–36, 553. Priests did exercise some quality controls. Father Anot, for reasons unknown, expelled three Catholics who lived at Dengjia. *JWJAD*, III/2/619, 807, 814, 828.

[44] *JWJAD*, III/2/587, 678.

[45] *JWJAD*, III/2/591, 683; *JWJAD*, IV/1/367, 457; and *JWJAD*, IV/2/379, 515–16.

[46] On March 15, 1899, an imperial decree gave missionaries equivalents of official status and the privilege to visit and correspond with Chinese officials of corresponding rank. Hosea Ballou Morse, *The International Relations of the Chinese Empire*, vol. 3, *The Period of Subjection, 1894–1911* (New York: Longmans, Green, and Co., 1910-1918), 160.

[47] Catholics, in some provinces, also used firecrackers at the start and the end of Mass. Latourette, *History of Christian Missions*, 335.

[48] For one example, see *JWJAD*, IV/1/379, 514, 522.

[49] Latourette, *History of Christian Missions*, 308, 322–23. The French had only obtained control over this cemetery in 1861.

[50] Any number of sources could be cited, but this may the best: Cohen, "Christian Missions," 550–73.

[51] During the late 1860s, Father Fu Ruhan had at least a three-prefecture circuit. Presumably, as missionary numbers increased there may have been several priests in one prefecture. However, the concomitant increase in Catholics meant that the convert-priest ratio stayed greatly out of balance. Latourette in *History of Christian Missions* (page 335 n. 186), writes about a Jesuit missionary in Jiangnan in 1845 who found that visits to sick Catholics anxious for extreme unction took over half of his time.

[52] *JWJAD*, III/2/606, 708. This of course gave missionaries time to handle other matters, but made them dependent upon second-hand information.

[53] Lü Shiqiang, *Zhongguo guanshen*, 162–70.

[54] *ACM* 38 (1873), 289. Father Anot implies that although some may have considered those who had expressed interest in the faith as conversions, he believed they "are not precisely conversions." The statistical records kept by missionaries distinguished between catechumens and Catholics generally.

[55] According to Wolferstan's statistics for 1907 (*Catholic Church*, 436–37), in the eastern and southern vicariates apostolic there were 170 and 53 catechists, respectively. For the northern vicariate there were 101, but this figure included an unknown number of European and Chinese brothers and sisters.

[56] *ACM* 18 (1853), 171.

[57] Latourette, *History of Christian Missions*, 128.

[58] For example, they are mentioned by one missionary in Guangzhou (1722) and one in Sichuan (1782). Latourette, *History of Christian Missions*, 191.

[59] *APF* old ser., 2 (1839), 7–8.

[60] *APF* old ser., 1 (1838), 375.

[61] *ACM* 3 (1837), 91–92. Father Li's full Chinese name is not known.

[62] *ACM* 52 (1887), 433

[63] *ACM* 11 (1846), 498.

[64] *ACM* 58 (1893), 247.

[65] Latourette, *History of Christian Missions*, 191.

[66] Latourette, *History of Christian Missions*, 334–35.

[67] Similarities between catechists and congregational leaders (*huizhang*) are noted by R. G. Tiedemann in "Indigenous Agency, Religious Protectorates and Chinese Interests: The Expansion of Christianity in Nineteenth-Century China" (paper presented at the North Atlantic Missiology Project Consultation, Indigenous Agents and Indigenous Interests, University of Edinburgh, September 1997), 4. Cited with the author's permission.

[68] Beginning sometime in the early twentieth century, the term used in Jiangxi for catechist became *xiansheng*, that is, "teacher." In Church records at the end of the century they were listed in English as "Catechists, Men ...; School Masters" and "Women ...; School Mistresses." *ACM-E* 7 (1900), 212.

[69] *JWJAD*, III/2/617, 794.

[70] Three men specifically mentioned establishing a teacher-student relationship. *JWJAD*, III/2/617, 790, 792, 794.

[71] *JWJAD*, III/2/617, 785.

[72] Wang Jiarui was referred to as a priest in one official report, *JWJAD*, III/2/571, 644; his *jiansheng* degree status is noted on page 648. In another report, local officials identified Wang as a *jiaotou*. *JWJAD*, III/2/578, 657. Wang apparently started out as a *jiaotou* at a church in Jiujiang, *JWJAD*, III/2/582, 670.

[73] *JWJAD*, III/2/617, 782, 799; and *JWJAD*, III/2/618, 802.

[74] *JWJAD*, V/2/1087, 991. In 1896 a Shandong Catholic and a non-Catholic became embroiled in an argument over an unpaid loan. Eventually, the Catholic and a relative sought protection and revenge through a catechist of the local church who responded by arming a group from his congregation. Esherick, *Origins*, 114.

[75] There are far too many examples to cite, so a mere sampling will be given here. For *huizhang*, see *JWJAD*, III/2/615, 748. For *jiaozhang*, see *JWJAD*, VI/2/727, 1077. For a *guanshiren* who lived at the church, see *JWJAD*, II/2/765, 978; for *guanshi*, *JWJAD*, III/2/583, 670; for a *dongshi* who held the *jiansheng* degree, *JWJAD*, IV/1/367, 472; for *jiaodongshi*, *JWJAD*, V/2/1100, 1011.

[76] This is one example where it seems that families stayed at the church. *JWJAD*, V/2/1087, 993.

[77] Charles A. Litzinger, "Patterns of Missionary Cases Following the Tientsin Massacre, 1870–1875," *Papers on China* 23 (July 1970): 99.

[78] Latourette, *History of Christian Missions*, 332.

[79] Latourette, *History of Christian Missions*, 332.

[80] Latourette, *History of Christian Missions*, 332.

[81] Latourette, *History of Christian Missions*, 333.

[82] Latourette, *History of Christian Missions*, 331–33, 335–36.

[83] *ACM* 3 (1837), 93.

[84] *ACM* 8 (1842), 175.

[85] Robert E. Entenmann, "Catholics and Society in Eighteenth-Century Sichuan," in *Christianity in China: From the Eighteenth Century to the Present*, ed. Daniel H. Bays (Stanford: Stanford University Press, 1996), 22.

[86] *ACM* 26 (1861), 270–75.

[87] *ACM* 18 (1853), 170.

[88] *ACM* 24 (1859), 372.

[89] *ACM* 38 (1873), 108.

[90] *ACM* 45 (1880), 291; and "Vincentian Missions," 78.

[91] *JWJAD*, II/2/721, 925–26.

[92] The expression "*chile*" was colloquial and used just this one time in the *jiao'an* documents for Jiangxi. I do not believe anything negative can be inferred from it. *JWJAD*, II/2/712, 904.

[93] *JWJAD*, II/2/712, 904–5.

[94] *JWJAD*, III/2/617, 785–94.

[95] For *jinjiao*, see *JWJAD*, II/2/704, 882; *fengjiao*, *JWJAD*, II/2/704, 883–85, 889; for *rujiao*, *ru Tianzhujiao*, *tourujiao*, and *touru Tianzhujiao*, see *JWJAD*, III/2/617, 780–801. Father Louis Boscat wrote from Ji'an in 1883 that people said to him "*Iao fongkiao* [*yao fengjiao*], c'est-à-dire, je veux me faire chrétien." *ACM* 49 (1884), 289.

[96] *JWJAD*, II/2/712, 903.

[97] *JWJAD*, II/2/712, 904.

[98] *JWJAD*, II/2/704, 885.

[99] *JWJAD*, III/2/597, 689–90.

[100] *JWJAD*, I/2/1082, 974–75.

[101] *JWJAD*, III/2/597, 690.

[102] Robert E. Entenmann, "Christian Virgins in Eighteenth-Century Sichuan," in *Christianity in China: From the Eighteenth Century to the Present*, ed. Daniel H. Bays (Stanford: Stanford University Press, 1996), 180–93.

[103] *ACM* 13 (1848), 302–3.

[104] *ACM* 45 (1880), 288; and "Vincentian Missions," 75.

[105] "Vincentian Missions," 63–64.

[106] *ACM* 45 (1880), 290; and "Vincentian Missions," 77.

[107] *ACM-E* 3 (1896), 340.

[108] The *Jiaowu jiao'an dang* for the period 1860–1900 does not identify a single all-Catholic village in Jiangxi in connection with any case. There is only one brief and passing statement regarding an unidentified rural village somewhere in Gan County that had been all Catholic for some time. Unfortunately, the documents provide no details. *JWJAD*, VI/2/667, 1006.

Nor did missionaries serving in Jiangxi mention any all-Catholic villages. However, the village of Sanqiao in northern Jiangxi's Gao'an County had become over a long period of time mostly, but not entirely, Catholic. From 1845 to 1855 Sanqiao was the site of Jiangxi's only seminary. For a time, it was also the site of the bishop's official residence. Missionaries seemed to like this village area and gave it considerable attention. Fighting during the Taiping Rebellion destroyed Sanqiao but afterwards missionaries returned, repaired the church, and gradually rebuilt the congregation. "Vincentian Missions," 80.

[109] Jean-Paul Wiest notes that these people were actually catechumens; they had not been baptized. He does not identify by name the villages nor does he provide hard data. See his "Catholic Activities in Kwangtung Province and Chinese Responses, 1848–1885" (Ph.D. diss., University of Washington, 1977), 122–23.

[110] Esherick, *Origins*, 87–88.

[111] In the early period, detailed reports are not available for every year. Later, the regular reports made by various bishops in Jiangxi indicate numbers of those who had been baptized and confirmed, and catechumens (those studying doctrine but not baptized).

[112] *ACM* 9(1843), 169–91.

[113] For the bishop's report see *ACM* 9 (1843), 170–89; the figure for Jiudu comes from Father Évariste-Régis Huc who visited the village in 1842.

[114] The number of catechumens in 1842 is unknown, but there probably were not many judging by the 177 reported for 1850. This small number barely affects the averages I compute. Archives, CM, "1850—Etat de la Province du Kiang-Si," C179-II-a-2-g.

[115] For 1881 the bishop of the Vicariate of Northern Jiangxi reported 11,446 Catholics living in 232 congregations, which he called "parishes." That same year the bishop for the Vicariate of Southern Jiangxi reported three thousand Catholics dispersed in more than fifty different villages. ACM 47 (1882), 126, 269. The figures for the south appear to have been rounded off. Regardless, the congregations in the two vicariates ranged from forty-nine to sixty Catholics per location. These figures are close to my provincewide estimate of forty-three to forty-four Catholics or eight Catholic families per congregation.

[116] These are Church figures for 1898–1899 and the "Presumed Number of Catholics." Catechumens were listed separately. The number of congregations is based on the figures listed for "Localities where annual Missions are given" and may be low because priests were unable to visit every locality. *ACM-E* 7 (1900), 212–13. Many but not all reports include the number of congregations. The figures used for 1898–1899 are consistent for the period under study. See, for one example, statistics for 1852: 8,925 Catholics living in 170 congregations or about 52 per congregation. *ACM* 18 (1853), 446–47.

[117] For family size see, Ping-ti Ho, *Studies on the Population of China*, 56. My calculations actually range from seven to nine Catholic families per village, depending on the year.

[118] See Kung-chuan Hsiao, *Rural China: Imperial Control in the Nineteenth Century* (Seattle: University of Washington Press, 1960), 14–17.

[119] For information on Sanqiao, see *ACM* 50 (1885), 119.

[120] *ACM* 50 (1885), 125; and *ACM* 51 (1886), 416. Bishop Rameaux wrote in 1842 that in one (unidentified) village in Nanfeng County fifty of one hundred families were Catholic. *ACM* 9 (1843), 173.

[121] A biography of Bishop Rouger published in 1888 stated that three hundred adult Catholics lived in Jiudu and in another nearby congregation, probably Qidu. *ACM* 53 (1888), 477.

[122] For example, see *ACM* 52 (1887), 436.

[123] *JWJAD*, IV/1/379, 515. The six families included some forty men, women, and children, all of whom were Catholics. They had a chapel for religious services. *JWJAD*, IV/1/380, 525.

[124] Frederic Wakeman, Jr., *Strangers at the Gate: Social Disorder in South China, 1839–1861* (Berkeley: University of California Press, 1966), 109–16. The author discusses Guangdong lineages and how they split along socioeconomic lines during the 1840s.

[125] For example, see *JWJAD*, II/2/715, 906, 908; and *JWJAD*, IV/1/367, 472.

[126] There was one instance of a *juren* who masterminded the fraudulent sale of property to a priest. It is unclear from the material if the degree holder was a Catholic or not. I believe he was not. *JWJAD*, V/2/1146, 1074.

[127] *JWJAD*, III/2/537, 689.

[128] As one example, see an explicit statement by a priest regarding the occupations of Catholics and their contact with non-Catholics. *ACM* 3 (1837), 93; for another, see *JWJAD*, II/2/712, 904.

[129] According to Latourette, *History of Christian Missions* (page 334), "Often Christians were gathered into villages, where ... they could be kept from idolatrous community practices and their entire life be supervised by the Church." Cohen used more figurative language to express the same view in "Christian Missions," 557.

[130] *JWJAD*, II/2/715, 908.

[131] *JWJAD*, III/2/614, 733.

[132] *JWJAD*, III/2/617, 790, 792, 794. Conversion is, here, the men's perspective, not that of the Church. Several of the men in the group had established a teacher-student relationship with various people, one of whom was a *jiaotou*. This kind of teacher-student bond, it should be noted, was organizationally important among some sectarian groups. Susan Naquin, *Millenarian Rebellion in China: The Eight Trigrams Uprising of 1813* (New Haven: Yale University Press, 1976), 39–46; also see Overmeyer, *Folk Buddhist Religion*, 39, 174–75.

Notes to Chapter 3

[1] Wiest, "Catholic Activities in Kwangtung Province," 60. Wiest writes that in Guangdong before 1860 Catholic missionaries chose to establish themselves mainly in small villages. They stayed away from cities and market towns in order to avoid trouble with local officials.

[2] "Vincentian Missions," 64–66.

[3] Entry into some large cities proved to be a problem. For example, in the 1840s British diplomats and their military encountered opposition when they tried to enter Canton. See Morse, *International Relations,* vol. 1, *The Period of Conflict, 1834–1860,* 367–99; and Wakeman, *Strangers at the Gate,* 71–80.

Missionaries had a particularly difficult time gaining access to Changsha, Hunan's capital, not succeeding until 1897. This is discussed by Joseph W. Esherick, *Reform and Revolution in China: The 1911 Revolution in Hunan and Hubei* (Berkeley: University of California Press, 1976), 34–37; and Charlton M. Lewis, *Prologue to the Chinese Revolution: The Transformation of Ideas and Institutions in Hunan Province, 1891–1907* (Cambridge, Mass.: East Asian Research Center, Harvard University, 1976), 110–33.

[4] *JWJAD,* VI/2/667, 1006.

[5] I have not seen in Catholic sources for Jiangxi a clear definition of church and chapel. Records from the early and mid-nineteenth century tend not to distinguish exactly between the two and priests seem to use the terms interchangeably. Later in the century there are numbers for categories labeled as churches, public chapels, and oratories. It appears that churches were buildings consecrated solely for that purpose while a public chapel might have been a designated worship space occupying a special area of a building that was used sometimes for other purposes, for example, in an orphanage. Private chapels were also located in seminaries. Oratories were probably located in a small room or in part of a room in a Catholic's home that continued to be used for other functions.

[6] *ACM* 6 (1840), 353; and *ACM-E* 7 (1900), 212–13. Depending on the source, the figures vary: Latourette in his *History of Christian Missions* (page 238) states that in 1849 Jiangxi had twenty chapels. From another source, Latourette (page 323) obtained figures for 1890: one seminary, six schools, five orphanages, four churches, and twenty-one chapels. Wolferstan, *Catholic Church,* 436–37, has totals for 1907: 34 churches, 136 chapels, 132 oratories and stations, 21 orphanages and asylums, 18 hospitals, and 8 dispensaries.

[7] Altogether, in this one prefecture, there were seven churches of various sizes; the smaller ones could have been chapels. *JWJAD,* II/2/770, 986–87.

[8] *ACM* 24 (1859), 339–40.

[9] *ACM* 23 (1858), 372.

[10] *JWJAD*, VI/2/732, 1083; and *JWJAD*, VI/2/733, 1084.

[11] *ACM* 47 (1882), 130.

[12] *ACM-E* 1 (1894), 533.

[13] *JWJAD*, V/2/1126, 1055. Another fraudulent sale of property to a missionary occurred outside the Poyang county seat's east gate. *JWJAD*, V/2/1146, 1074–79.

[14] *JWJAD*, IV/1/367, 453, 455.

[15] An anonymous placard posted in the county seat of Yihuang in 1875 threatened bodily harm to anyone leasing or selling property to Catholics. *JWJAD*, III/2/606, 716. In 1884 an anonymous placard posted at the county seat of Longquan called for a boycott to stop the construction of a church. *JWJAD*, IV/1/376, 511.

[16] Westel W. Willoughby, *Foreign Rights and Interests in China*, rev. ed. (Baltimore: Johns Hopkins Press, 1927), vol. 2, 706–10; and Henri Cordier, *Histoire des relations de la Chine avec les puissances occidentales, 1860–1900* (Paris: Ancienne Librairie Germer Bailliere, 1901–1902), vol. 1, 68–77.

[17] *JWJAD*, III/2/606, 710.

[18] For example, the Tianjin Catholic church, destroyed in 1870, was rebuilt with an indemnity of 130,000 taels. Many Protestant missionaries also sought indemnification for destroyed property. Latourette, *History of Christian Missions*, 351, 473. After a village chapel was destroyed in Nanchang County officials ordered compensation to be collected from the people living in that immediate area. *JWJAD*, V/2/1095, 1003.

[19] *JWJAD*, I/2/969, 907. According to Latourette, *History of Christian Missions* (page 330), Catholic missionaries from various orders and congregations had investment properties, which generated profits to fund ecclesiastical expenses.

[20] *ACM* 31 (1866), 12.

[21] "Vincentian Missions," 67–68.

[22] *JWJAD*, V/2/1145, 1065.

[23] *JWJAD*, II/2/712, 902–4. Even if the amounts were minuscule, still the symbolic importance of such donations is worth noting. Latourette makes little or no mention of Chinese Catholic donations during the period 1856–1897. For example, see pages 323–31 in his *History of Christian Missions*. Chinese Protestants during the early decades of the twentieth century also contributed to the rural churches. Price, *Rural Church*, 142–69.

[24] *ACM-E* 3 (1896), 463–65. This sum equaled twenty thousand francs. Also, see "Vincentian Missions," 48–49.

[25] "Vincentian Missions," 101.

[26] "Vincentian Missions," 108.

[27] *ACM-E* 1 (1894), 533.

[28] *JWJAD*, III/2/604, 700.

[29] This also may be applied to Protestant churches built during the early twentieth century. Frank Price, based on a 1936–1937 survey of Protestant churches in Anhui, Jiangsu, and Zhejiang, found that 629 (34.4 percent) of 1,824 churches were located in market towns. The author defined the natural rural community as the "market or trade area or other natural grouping of villages, in which the church is located." Price commented incisively: "Our studies show that rural parishes in China tend to follow the lines of natural communities . . . rather than the boundaries of artificial political divisions." Furthermore, "the market area or natural community seems to be the best unit for programs of rural service which depend chiefly upon social organization and the efforts of the people themselves." Price, *Rural Church*, 15, 37, 39, 221–22.

[30] *JWJAD*, V/2/1086, 990; and *JWJAD*, V/2/1100, 1010.

[31] *JWJAD*, IV/1/372, 503–4.

[32] *ACM* 48 (1883), 387.

[33] *ACM* 47 (1882), 130.

[34] *JWJAD*, V/2/1087, 991; and *JWJAD*, V/2/1095, 1006.

[35] *JWJAD*, II/2/694, 870–71.

[36] *JWJAD*, V/2/1087, 991.

[37] *JWJAD*, IV/1/379, 515, 517. The people involved said there were six Catholic families, but a missionary argued that there were twenty or so. If the average family size was approximately five people, then there were between thirty and one hundred Catholics in the area.

[38] *ACM* 48 (1883), 380–83.

[39] "Vincentian Missions," 79.

[40] Throughout this book, peoples' ages are cited in *sui*, the Chinese measure for calculating age. That is, at birth a person is one *sui*, and at the next lunar new year, two *sui*. This means a one-to-two-year discrepancy with Western age calculation.

[41] According to Chinese sources, Father Fu Ruhan was French. *JWJAD*, II/2/708, 895. I have not found biographical information on him in any of my sources, nor have I been able to determine his French name.

[42] *JWJAD*, II/2/712, 901–5. For Wu Aiyao's deposition, see 903–4.

[43] *JWJAD*, II/2/712, 904–5.

[44] Lineage regulations explicitly condemned religious services held in mixed company. See Hui-chen Wang Liu, "An Analysis of Chinese Clan Rules: Confucian Theories in Action," in *Confucianism and Chinese Civilization*, ed. Arthur F. Wright (New York: Atheneum, 1964), 91.

[45] *JWJAD*, II/2/708, 895–96. Exactly how the examination candidates and local people came together is unknown. The report noted, in a perhaps self-serving manner, that officials and cooperative local gentry had successfully protected the church during an earlier prefectural examination.

[46] Price, *Rural Church*, 114; and Latourette, *History of Christian Missions*, 335. I would also add that this holds true for contemporary Taiwan based on my own observations and travel over five years. For example, in 1970 I visited a Maryknoll chapel in Taidong. The chapel's interior had a Chinese ambiance and some similarity to the one described in the text.

[47] Price, in *Rural Church*, 113, points out that some Protestant churches had adopted "the use of a special name for the church, with an appealing meaning and sound, e.g., 'Shangai Tang' or 'Hall of Love.'" Catholic churches were usually identified as *Tianzhu tang*, and this is still the practice today in Jiangxi.

[48] *JWJAD*, IV/1/379, 515. Reading between the lines, I estimate the village to have been as large as nine hundred people.

[49] "Vincentian Missions," 92. The author calls the place of worship an oratory, but it seems to have been a very modest chapel. The author also calls Longquan a village of Ganzhou Prefecture. In fact, it was a county seat and part of Ji'an Prefecture.

[50] *JWJAD*, IV/1/380, 525. The bishop wrote that he went to the village for repair of the chapel. *ACM* 50 (1885), 132. Perhaps the local Catholics hoped the chapel would become a large and formal church building.

[51] "Vincentian Missions," 92; and *ACM* 50 (1885), 132. This association was also known as that of the Holy Infancy.

[52] *JWJAD*, IV/1/376, 511.

[53] *JWJAD*, IV/1/379, 517.

[54] *JWJAD*, IV/1/380, 526.

[55] *JWJAD*, IV/1/380, 527; and *JWJAD*, IV/2/666, 993–94.

[56] *JWJAD*, IV/1/380, 527.

[57] *JWJAD*, IV/1/380, 526; and *JWJAD*, IV/2/666, 998.

[58] *JWJAD*, IV/1/380, 525.

[59] *JWJAD*, IV/1/380, 525. For details on the Berthemy Convention, see chapter 4.

[60] *JWJAD*, IV/1/380, 526.

[61] *JWJAD*, IV/1/380, 526.

[62] *JWJAD*, IV/1/380, 526, 528.

[63] *JWJAD*, IV/1/379, 520; and *JWJAD*, VI/2/666, 995.

[64] *JWJAD*, IV/1/379, 516. In subsequent official citations of lineage members' comments and in the official summation of the case this statement was deleted. For example, see *JWJAD*, IV/1/380, 526; and *JWJAD*, IV/2/666, 995.

[65] *JWJAD*, IV/1/380, 526.

[66] *JWJAD*, IV/1/379, 518–19; and *JWJAD*, IV/1/380, 525–27.

[67] *JWJAD*, IV/1/379, 517.

[68] *ACM* 50 (1885), 132–33; and "Vincentian Missions," 92.

[69] *ACM* 49 (1884), 609.

[70] *ACM* 50 (1885), 136.

[71] *JWJAD*, IV/1/379, 514, 522. The bishop returned quickly to Ji'an and then went to Shanghai. Given the distances he traveled, the bishop did not seem to be seriously injured, if at all. Chinese officials noted this and also that the bishop refused to meet with them for verification of his alleged injuries.

[72] *JWJAD*, IV/1/380, 529.

[73] *JWJAD*, IV/1/380, 528. To what degree the gentry were involved in the local *baojia* system is not known, but *baojia* headmen certainly had responsibility for knowing about and reporting problems in their local areas.

[74] *JWJAD*, IV/1/380, 527.

[75] *JWJAD*, IV/1/376, 512–13; *JWJAD*, IV/1/377, 513–14; and *JWJAD*, VI/2/666, 993, 998.

[76] *JWJAD*, IV/1/379, 516.

[77] *JWJAD*, VI/2/666, 992, 997.

[78] Cohen, *China and Christianity*, 149–69, 186–228.

[79] Morse, *International Relations*, and Cordier, *Histoire des relations*, provide good general treatment, but both are very dated. Other studies include: Paul A. Varg, *Missionaries, Chinese, and Diplomats: The American Protestant Missionary Movement in China, 1890–1952* (Princeton: Princeton University Press, 1958); Edmund S. Wehrle, *Britain, China, and the Antimissionary Riots, 1891–1900* (Minneapolis: University of Minnesota Press, 1966); and Chester C. Tan, *The Boxer Catastrophe* (New York: Columbia University Press, 1967).

[80] Esherick's *Origins*, which focuses on the Boxers in Shandong (and border areas) is a model study. Similar research will be difficult for other provinces due to the lack of primary source materials.

[81] *JWJAD*, III/2/568, 641–42; *JWJAD*, III/2/571, 645–47; and *JWJAD*, III/2/573, 653.

[82] *JWJAD*, III/2/597, 687, 690.

[83] *JWJAD*, III/2/597, 687–88. I presented these cases in my article, "Catholic Converts in Jiangxi Province: Conflict and Accommodation," in *Christianity in China: From the Eighteenth Century to the Present*, ed. Daniel H. Bays Stanford: Stanford University Press, 1996, 24–40.

[84] *JWJAD*, III/2/597, 688.

[85] *JWJAD*, III/2/597, 689.

[86] *JWJAD*, III/2/597, 690.

[87] *JWJAD*, III/2/606, 708–11.

[88] *APF* 37 (1876), 190; also see *ACM* 41 (1876), 565–75.

[89] *JWJAD*, III/2/610, 721; and *JWJAD*, III/2/619, 803–28.

[90] In several instances people complained because of mistaken circumstances or identity. In a few complaints, the plaintiff used a fictitious name, and someone used the name of a Catholic without permission. *JWJAD*, III/2/619, 804–7, 811–12, 820, 823–24, 827.

[91] *JWJAD*, III/2/610, 721.

[92] *JWJAD*, III/2/619, 828.

[93] Also see Sweeten, "Catholic Converts in Jiangxi Province," 24–40.

[94] *JWJAD*, VI/2/710, 1062.

[95] *JWJAD*, VI/2/730, 1078–83; and *JWJAD*, VI/2/736, 1089–93.

[96] *JWJAD*, VI/2/730, 1079–80.

[97] *JWJAD*, VI/2/730, 1080–81.

[98] It should be noted that at some point during the proceedings Yan tried unsuccessfully to involve the Church at Hekou on his side. *JWJAD*, VI/2/730, 1081–82.

[99] Wang evidently tried without success to get Church intervention on his behalf. *JWJAD*, VI/2/730, 1082–83.

[100] *JWJAD*, VI/2/736, 1091–92.

[101] *JWJAD*, VI/2/736, 1092–93. *Shoukui* has a range of meanings and can be taken to mean here either a social (i.e., loss of face) setback or a financial loss or perhaps both.

[102] *JWJAD*, VI/2/736, 1093.

[103] *JWJAD*, VI/2/739, 1095.

[104] *JWJAD*, VI/2/739, 1096–97.

[105] *JWJAD*, VI/2/739, 1095–96.

[106] *JWJAD*, VI/2/739, 1096–97.

[107] *JWJAD*, VI/2/739, 1096–97.

[108] *JWJAD*, VI/2/739, 1096.

[109] The *dibao* had died from an illness and no one else acted in his place or independently to report the murder. *JWJAD*, VI/2/739, 1095.

[110] *JWJAD*, VI/2/739, 1095–96.

[111] *JWJAD*, VI/2/739, 1096.

[112] Officials ordered underlings to return Li Jingzheng to Fengcheng County for detention in jail there until they apprehended Cai Mingliu and brought him to trial. It is not known if officials ever arrested Cai or how long they held Li before administering his sentence. *JWJAD*, VI/2/739, 1099–100.

[113] *JWJAD*, VI/2/700, 1041–42.

[114] *ACM-E* 3 (1896), 56–60.

[115] *ACM-E* 3 (1896), 60–61; and "Vincentian Missions," 117–18.

[116] *ACM-E* 3 (1896), 61.

[117] *JWJAD*, VI/2/671, 1016; and *ACM-E* 5 (1898), 85.

[118] *JWJAD*, VI/2/671, 1016.

[119] *JWJAD*, VI/2/671, 1016.

[120] *JWJAD*, VI/2/672, 1016.

[121] Centre des Archives Diplomatiques de Nantes (hereafter CADN), Pékin, Ambassade, Série A, carton 32, dossier 1895, 1896. The placard was included as an enclosure in a letter written by Bishop Casimir Vic and dated August 10, 1896.

[122] *ACM-E* 5 (1898), 85.

[123] *ACM-E* 5 (1898), 86; and "Vincentian Missions," 118–19.

[124] *ACM-E* 4 (1897), 238.

[125] For several examples, see *JWJAD*, II/2/706, 893; *JWJAD*, V/2/1048, 935–36; *JWJAD*, V/2/1100, 1010, 1012–13; and *JWJAD*, V/2/1112, 1048.

Notes to Chapter 4

[1] *JWJAD*, II/2/708, 895.

[2] Paul Cohen mentions this as a possibility for the gentry. See "Christian Missions," 585.

[3] *JWAD*, I/2/1082, 974–75.

[4] The acting magistrate also left room for people to refuse to participate. *JWJAD*, III/2/597, 688.

[5] *JWJAD*, III/2/602, 694; and *JWJAD*, III/2/604, 697.

[6] *JWJAD* V/2/1095, 1005.

[7] Social historians rightfully lament the lack of data for the common people during the Qing period. An especially good statement of the problem appears in the introduction to *Women in Chinese Society*, ed. Margery Wolf and Roxanne Witke (Stanford: Stanford University Press, 1975), 11.

[8] From June 8 to November 16, 1868, twenty petitions (*bing*) were sent to the magistrate and the prefect: Yan Bingyi submitted sixteen of these; Li Shangsong (one of Yan Bingyi's tenants) submitted one; and Huang Daojin (a relative by marriage to Yan Bingyi) submitted three. Besides these, there was a petition to the Zongli Yamen from Yan Bingyi explaining the overall situation and a copy of the statement that Yan Bingyi claimed the Yan lineage forced him to make. Yan made the first petition to the magistrate with the assistance of "agents for the plaintiff" Zhou Xuchun (a *ba gongsheng* degree holder) and Liu Zaiji (a *juren*). They also assisted Yan in making the petition to the Zongli Yamen. *JWJAD*, II/2/704, 880–92.

[9] Yan Bingyi appealed to Father Anot soon after he concluded that the magistrate would not reply to his petition of June 15.

[10] The Zongli Yamen took the position that local officials must not be lenient to litigants simply because they were Catholics. Even if some Chinese converted to Catholicism, "still the people are Chinese and Chinese laws are used to govern Chinese." Moreover, the Zongli Yamen considered it improper for the French minister to hand over petitions to the Chinese government on the behalf of Chinese Catholics. *JWJAD*, II/2/706, 893–94.

[11] Yan lineage degree holders (*gongsheng, jiansheng,* and *shengyuan*) condescendingly referred to Yan Bingyi as a "rural farmer," a label that the prefect adopted, too. I do not think this description should be taken literally, even though it is clear that Yan Bingyi did live in the countryside. *JWJAD*, II/2/718, 918, 923.

[12] *JWJAD*, II/2/718, 921; and *JWJAD*, II/2/704, 885.

[13] *JWJAD*, II/2/718, 915–16.

[14] *JWJAD*, II/2/718, 919.

[15] *JWJAD*, II/2/718, 919.

[16] *JWJAD*, II/2/718, 916. The only protection a wife had against mistreatment by her husband and his relatives was her own parents. C. K. Yang, *A Chinese Village in Early Communist Transition* (Cambridge, Mass.: The Technology Press, 1959), 90.

[17] Although the lineage deliberated on these matters, it is not known how it reached its decisions. Presumably, the lineage head and degree-holding members played leading roles. For general comments on lineage judiciary power, see Hui-chen Wang Liu, *The Traditional Chinese Clan Rules* (Locust Valley, N.Y.: J. J. Augustin, 1959), 39.

[18] *JWJAD*, II/2/718, 919.

[19] The widow's personal belongings included clothing and farming utensils, probably all part of her dowry. *JWJAD*, II/2/718, 917, 919. The acting prefect commented that widows should be commended for not remarrying because this bestowed honor on the widow's lineage. *JWJAD*, II/2/718, 917.

[20] *JWJAD*, II/2/718, 919. *Jiafa* may have referred to the bamboo instrument used for the beating; see Liu, *Traditional Chinese Clan Rules*, 41.

[21] *JWJAD*, II/2/718, 917. Regarding lineage fines, see Liu, *Traditional Chinese Clan Rules*, 40–41. According to Yan Bingyi, his lineage also implied that he was connected with Vegetarian sect bandits. *JWJAD*, II/2/704, 880.

[22] *JWJAD*, II/2/718, 917, 920.

[23] *JWJAD*, II/2/718, 917.

[24] *JWJAD*, II/2/718, 917.

[25] Some lineages had rules prohibiting members from joining various religious sects because of possible harm to family and lineage institutions. Liu, "Analysis of Chinese Clan Rules," 44.

   The Yans feared that additional lineage converts to Catholicism would disrupt ancestor veneration. *JWJAD*, II/2/718, 921. According to Huang Daojin, a relative of Yan Bingyi, Yan's conversion to Catholicism had not influenced other Yans to convert. Other Catholics in the area came from families not bearing the Yan surname. *JWJAD*, II/2/704, 889.

[26] *JWJAD*, II/2/704, 844. Technically, Yan Shanqing was a *ling gongsheng*. That is, he had formerly been a *shengyuan* on stipend, the most powerful and privileged of that degree group. Chung-li Chang, *The Chinese Gentry: Studies on Their Role in Nineteenth Century Chinese Society* (Seattle: University of Washington Press, 1955), 18, 20 n. 71.

[27] *JWJAD*, II/2/704, 880–81.

[28] Although Yan Bingyi called the Yans armed military thugs, there is no indication that local officials investigated this accusation. *JWJAD*, II/2/704, 880, 882, 886.

[29] *JWJAD*, II/2/704, 882.

[30] *JWJAD*, II/2/704, 885.

[31] *JWJAD*, II/2/704, 883–84, 887, 892. Only Yan Bingyi, and then only on one occasion, mentioned local public security personnel. He stated in a petition that the neighborhood *dibao* did not know why the August 7 incident had occurred. *JWJAD*, II/2/704, 887. There is no record that this functionary ever reported it to officials or that officials ever sought information from him.

[32] Yan Bingyi blasted local officials repeatedly and claimed that their inaccessibility, prejudice, and corruption had aggravated Yan lineage feelings and made his kin more hostile towards him than ever. Yan Bingyi also rebuked the magistrate for not acting as the "parent of the people" (a Confucian metaphor to describe the closeness and concern officials should have for the people). *JWJAD*, II/2/704, 887, 889–91 provide some examples. Such criticisms did not seem to bother either the magistrate or the prefect. The prefect curtly remarked that Yan Bingyi had offered no real proof for his charges. *JWJAD*, II/2/704, 889.

[33] *JWJAD*, II/2/704, 892.

[34] *JWJAD*, II/2/718, 922–24. Representatives of the Yan lineage also indicated that they really did not care about collecting the fine itself. They had levied it only to bring Yan Bingyi into line. *JWJAD*, II/2/718, 923.

[35] *JWJAD*, II/2/718, 923–24.

[36] *JWJAD*, II/2/718, 920. Indeed, the Yan lineage used corporal punishment to deal with kinsmen who turned outlaw and committed crimes such as robbery and murder in mountain areas. *JWJAD*, II/2/718, 917.

For a general statement regarding lineage trials, see Hsien Chin Hu, *The Common Descent Group in China and Its Functions* (New York: The Viking Fund, 1948), 55–59.

[37] *JWJAD*, II/2/718, 920.

[38] *JWJAD*, II/2/718, 918. Huang Daojin, however, claimed that Yan kinsmen had been at the county yamen to prevent others from lodging complaints. *JWJAD*, II/2/704, 888. If this was true then it is unknown why no one came forward during the subsequent investigation and trial.

If Yan Bingyi won, getting his allegations investigated and his punishments reversed, his victory was not decisive. The prefect upheld the Yan lineage's management of the disputes and its right to try and to punish offenders. Since lineage control of its members served the government's own security interests, it was only fitting that the government support these efforts. This symbiotic relationship was imperfect, however, a fact played upon by Yan Bingyi with his demand for a government investigation and trial. The lineage not only needed to deal effectively with Yan Bingyi as an example to others, but also needed to prevent external bureaucratic interference and trial expenses. Apparently, stymieing the official investigation was the Yans' answer. There seems no doubt that Yan lineage leaders, through connection with or bribery of county bureaucrats, succeeded in convincing local officials to disregard Yan Bingyi's petitions from June 8 to November 16, 1868. Although Yan Bingyi alleged the lineage had influenced officials for other reasons, the result was the same.

[39] Stanley Wright gives a picturesque description of the Jingdezhen area and its kilns in his *Kiangsi Native Trade and Its Taxation* (Shanghai, 1920), 20–25.

[40] Wright, *Kiangsi Native Trade*, 84; and Latourette, *History of Christian Missions*, 158.

[41] The process of segmentation is described by Maurice Freedman, *Chinese Lineage and Society: Fukien and Kwangtung* (London: The Athlone Press, 1971), 37.

[42] *JWJAD*, III/2/615, 744.

[43] Hu Bayi and Hu Wenpin were third cousins and not part of the same mourning circle. Hu Wenpin obtained his degree in 1866 in return for making a sizable rice contribution to the dynasty. Hu Bayi apparently held no degree. *JWJAD*, III/2/615, 754.

[44] *JWJAD*, III/2/615, 744, 754.

[45] *JWJAD*, III/2/615, 744, 754.

[46] *JWJAD*, III/2/615, 749–51.

[47] No relationship between the *dibao* and either disputant was indicated in the documents. *JWJAD*, III/2/615, 743–44.

Regarding the role of *dibao*, see Alan Richard Sweeten, "The *Ti-pao* as Bottom-level Bureaucrat: Evidence from Local Criminal Cases in South China, 1860–1877," *Jindaishi yanjiushu jikan* 7 (June 1978): 634–40; and "The *Ti-pao*'s Role in Local Government as Seen in Fukien Christian 'Cases,' 1863–1869," *Ch'ing-shih wen-t'i* 3.6 (December 1976): 1–27.

[48] *JWJAD*, III/2/615, 743.

[49] The two *jiansheng* were Hu Wangguo and Li Weixian. They had degree status because of rice contributions made to the government during the 1860s. Both men were distant relatives of Hu Bayi and Hu Wenpin. *JWJAD*, III/2/615, 745–46.

[50] *JWJAD*, III/2/615, 743, 746.

[51] *JWJAD*, III/2/615, 751–52. Father Li Yuqing was Chinese and probably a secular priest.

[52] *JWJAD*, III/2/615, 752, 753.

[53] *JWJAD*, III/2/615, 742–44. In the *jiao'an* documents for Jiangxi, no official ever reported another priest involved in a case of extortion. The allegation is either untrue or an anomaly.

[54] In the report submitted to Governor Liu Bingzhang by the acting judicial commissioner, which was based on the magistrate's report, the *dibao*'s statement was given before all others. *JWJAD*, III/2/615, 742–43.

Hu Yuanji, according to officials, was responsible for reporting the murder of Hu Bayi since it occurred within his jurisdiction (*dijie*). But because he did not fulfill his duty he was sentenced to eighty blows with the heavy bamboo and dismissed from service. *JWJAD*, III/2/615, 762. The extenuating circumstances and the fact that he did not live in Huzhai, but a good distance away, made no difference whatsoever. *JWJAD*, III/2/615, 743.

As for other punishments, Hu Wenpin was sentenced to strangulation, but was released because of the two imperial pardons. Government authorities stipulated that if he ever committed another offense, his punishment for it would automatically be one degree stiffer than otherwise. During the trial, his *jiansheng* degree status (and that of Hu Wangguo and Li Weixian) had been rescinded. All three were later returned to the lists of degree holders. *JWJAD*, III/2/615, 761–63.

[55] *JWJAD*, IV/1/366, 448.

[56] *JWJAD*, IV/1/366, 448.

[57] *JWJAD*, IV/1/366, 448.

[58] *JWJAD*, IV/1/366, 448–49.

[59] *JWJAD*, IV/1/366, 449.

[60] *JWJAD*, IV/1/366, 449.

[61] *JWJAD*, IV/1/366, 449.

[62] The magistrate's source of information cannot be determined from the documents.

[63] The magistrate who learned of the extortion tried Gong first. When the Nanchang prefect requestioned Gong, he found discrepancies in his testimony and ordered the new magistrate of Fengcheng County to retry the case. Again the prefect reviewed the testimony and was dissatisfied. Therefore, Magistrate Leng Dingheng of Xinjian County was commissioned to try the case; he forwarded the results to the prefect for endorsement. The prefect questioned Gong again. Then a second deputy, (the acting magistrate of Nanchang County) Cui Guobang, was ordered to reinvestigate the case. The prefect and the judicial commissioner each approved Cui's report. *JWJAD*, IV/1/366, 450–51.

[64] Officials judged the headmen, referred to as *paijia*, guilty of negligence but innocent of the more serious charge of concealment. *JWJAD*, IV/1/366, 448, 451.

[65] *JWJAD*, IV/1/366, 451.

[66] Apparently Nie and Gong did not know or care that, according to Qing law, for the false complaint of a crime, the applicable punishment was administered to the plaintiff instead of the defendant. They could have pointed this out and called Gong Gaozi's bluff about going to the magistrate.

[67] Some village bullies became well acquainted with yamen runners and cooperated with them in order to snare victims. See Arthur Smith's chapter-length

discussion of the village bully in his *Village Life in China: A Study in Sociology* (New York: Fleming H. Revell Co., 1899), 211–25.

[68] *JWJAD*, VI/2/683, 1030–31.

[69] *JWJAD*, VI/2/704, 1046.

[70] See the chapter entitled "The Widow" in Jonathan D. Spence, *The Death of Woman Wang* (New York: The Viking Press, 1978), 59–76.

[71] *JWJAD*, III/2/620, 828–38. This case and the one that follows it first appeared in my article "Women and Law in Rural China: Vignettes from 'Sectarian Cases' (*chiao-an*) in Kiangsi, 1872–1878," *Ch'ing-shih wen-t'i* 3.10 (December 1978): 49–68.

[72] Information from the *dibao* was given citational prominence at the beginning of the magistrate's dispatch to the judicial commissioner and in the latter's communication to the governor, who forwarded it under his name to the Zongli Yamen. *JWJAD*, III/2/620, 828–29.

[73] *JWJAD*, III/2/620, 831.

[74] *JWJAD*, III/2/620, 833.

[75] *JWJAD*, III/2/620, 828–29. Mrs. Wu and her son confirmed this point regarding the *dibao* (here called *baolin*) in their depositions. *JWJAD*, III/2/620, 831, 833. It was also repeated in the official summation of the case. *JWJAD*, III/2/620, 835.

[76] *JWJAD*, III/2/620, 831.

[77] *JWJAD*, III/2/620, 831–32.

[78] *JWJAD*, III/2/620, 832–34.

[79] *JWJAD*, III/2/620, 834.

[80] *JWJAD*, III/2/620, 828.

[81] *JWJAD*, III/2/620, 829.

[82] *JWJAD*, III/2/620, 837.

[83] *JWJAD*, III/2/620, 837. Monetary redemption was allowed as a substitute for punishment for certain categories of wrongdoers, women included. Also, for bamboo beatings the nominal number of blows differed from the actual number given. Derk Bodde and Clarence Morris, *Law in Imperial China: Exemplified by 190 Ch'ing Cases* (Cambridge, Mass.: Harvard University Press, 1967), 77–79.

There was one technical legal point, the Wu inheritance, that was never raised by anyone with an interest in it. Although Wu Leixia did not assume control of the family property upon maturity, his legal status as heir was not in question. Moreover, he had already received the property deed from his mother. In the settlement of the case, authorities decided that "Zhang Chunxing had occupied by force building and field of the Wu family, which were to be returned to Wu Leixia [i.e., his family, who will assume] control of the property." *JWJAD*, III/2/620, 838. This judgment constitutes an unusual case indicating an uxorilocal husband's (and his relatives') lack of claim to property of the wife when the latter had an heir. This detail illustrates the *Jiaowu jiao'an dang's* value to the study of Qing law.

Regarding the inheritance position of widows, see T'ung-tsu Ch'u, *Law and Society in Traditional China* (Paris: Mouton, 1961), 104; George Thomas Staunton, trans., *Ta Tsing Leu Lee; Being the Fundamental Laws ... of the Penal Code of China* (London: Cadell and Davies, 1810), 84–85 and 526; Guy Boulais, trans., *Manuel du code chinois* (Shanghai: Mission Catholique, 1924), 189–90; and Spence, *Woman Wang*, 72–73. Some lineage regulations stated specifically that a widow who took a second husband by uxorilocal marriage was not allowed to keep her first husband's property. Liu, *Traditional Chinese Clan Rules*, 92.

[84] The *sancong* principle stripped a woman of autonomy. Obedience was required: first, to one's father during childhood, then to one's husband during marriage, and finally, to one's son during widowhood. Ch'u, *Law and Society*, 102–3.

To be sure, when Mrs. Wu's husband died Wu Leixia was only sixteen *sui* old. He was the older of two sons. At an early age, the younger brother had been adopted by an uncle as heir and lived separately from his natal family. By the time of the love affair in 1872, Wu Leixia was a grown man with a wife and son. *JWJAD*, III/2/620, 831, 833.

[85] Normally, one would expect to find matters such as moral conduct under the purview of lineage or village elders. Ch'u, *Law and Society*, 20–41; Hu, *Common Descent Group*, 53–63; and Hsiao, *Rural China*, 184–205, 342–43. Village leadership may have been weak, giving the *dibao* authority over adultery and other improper behaviors. Certainly, Zhang went to a great deal of trouble to legitimize the nature of this relationship with the widow because of the *dibao's* role and power as he and other villagers perceived it. The lowly *dibao*, categorized as one of the "mean people," and thus permanently denied entrance into the elite world, ironically enforced one of the elite's traditional ideals.

[86] *JWJAD*, III/2/616, 770–80.

[87] *JWJAD*, III/2/616, 770–72, 774.

[88] The husband could go unpunished for the murder of his wife and her lover only if he caught them *in flagrante delicto*. Whether then or later, the husband remained liable for punishment should he kill just the wife. Ch'u, *Law and Society*, 110.

[89] *JWJAD*, III/2/616, 773.

[90] *JWJAD*, III/2/616, 774–75.

[91] *JWJAD*, III/2/616, 770–71, 773.

[92] *JWJAD*, III/2/616, 770–71.

[93] *JWJAD*, III/2/616, 777–79.

[94] Sybille van der Sprenkel, *Legal Institutions in Manchu China: A Sociological Analysis* (London: The Athlone Press, 1966), 80–89; and Hu, *Common Descent Group*, 56. A lineage grandfather and grandson were two generations apart and of different mourning circles.

[95] Of the three accomplices who appeared for trial, two were thirty *sui* and one was thirty-two *sui*. *JWJAD*, III/2/616, 773.

[96] Qing law specified a punishment (one hundred blows of the heavy bamboo) for distant relatives who broke the sexual taboos. If the offenders were of the same mourning circle, the crime was incest and the sentence was death. Ch'u, *Law and Society*, 64–67. Also see Sommer, *Sex, Law, and Society*, 30–38.

[97] The communication from Governor Li Wenmin to the Zongli Yamen included a summation of the case as reported by Magistrate Yang Huibi. The Fuzhou prefect endorsed the magistrate's report, which was in turn reviewed and approved by the acting judicial commissioner. The latter also wrote a summation. These two official summations were clearly based on depositions taken from Xu family members, although no depositions were quoted directly. *JWJAD*, IV/1/365, 445–47.

[98] *JWJAD*, IV/1/365, 445.

[99] *JWJAD*, IV/1/365, 445. This was a harsh punishment because removal of one's name from the lineage genealogy specifically meant loss of lineage membership and all lineage privileges as well as material benefits. Hu, *Common Descent Group*, 61.

[100] The way the Xus handled their problem concretely supports Hui-chen Wang Liu's general discussion of the various levels of lineage punishment. She states that "Forfeit of clan privileges, expulsion from the clan, and exclusion from the geneaology are the severe level of punishment. They involve the suspension or cancellation of the status of the offender. Such punishment is used when physical coercion or medium-level punishment is insufficient to rectify or remedy the situation, when the status of another member is threatened or violated, when the offender compromises his own proper status, or when he disgraces the lineage. These punishments represent the enforcement of status-ethics: a retaliation in status as punishment of misconduct that flagrantly violates status." Liu, *Traditional Chinese Clan Rules*, 36–46, especially 46.

[101] *JWJAD*, IV/1/365, 445.

[102] *JWJAD*, IV/1/365, 445–46.

[103] *JWJAD*, IV/1/365, 446.

[104] How the magistrate learned of the case remains a mystery. Because the local *dibao* did not make a report, as was his duty, the magistrate ordered him dismissed from service. *JWJAD*, IV/1/365, 446.

[105] *JWJAD*, IV/1/365, 446. Regarding the use of analogy to determine appropriate punishment, see Fu-mei Chang Chen, "On Analogy in Ch'ing Law," *Harvard Journal of Asiatic Studies* 30 (1970): 212–24.

[106] Xu Ruilong's offer to take care of Mrs. Xu was probably made because she had lost her two sons and did not have a husband.

[107] *JWJAD*, IV/1/365, 446.

[108] He was probably a Chinese secular priest.

[109] *JWJAD*, VI/2/725, 1076.

[110] *JWJAD*, VII/2/614, 718.

[111] The documents on this case clearly indicate that Feng and Huang tried to force the widow to remarry. It is implicit that the intended marriage was to another man with the surname Huang. Thus the involvement of the Huang lineage.

[112] *JWJAD*, VI/2/727, 1077.

[113] *JWJAD*, VII/2/614, 720.

[114] *JWJAD*, VI/2/727, 1077.

[115] *JWJAD*, VII/2/614, 721.

[116] An official awaiting appointment to a substantive post was designated as an "expectant" for that position. Expectants often received temporary assignments such as the investigation of *jiao'an* under the title of deputy (*weiyuan*). H. S. Brunnert and V. V. Hagelstrom, *Present Day Political Organization of China*, trans. A. Beltchenko and E. E. Moran (Shanghai: Kelly and Walsh, 1912), 510–11.

[117] Feng and Huang had fled the area and officials were unable to arrest them. *JWJAD*, VII/2/614, 720–21.

[118] These men were the ones who went to invite the missionary to the lineage hall. One of the two men, judging by his generational given name, was either Huang Bangyi's brother or cousin. *JWJAD*, VII/2/614, 719, 721.

[119] *JWJAD*, VII/2/614, 721–22.

[120] The Huangs probably stood to gain either a fee or property by pressing the widow to remarry. *JWJAD*, VII/2/614, 721.

[121] *JWJAD*, VI/2/743, 1106.

[122] *JWJAD*, VI/2/743, 1106.

[123] *JWJAD*, VI/2/743, 1106.

[124] *JWJAD*, VI/2/743, 1106.

[125] *JWJAD*, VI/2/743, 1106.

[126] Huang, *Civil Justice*, 110–37.

Notes to Chapter 5

[1] See Huang, *Civil Justice*, 36, and 36–42 for examples.

[2] D'Elia, *Catholic Missions*, 98.

[3] Wiest, "Catholic Activities," 60. Although Wiest directed his comments at missionary activity in Guangdong, they may also be applied to other provinces.

[4] *JWJAD*, VI/2/667, 1004, 1008.

[5] *JWJAD*, I/2/969, 907.

[6] Willoughby, *Foreign Rights*, vol. 2, 702–3; Morse, *International Relations*, vol. 1, *Period of Conflict, 1834–1860*, 312; also, see Godfrey E. P. Hertslet and Edward Parkes, eds., *Treaties, &c., between Great Britain and China; and between China and Foreign Powers; and Orders in Council, Rules, Regulations, Acts of Parliament, Decrees, &c., affecting British Interests in China*, vol. 1 (London: His Majesty's Stationery Office, by Harrison and Sons, 1908).

[7] Morse, *International Relations*, vol. 1, *Period of Conflict, 1834–1860*, 691.

[8] Morse, *International Relations*, vol. 1, *Period of Conflict, 1834–1860*, 692.

[9] See Hertslet and Parkes, *Treaties*, vol. 1, 273–74, for Article XIII of the Sino-French Treaty of 1858.

[10] Willoughby, *Foreign Rights*, vol. 2, 706–7.

[11] Willoughby, *Foreign Rights*, vol. 2, 707.

[12] *JWJAD*, I/1/84, 50.

[13] Hertslet and Parkes, *Treaties*, vol. 1, 320–21. For the Chinese version of the Berthemy Convention, see *JWJAD*, I/1/86, 52. For the French text of the Berthemy Convention and an extended discussion, see Cordier, *Histoire des relations*, vol. 1, 68–71.

[14] According to Willoughby, "The text of this Berthemy Convention has never been officially published or, indeed, its existence explicitly and formally announced." He does quote, however, a communication from the Zongli Yamen that includes the Berthemy Convention and the addition to it negotiated by Minister A. Gérard. At times the French position may have seemed ambiguous. See *Foreign Rights*, vol. 2, 707–9.

The archives of French diplomatic correspondence, however, include both conventions printed in booklet format. The French legation in Beijing printed the two booklets in Chinese and French probably in 1895. See CADN, Pékin, Ambassade, Série A, Carton 415. The *Jiaowu jiao'an dang* documents and specific cases discussed in this chapter make it clear that the French considered the Berthemy Convention a binding agreement.

[15] Willoughby, *Foreign Rights*, vol. 2, 709–10; and Hertslet and Parkes, *Treaties*, vol. 1, 321.

[16] *JWJAD*, I/1/86, 53.

[17] According to the arrangement between China and France spelled out in the collection by Hertslet and Parkes, "It was further stipulated that owners of property should, before disposing of it in this way, intimate their intention to the local authorities and solicit the instructions of the latter as to whether the sale was permissible or not. On receiving the sanction of the authorities they would be at liberty to complete the transaction, but no direct sale of private property would be allowed." Hertslet and Parkes, *Treaties*, vol. 1, 321.

[18] *JWJAD*, II/3/1281, 1771.

[19] *JWJAD*, V/1/259, 192.

[20] *JWJAD*, V/1/235, 166–67. Also, see Cordier, *Histoire des relations*, vol. 1, 71–73.

[21] *JWJAD*, V/4/Chronology of Major Events, 19.

[22] *JWJAD*, V/4/Chronology of Major Events, 25.

[23] *JWJAD*, V/3/1613, 1632–33; and Cordier, *Histoire des relations*, vol. 1, 73–74. Cordier provides basic information on pages 74–77 regarding the sequence of the discussions between the French and the Chinese.

[24] *JWJAD*, V/3/1614, 1634.

[25] *JWJAD*, V/1/235, 167.

[26] *JWJAD*, V/1/241, 171.

[27] *JWJAD*, V/1/247, 174.

[28] *JWJAD*, V/1/236, 169.

[29] *JWJAD*, V/1/256, 185.

[30] *JWJAD*, V/1/259, 191. Quoted in Willoughby, *Foreign Rights*, vol. 2, 708–9 and in Cordier, *Histoire des relations*, vol. 1, 74, 78.

The version in Hertslet and Parkes reads as follows: "Hereafter, if French missionaries go into the interior to purchase land or houses, the title deed shall specify clearly the name of the seller, and shall state that the property has been sold to become part of the collective property of the Catholic Mission in the locality where it is situated. It will be unnecessary to record on the deed the name of the missionary or of a native Christian. After the deed has been completed, the Catholic Mission will pay the cost of registration as fixed by Chinese law. The seller shall not be required to inform the local authorities of his intention to sell nor need he ask beforehand their authorization of the sale." Hertslet and Parkes, *Treaties*, vol. 1, 321.

[31] *JWJAD*, V/1/265, 198.

[32] *JWJAD*, V/1/267, 201; and *JWJAD*, V/1/271, 202.

[33] A copy of one of the booklets printed by the French legation is preserved at the Archives, CM.

[34] See CADN, Pékin, Ambassade, Série A, Carton 415.

[35] *ACM* 51 (1886), 580–82.

[36] *JWJAD*, IV/1/382, 532.

[37] *JWJAD*, IV/1/384, 537.

[38] *JWJAD*, IV/1/382, 532; and *JWJAD*, IV/1/385, 545, 549. The governor knew that the complexity of the Pinglushang case and the distance between Nanchang and Ganzhou made supervision difficult. Significantly, Cai Shichun did not come from a pool of expectant officials but was a tenured official. For the investigation of certain *jiao'an*, deputies were selected with care.

[39] *JWJAD*, IV/1/382, 533–36.

[40] Yang Jusan had lodged complaints against the Xies for several reasons: (1) At one time the Xies contracted to pay taxes on hillside property belonging to the Yangs in exchange for its use. Now descendants of the original party refused to pay Yang the money due. (2) The Xies constructed, without authorization, a building on Yang property thereby rupturing the site's geomantic features. (3) Xie Lanyu owed the Yang lineage hall grain rent. (4) Xie Lanyu's women folk had cut and taken wood from property belonging to the Yangs. *JWJAD*, III/2/591, 681–82.

[41] *ACM* 39 (1874), 296.

[42] The Xies stated that forebears had actually contracted to purchase the property where construction had started; thus, they considered it permissible. However, to the west of this site, the Yangs had property for which another Xie ancestor had agreed to pay taxes. Thereafter, the Xies had planted and cut trees there. When the Yangs later reclaimed that property, they still tried to collect taxes for it from the Xie family. *JWJAD*, III/2/591, 681–82.

[43] *JWJAD*, VI/2/667, 1006.

[44] *ACM*, 43 (1878), 179–80.

[45] *JWJAD*, VI/2/667, 1004, 1008.

[46] *JWJAD*, VI/2/667, 1008.

[47] *ACM* 42 (1877), 282–84.

[48] *ACM*, 43 (1878), 179–80.

[49] This case contained factual discrepancies that the various Chinese investigatory officials recognized and were able to resolve. This researcher also resolved some discrepancies based on the complete documentation of the case. Regarding the

yixue, see *JWJAD*, IV/1/382, 533. For clarification of place names used in this case, see *JWJAD*, IV/1/384, 538; and *JWJAD*, V/2/1054, 967–68.

[50] *JWJAD*, IV/1/382, 533–34; and Archives of the Institute of Modern History, Academia Sinica, Taibei, Taiwan (hereafter Archives, IMH), Zongli Yamen shoudianbu, March 11, 1891 (GX17/2/2), the governor of Jiangxi, Dexing, to the Zongli Yamen. This communication is missing from the *JWJAD* collection and indicated as such for *JWJAD*, V/2/1071.

[51] The *sui* examination determined if *shengyuan* degree holders should be promoted, demoted, or dismissed. Chang, *Chinese Gentry*, 75.

[52] *JWJAD*, IV/1/382, 533.

[53] *JWJAD*, IV/1/382, 536. In a later communication it was stated that the magistrate ordered gentry and elders (*shenqi*) to sternly restrain the local people, prevent another incident, and calm all parties. *JWJAD*, IV/1/385, 549.

[54] *JWJAD*, IV/1/382, 534.

[55] *JWJAD*, IV/1/384, 537–38; and *JWJAD*, V/2/1039, 925. According to Chinese accounts, the incident occurred on either June 25, 26, or 27 and the magistrate arrived to investigate on June 28. According to Bishop Rouger, the trouble began on the night of June 28 and continued the next day. *ACM*, 51 (1886), 582. I have no explanation for the discrepancy in dates.

[56] *JWJAD*, IV/1/384, 542–43.

[57] *JWJAD*, IV/1/382, 535; and *JWJAD*, IV/1/386, 551. The functionary was referred to as *dilin jiebao*, but the exact meaning of this term is unclear because this is the only instance of its use in Jiangxi *jiao'an*. However, since officials sometimes used the term *dilin* in reference to *dibao*, I believe this is also the case here.

[58] *JWJAD*, IV/1/382, 535.

[59] *JWJAD*, IV/1/384, 538.

[60] *JWJAD*, IV/1/384, 538.

[61] *JWJAD*, V/2/1051, 964–66. This communication included a copy of the Xies' deed; see pages 965–66. According to Bishop François-Adrien Rouger, the Xies had first leased the property in 1796. *JWJAD*, VI/2/667, 1004.

[62] *JWJAD*, V/2/1054, 967–73. This communication included copies of the academy's deeds; see pages 969–72.

[63] An on-the-scene investigation of the boundaries indicated in the various deeds and careful comparison of the deeds led officials to conclude that the academy held valid ones. *JWJAD*, V/2/1054, 967–69. Other officials later declared that the Xies possessed a counterfeit deed. *JWJAD*, V/2/1077, 988.

[64] *JWJAD*, IV/1/384, 539. Earlier the matter of rent amount had also been unsuccessfully litigated by the academy.

[65] *JWJAD*, V/2/1054, 967; *JWJAD*, V/2/1055, 973; and *JWJAD*, V/2/1061, 978–79.

[66] *JWJAD*, IV/1/384, 539. The Xies evidently felt they had "the right of perpetual cultivation." This practice prevailed in the lower Yangzi valley area. It gave tenants a bit more security and eased, to a degree, the hardships faced by tenant farmers. Albert Feuerwerker, *Rebellion in Nineteenth-Century China* (Ann Arbor: Center for Chinese Studies, University of Michigan, 1975), 97.

[67] *JWJAD*, IV/1/384, 539, 541.

[68] *JWJAD*, VI/2/667, 1005.

[69] *JWJAD*, IV/1/386, 550.

[70] *JWJAD*, IV/1/386, 551.

[71] *JWJAD*, V/2/1044, 933; *JWJAD*, V/2/1047, 934; and *JWJAD*, V/2/1049, 962.

[72] *JWJAD*, V/2/1061, 979.

[73] Archives, IMH, Zongli Yamen shoudianbu, March 18, 1891 (GX17/2/9), the governor of Jiangxi, Dexing, to the Zongli Yamen. This communication is missing from the *JWJAD* collection and indicated as such for *JWJAD*, V/2/1074; also, see *JWJAD*, V/2/1077, 988.

[74] *JWJAD*, V/2/1049, 962–63; also see *JWJAD*, V/2/1050, 963.

[75] *JWJAD*, V/2/1077, 989.

[76] *JWJAD*, V/2/1076, 986; and *JWJAD*, V/2/1077, 987–89.

[77] *JWJAD*, V/2/1060, 977.

[78] Paul Cohen elaborates on this contention for the 1860s. See his *China and Christianity*, 180–85.

[79] Who these deputies were and if local officials had commissioned them cannot be determined. *JWJAD*, V/2/1077, 988.

[80] *JWJAD*, V/2/1077, 987–88.

[81] *JWJAD*, V/2/1082, 990.

[82] *JWJAD*, VI/2/667, 1007–9.

[83] Evidently, the deed was destroyed when one of the Nanchang churches burned in 1862. The various churches of Jiangxi kept certain important documents, including property deeds, in Nanchang. *JWJAD*, VI/2/667, 1007–8, 1010.

[84] *JWJAD*, VI/2/667, 1010–11.

[85] *JWJAD*, IV/1/382, 533; and *JWJAD*, IV/1/386, 551.

[86] The property and related disputes at Pinglushang sheds light on how provincial-level officials approached the settlement of difficult *jiao'an*. However, it is not possible to separate precisely the roles played by the different officials.

After the arrival of Subprefect Cai Shichun, he and the Ganzhou prefect dominated the investigation. Although two other deputies were assigned locally, they did not assume prominent roles. The prefect and Cai worked smoothly and efficiently together. More importantly, they conducted a thorough investigation and a fair trial. The governor had confidence in their decisions, which he supported completely in the face of the bishop's challenge. In my evaluation, the subprefect and prefect served the provincial-level officials well.

[87] *JWJAD*, VI/2/736, 1090–91.

[88] *JWJAD*, VI/2/736, 1090.

[89] *JWJAD*, VI/2/736, 1090.

[90] *JWJAD*, VI/2/736, 1091.

[91] *JWJAD*, VI/2/736, 1091.

[92] *JWJAD*, VI/2/736, 1091.

[93] *JWJAD*, VI/2/663, 990.

[94] Edward S. Little, *The Story of Kuling* (Shanghai: Presbyterian Mission Press, 1899), 4. Little stated that a *juren* degree holder named Wan, who was the most powerful of the local gentry, wrote the lease. I do not believe that this man should be confused with Wan Dongfu since officials indicated the degree status of people involved in *jiao'an* and they made no mention of Wan Dongfu holding any degree.

[95] *JWJAD*, VI/2/663, 988. Little alleged that some gentry instigated the incident because they resented the fact that they had not been consulted, nor shared in any extra-legal payments. Little, *Story of Kuling*, 8. I find nothing in the *jiao'an* documents to substantiate this.

[96] *JWJAD*, VI/2/663, 987.

[97] *JWJAD*, VI/2/663, 989–90.

[98] *JWJAD*, VI/2/663, 987–88, 990.

[99] However, Little said the gentry later sponsored anonymous placards that raised fengshui as a reason to oppose the lease. See his *Story of Kuling*, 4, 8. Since the property was "waste land," how believable and convincing could the gentry's claim have been? Moreover, Chinese officials stated explicitly the gentry had no objections based on geomancy. *JWJAD*, VI/2/663, 990.

[100] Archives, MSSC, "Mullen's Manuscript," 148–49.

[101] *JWJAD*, VI/2/673, 1017.

[102] *JWJAD*, VI/2/673, 1017.

[103] *JWJAD*, VI/2/680, 1024. Chinese officials also referred to Zhanghuwei as Zhanghutian.

[104] *JWJAD*, VI/2/681, 1029.

[105] *JWJAD*, VI/2/683, 1032.

[106] *JWJAD*, VI/2/704, 1043.

[107] In 1885 Chinese destroyed a church in Zhanghuwei. It seems likely that the Catholics intended the property purchased in 1896 to replace that lost earlier and for which they were indemnified. High and low Chinese officials alike believed that the bishop was using the 1885 incident to coerce a favorable settlement for the current case. *JWJAD*, VI/2/704, 1044–45.

[108] *JWJAD*, VI/2/704, 1045.

[109] *JWJAD*, VI/2/704, 1045.

[110] *JWJAD*, VI/2/735, 1085–86.

[111] *JWJAD*, VI/2/735, 1086.

[112] *JWJAD*, VI/2/735, 1086–87.

[113] *JWJAD*, VI/2/735, 1088–89.

[114] Feuchtwang, *Anthropological Analysis*, 172–75, 236–54.

[115] *JWJAD*, IV/1/367, 453–54. In another example, the gentry and people of Lüqi's county seat indicated in 1894 that "if a church were built there, it would involve the fengshui of the entire city." *JWJAD*, V/2/1145, 1070.

[116] *JWJAD*, IV/1/367, 489.

[117] *JWJAD*, IV/1/367, 458.

[118] For example, at Dengjia marketplace in a rural part of Anren County during the 1870s, no geomantic obstacles surfaced when Catholics used several old houses originally belonging to commoners as their church. *JWJAD*, III/2/605, 706.

[119] *JWJAD*, IV/1/379, 514.

[120] *JWJAD*, VI/2/705, 1049.

[121] *JWJAD*, IV/1/379, 514.

[122] *JWJAD*, IV/1/379, 523.

[123] *JWJAD*, VI/2/705, 1047.

[124] *JWJAD*, VI/2/705, 1047.

[125] *JWJAD*, IV/1/379, 523; and *JWJAD*, VI/2/705, 1047. The French minister claimed that because the missionary made no report of the purchase to local officials, they were using this as a pretext to block the purchase. *JWJAD*, IV/1/376, 509. This contention, however, was not supported by the facts of the case.

[126] *JWJAD*, IV/1/379, 523–24; and *JWJAD*, IV/1/381, 531. Father Anot may have retained the deeds because the magistrate had not received the full amount of purchase money. *JWJAD*, VI/2/705, 1050.

[127] *JWJAD*, VI/2/705, 1048.

[128] *JWJAD*, VI/2/705, 1048.

[129] *JWJAD*, VI/2/705, 1048.

[130] *JWJAD*, VI/2/705, 1048.

[131] *JWJAD*, VI/2/705, 1049–50.

[132] Among the Gui lineage, it appears that only one man held a civil service degree, that of *jiansheng*. *JWJAD*, IV/1/379, 523.

[133] *JWJAD*, VI/2/705, 1050.

[134] *JWJAD*, VI/2/733, 1084.

[135] Gui Caohua's family was poor and unable to pay the 102 taels compensation. The Gui lineage found it difficult not to help him and arranged to transfer land formerly donated to the subcounty yamen to the Catholic Church. Gui Caohua signed an irrevocable agreement to this effect on an auspicious day during April of 1897. *JWJAD*, VI/2/705, 1049, 1051.

[136] *JWJAD*, VI/2/705, 1050–51.

[137] *JWJAD*, VI/2/705, 1050.

[138] *JWJAD*, VI/2/707, 1052–53.

[139] *JWJAD*, VI/2/707, 1053–54.

[140] *JWJAD*, VI/2/707, 1053.

[141] *JWJAD*, VI/2/707, 1053.

[142] *JWJAD*, VI/2/709, 1059–61.

[143] *JWJAD*, VI/2/710, 1062.

[144] *JWJAD*, VI/2/720, 1067–69.

[145] *JWJAD*, VI/2/720, 1067.

[146] A variety of natural objects received attention and veneration by the Chinese. For an account of "tree-worship," see R. F. Johnston, *Lion and Dragon in Northern China* (New York: E. P. Dutton and Co., 1910), 377–84. Also, see V. R. Burkhardt, *Chinese Creeds and Customs*, vol. 2 (Hong Kong: South China Morning Post, 1955), 103–5.

[147] *JWJAD*, VI/2/720, 1068.

[148] *JWJAD*, VI/2/720, 1067.

[149] *JWJAD*, VI/2/720, 1068.

[150] *JWJAD*, VI/2/720, 1068.